Practitioner's Guide to Emotion Regulation in School-Aged Children

Practitioner's Guide to Emotion Regulation in School-Aged Children

by

Gayle L. Macklem

Licensed Educational Psychologist
Manchester, Massachusetts
USA

 Springer

Gayle L. Macklem
Licensed Educational Psychologist
Manchester, Massachusetts
USA

ISBN-13: 978-0-387-73850-5   e-ISBN-13: 978-0-387-73851-2

Library of Congress Control Number: 2007938962

Printed on acid-free paper.

9 8 7 6 5 4 3 2 1

springer.com

This text is designed for school psychologists and other mental health workers in schools to strengthen their capacity to help children and adolescents who must learn to regulate their emotions or strengthen their ability to do so. After thirty years in education working with children and adolescents, emotion regulation appears to me to be a key variable in student functioning that we have not fully understood or successfully addressed. The text is dedicated to the children who must frequently deal with intense emotion that they have difficulty controlling. Not only are these children and adolescents the most challenging and tiring for parents and school staff, they are also the most interesting and the most fun when their emotions are positive.

Contents

Figures

Informational figures are provided to help elucidate concepts, provide additional information and research of interest, or to provide an example of how concepts could be thought about or used. The Tools/Worksheets/Handouts are practical materials that can be used by practitioners in their day-to day work with students, teachers and/or parents.

Informational

Tools/Worksheets/Handouts

Introduction

After thirty years in education, a practitioner begins to step back and reflect upon the "big picture." What do we as mental health practitioners do well? What are the areas in which we have to develop more skills, strategies, and techniques in order to help students function more successfully? Why are some of our most frequent interventions not working? How can we do better? These questions are inevitable, and they are not easily answered.

One practice that is not working well is the training in social skills. School psychologists and other practitioners spend a lot of time attempting to train for social skills when there are considerable data to indicate that these efforts are often not successful. A major flaw in training for social skills is poor generalization. The skills that we teach, and that students appear to learn at least in the contexts in which we teach them, are not being exhibited in the environments in which students need them. In the fast-moving, confusing, often noisy, and complex peer world, all of our efforts to train social skills are invisible. The peer world is, of course, where young people need these skills the most, for fitting into that world is vitally important for their general emotional adjustment as well as for academic success!

When students are observed, the skills that were trained are not being used. One of the primary problems is the fact that many children who need social skills training cannot control their emotions well enough to think about using their skills, if in fact they can focus on them well enough to think about using them or even can recall them at all.

Emotion regulation is a critical missing piece in our training. Moreover, we must considerably change the way we deliver skills and strategies. Many of the ones that we teach are not developmentally appropriate, are not intensive enough, are not delivered often enough, or are not delivered in relevant contexts.

There are considerable data available to help us improve our training and the targeted and specific interventions that we want to deliver to help schoolchildren. Some of these data are ignored and some are not well known, but the information is available if we look for it. Regulating emotion is a fairly new focus of researchers, and we do not yet know enough about how to help children who are having difficulties. This book is designed to support the work of school psychologists and other mental health workers in schools in regard to understanding, facilitating, and strengthening students' emotion regulation.

Chapter 1 offers a basic introduction to the "hot topic" of emotion regulation. A broad view of the subject is helpful, although there does not yet seem to be a clear, agreed upon definition of emotion regulation among researchers. Several concepts related to emotion regulation are discussed along with the domains and components of emotion regulation. 'Good enough' ability to regulate one's emotions means physical and mental health for students, and in our culture learning to regulate emotion appropriately is critical for academic success, personal satisfaction, and a sense of competence and resilience. Current research dealing with the relevance of emotion regulation for students will help school psychologists and other mental health practitioners appreciate why they have to understand the science of emotion regulation as well as the clinical work needed to help students from preschool through high school.

The discomfort and pain that underdeveloped emotion regulation causes children and adolescents are covered in Chapter 2. Although dysregulation at a particular stage of development can be temporary with no long-term effects, repeated patterns of emotion regulation that strongly interfere with competence can place a student at risk for developing a disorder or can be the symptoms of a disorder. The chapter discusses the role of emotion dysregulation in physiological disorders and in the major disorders of childhood: borderline personality disorder, autism spectrum disorders, bipolar disorder, attention-deficit disorder, generalized anxiety disorder, and the depressive disorders. Considerations for interventions are introduced. The control of negative emotions is the key to helping children who have identified disorders or are at risk for developing disorders. It is also important to strengthen effortful control and attention.

A brief understanding of the connection between the brain and the body with the goal of making emotion less mysterious and possibly more controllable is delineated in Chapter 3. Children's emotional behavior may represent an "affective style" of responding. We have to appreciate that there are individual differences in the ways in which emotions are experienced, how often they are experienced, and to what degree.

The brain structures that are involved in emotional learning include the amygdala, the prefrontal cortex, and the hippocampus. The "stress response" is a brain-based reaction that triggers behavior. When a child who is already exhibiting poor emotion regulation is placed under stress, it will be especially difficult for him or her to regulate emotion and recover. The appeal of feeling better in the present may overcome the appeal of any longer-term goals. An improved understanding of the biology of emotion can help us in our search for interventions that will be helpful in several ways.

It is important to understand typical development, so that underdeveloped emotion regulation can be identified early and addressed. In Chapter 4, we see that the emotion regulatory aspects of temperament are helpful in appreciating an individual's response to his or her several primary environments. Children with different temperaments can be distinguished by the ways in which they regulate their emotions. Researchers trying to determine the relationship between a child's temperament and his or her growing ability to regulate emotions have explored how behaviors that reflect temperament influence styles of emotional control. The connection between emotion regulation, attention regulation, and temperament also affects a child's developing social competence. Development of emotion regulation during infancy and toddlerhood and the role of language are discussed as well as emotion regulation during the preschool period. Emotion regulation is a key developmental task of the early childhood period, yet significant numbers of children continue to have difficulty as they begin formal schooling.

The influence of parenting styles and practices on the development of emotion regulation and the various ways that children learn about emotions are described in Chapter 5. "Positive parenting" is a term that is used to describe parent-child interactions that are important for the study of the development of emotion regulation. Family expressiveness of positive emotion has been connected to emotion regulation as has family 'talk' about emotions.

Parents' reactions to children's negative emotions are particularly influential in regard to the development of emotion regulation. Children who are punished when they exhibit negative feelings associate their emotion with negative consequences, which increases their distress and the intensity of the emotion, and it is difficult for these children to regulate their emotions. Children whose parents who use an interactive style around expression of emotion that is similar to "coaching" can generally regulate their emotions and tend not to behave aggressively. Both parenting and child behavior can also be explored in terms of approach and avoidance motivation. Finally, a number of interventions have been developed to help parents increase positive behaviors when interacting with their children, and these are discussed as well.

Emotion in the classroom has recently been recognized as an area of interest by researchers. Chapter 6 examines a student's ability to regulate emotion and function in class. Anxiety is the most frequently experienced (and studied) academic emotion in the school setting. There is a body of research to indicate that anxiety decreases children's test performance as do their beliefs about their competency in various school subjects.

There is convincing evidence to indicate that early relationships with teachers as well as parents are important in determining whether or not a child will learn self-regulation skills and emotion regulation, take others' perspectives, and develop relationships. Classroom climate is also important. When it is ambiguous or negative, avoidance behaviors, disruption, and cheating are more likely. Evidence is provided that indicates that emotion regulation in children and adolescents can be improved. Programming is explored and its importance becomes clear when we realize that emotional and social skills are closely connected to academic performance.

Students may feel that their most important issues have to do with friendships and other peer relationships. Chapter 7 deals with peer relationships. Young people who are strong in effortful control of their emotions are socially competent and are liked by their peers. Emotion dysregulation places children at risk for isolation from or rejection by their peers. The peer group is a key source of emotional knowledge and practice. Boys and girls learn how and when to express emotion through social interactions with their peers, and display rules are learned within the context of the peer group. Children create their own rules about how emotions can or cannot expressed. Prosocial behavior is significantly reduced even when young people simply think that they may be excluded from the group. In order to avoid rejection, they must learn to keep anger under control and express it carefully. Emotion regulation is especially important when considering victims of bullying.

Students with varying abilities in emotion regulation and varying degrees of reactivity may respond differently to different types of interventions. The varieties of interventions available for consideration by school psychologists to deal with peer issues include curricula that feature empathy training and antibullying techniques, and these are reviewed.

School is stressful for many students. Chapter 8 deals with how students adapt to stress and how they can be helped to develop more effective strategies. Young people develop coping styles to deal with stress within and outside of school. Among the less adaptive strategies are suppression, rumination, avoidance, and negative self-thinking. More adaptive strategies include behavioral distraction, optimism, problem solving, positive reappraisal, and detached mindfulness. Cognitive behavioral therapy (CBT) has good support as an intervention for use with children and adolescents to improve self-regulation. Newer approaches include mindfulness, acceptance, and emotion coaching. Specialized interventions for coping with anxiety, depression, and anger management are reviewed.

Interventions are the focus of the next two chapters. Chapter 9 suggests various ways in which school psychologists and other mental health workers in schools can support teachers and parents. A particularly important variable in helping children develop good emotion regulation has to do with how adults react to children's negative emotions. It is clearly important for adults to correctly 'read' a child's temperament and emotional style and to respond appropriately. For example, researchers have paid particular attention to the parenting styles of those adults who have highly anxious children. These reticent children influence their parents, who then become overprotective. Parents and teachers have to teach emotion vocabulary and talk with students about emotions. Emotion coaching is a style of interacting that can be used by both parents and teachers.

Teachers also have to be more aware of differences among their students so that their reactions will be appropriate and helpful and not add to their students'stress. In classrooms where the climate is positive, these students are both supported and protected. Interventions that are helpful for children as they develop emotion regulation skills include stress reduction, emotion coaching, modeling, and direct teaching of coping skills. Today we have the added pressure of dealing with students from diverse backgrounds. When a child's family culture does not match the predominant culture of the school, considerable stress can be placed on the child, the family, and the school. Issues around culture, gender, and various student handicapping conditions make helping children develop emotion regulation a considerable challenge.

It is clear that the same tools, strategies, and techniques are not appropriate for students of all ages and ability levels. Tools used to assist children and adolescents to regulate emotion and behavior may have to be adapted to increase the likelihood that they will be used. It is particularly important to adapt tools for young children. Cognitive interventions have been shown to be particularly useful for adolescents and adults, and many of these tools can be easily adapted so that they can be used effectively with younger schoolchildren. Some easily adapted techniques involve, for example, number scales, mantras, self-talk, acceptance, problem solving, and fear hierarchies. A few tools designed for juveniles with autism spectrum disorders or learning disabilities can also be used for those with weak emotion regulation. Interventions described Chapter 10 range from 'quick' tools for young people with mild emotion regulation problems to more complex techniques for students with significant weaknesses in emotion regulation.

General and practical information for school psychologists who want to establish both targeted and intensive interventions for students with poor emotion regulation can be found in Chapter 11. Although boys and girls who have more extreme difficulty with emotional regulation stand out in the school setting, tools are needed to identify both the student who has more moderate needs and the more specific skills that a student may have to master. Generalization and transfer (carrying over skills taught in one environment to different environments) must be directly addressed. Finally, the major steps in providing treatment for problems in emotion regulation are specified.

Several individuals have been enormously helpful in the preparation of this text. Two young artists, Hunter Ward and Summer Ward, deserve special thanks. Sandra Ward, a talented medical editor, provided many ideas for organizing and strengthening the readability of the text. Janet Lemnah meticulously read and corrected the manuscript, identifying errors and changes that were needed. Few people have her ability to attend to detail in the same way. Most of all, Dick Macklem supported me in this project both emotionally and by reviewing text. Without his strong encouragement and support it would never have been completed. The work and support of these individuals is deeply appreciated.

It is hoped that this text will prove to be a practical tool for school psychologists and other mental health workers in school environments. The worksheets and handouts included may be copied for the use of the individual practitioner as long as the source is correctly identified. They may not be used for any purpose other than helping an individual student and his or her family and may not be reprinted or distributed for any other reason.

Chapter 1
The Importance of Emotional Regulation in Child and Adolescent Functioning and School Success

Emotion Regulation

Spending any time at all in or around a school provides ample opportunity to observe students who are having difficulty coping with the stresses of their daily lives. On a playground you might see a student with an angry expression pushing another student out of the way. Or, you might hear one yelling at his playmates about whether or not he is "in" or "out" of the game. You might spot yet another student sulking long after being reprimanded by a playground monitor, or one isolating herself from others on the edge of the playground avoiding interaction and even eye contact with any of the other children playing nearby.

Inside the school building you might see a parent or teacher trying to calm an hysterical student or a frustrated teacher trying to interact reasonably with one who has "shut down" completely and cannot hear anything that is being said to him. You might find an older student hiding in the restroom trying to calm down after having "escaped" temporarily from the teasing he was being subjected to in the cafeteria. Or you might observe a student who is frequently "scapegoated" by peers hugging the corridor walls, walking at the slowest pace possible toward her classroom. You may see a student scribble all over an almost finished paper or crumple it up because he has made an error.

You might see a student taking a test who is dealing with so much emotion that she cannot even begin to write. You may observe one who cannot focus or organize his thinking well enough to even begin to focus on the work in front of him. In a high school you may see a student turn to his locker and hit it hard with his fist after being reprimanded by a teacher or rejected by a girlfriend. You may suddenly realize how often a particular student is visiting the school nurse, especially around exam time. You may wonder why a student sits alone at lunch wearing a cap or hood to hide his face when others appear to be socializing comfortably.

None of these observations is unusual, although they may not be apparent to the casual observer or even seen regularly, depending on the awareness and expertise of staff and the general climate of a particular school. On the other

G. L. Macklem, *Practitioner's Guide to Emotion Regulation in School-Aged Children.* © Springer 2008

hand, you may observe students yelling, demoralized, or actually fighting in a school, or totally withdrawn, when the school's climate is less healthy and the staff less competent. Although none of these observations in and of itself points to pathology, all of these students are having difficulty controlling or "regulating" their emotions. At the very least, difficulty regulating one's emotions would result in unhappiness; at worst, it could result in serious emotional or behavioral problems.

Regulating our emotions involves a necessary and important set of skills that all of us must master to some degree in order to negotiate our day-to-day lives, and emotion regulation has become a "hot topic" in several disciplines. Interest, research, and knowledge around the construct of emotion regulation are expanding rapidly (Eisenberg, Champion, and Ma 2004). Researchers in a number of fields—social and personality psychology, child and normal development, cognition, neuroscience, psychopathology, education psychology, and now school psychology—now realize that the ability of individuals to regulate emotion is relevant to their specific academic areas. Emotion regulation has become an overriding theme in affective science (Rottenberg and Gross 2003) and a major and popular topic in developmental psychology (Eisenberg, Champion, et al. 2004). Cole, Martin, and Dennis (2004) consider emotion regulation to be "an exciting lens through which to study development" (p. 330).

Definitions of Emotion Regulation

Researchers and theorists have not as yet settled on an agreed upon definition of emotion regulation. In fact, there is considerable discussion and debate around it—to the extent that questions have been raised in regard to its usefulness as a scientific construct (Cole, Martin, et al. 2004). Although one area of agreement is the idea that emotion regulation involves internal processes that have to do with emotions, not everyone considers intent or overt behavior as a consequence of emotion regulation or lack thereof in their definition. There is disagreement in regard to whether or not the concept includes external regulation of a child by parents or teachers and if both voluntary and involuntary regulation can be included. Nor is there total agreement in regard to anticipatory emotion regulation as an important component of emotion regulation.

The literature provides a number of definitions. Cole, Martin, et al. (2004) wrote about emotion regulation as the changes that are associated with emotions once they are triggered by some event or situation. Bridges, Margie, and Zaff (2001) consider emotion regulation to be a group of processes that a person might use to call up a positive or negative emotion, hold onto the emotion, control it, or change it, and they differentiate between the *feelings* of emotion and how emotion might be *displayed*. Thompson (1991) was interested in both extrinsic and intrinsic actions associated with behavioral reactions as a result of experiencing emotions. Dahl (2001) looked at emotion regulation as the individual's effort toward managing emotion so that a particular emotion could be used for a purpose. A simple way to think about emotion regulation is to think of it as the action an individual might take to control: (a) *which* emotions are experienced; (b) *how and when* they are felt by the individual; and (c) the *ways* they are expressed or might be observed by others (Gross 1998b; Westphal and Bonanno 2004). Gross and Thompson (2007) write that the term emotion regulation could mean regulation by emotions or it could refer to how emotions are controlled (pp. 8–9). They use the term emotion regulation to explain how emotions are regulated, and that is how the term is used here.

It is not only the definition of emotion regulation that has complicated the study of these processes, but the fact that it is very difficult for researchers to separate emotion from emotion regulation. They use different definitions (if they use any definition at all) and different tools or measures to determine a child's ability to self-regulate. Much of the research on emotion regulation has focused on very young children or on mother-child dyads. Fortunately, this is changing because practitioners who are struggling with children's problems on a day-to-day basis cannot wait for theorists and researchers to come to full agreement. Thus, it makes the most sense for practitioners to take a broad view of emotion regulation as they acquire a deeper understanding of the phenomenon and develop interventions to prevent difficulties with emotion regulation in the children they are working with and to find ways to strengthen children's emotional competency.

Emotion Regulation and Related Concepts

Our emotions serve important functions, including preparing us for action, helping drive decision making, helping us make judgments about the environment or the context in which we find ourselves, and giving us cues about others' intentions (Gross, 1998). Increasing, decreasing, or maintaining a particular emotion is the action we take in order to regulate emotion. Emotions can involve positive as well as negative affect. They tend to involve specific objects or goals and are aimed toward action or behavior. Emotion regulation, emotional regulation, affect regulation, mood, coping, stress reduction, self-regulation, effortful control, and self-control are the several concepts that have been closely associated in the literature.

Emotion Regulation versus Emotional Regulation

The terms emotion regulation and emotional regulation are often used interchangeably, although semantics might make a distinction between them. Lévesque and colleagues (2003) use the term emotio*nal* self-regulation to refer to modulating behavioral and physical aspects of emotion. They (Lévesque et al. 2004) describe emotional self-regulation as one of the "cornerstones of socialization and moral development" (p. 361). Gross and Thompson (2007) prefer the term "emotion regulation" (p. 8).

Affect Regulation

Affect can be considered the most general and categorical term (Schutz, Hong, Cross, and Osbon 2006). Within the broad, general category of affect we might include emotions, feelings, moods, attitudes, affective style, and temperament (Davidson, Scherer, and Goldsmith 2003). Gross (1998b) uses the term affect as the "superordinate category," which includes: (a) emotions, (b) emotion episodes (including the context in which emotions occur), (c) moods, (d) dispositional states, and (e) traits. More recently, Gross and Thompson (2007) wrote that affect regulation is the overriding category. Coping, emotion regulation, mood regulation, and psychological defenses would be subcategories.

Mood

The terms "affect," "mood," and "emotion" are often used without distinguishing one from the other. Part of the problem is that words such as "emotion" and "mood" are part of our everyday language, but there is an important distinction between emotions and moods. Moods last longer than emotions and may not have an easily identifiable trigger. Emotions are mostly of short duration and arise in conjunction with a trigger or stimulus of some kind. Several researchers have described moods as low-intensity emotions (Linnenbrink, 2006; Pekrun 2006; Schutz et al. 2006), but moods are pervasive and sustained and can bias our thinking more than our behavior.

Moods are diffuse, occur over time, and give rise to actions such as approach or avoidance. Efforts to regulate mood or to repair mood are directed at changing feelings rather than behavior because moods change slowly. Rottenberg and Gross (2003) suggest a helpful analogy: "If emotional reactions are like storms then moods are like seasonal climate change" (p. 228). Defenses are stable and automatic and are involved with the experience of emotion. Because emotion is malleable, regulation is possible, and individuals can learn to intensify, depress, or maintain emotion.

Coping and Stress Reduction

Coping and stress deal with decreasing negative affect. Pardini, Lochman, and Wells (2004) listed three components of negative affect: (a) depressed mood, (b) fear, and (c) anger. When exposed to stressful events or situations, students may experience anxiety or anger. Anger is experienced in relation to events that are interpreted as threatening, such as a cutting remark by a popular peer, a brief physical contact perceived as a threat, or a perceived attack on one's self esteem. Sadness may be experienced in reaction to a loss or a disappointment. Anxiety may be felt in situations that are novel or when one feels exposed. Young people attempt to decrease the intensity of negative emotions with various coping and stress reduction strategies; i.e., thinking of something else, trying to relax, speaking assertively, or walking away from the situation.

Self-Control

Self-control is our ability to make ourselves fit better into our environments by overriding impulses and responses so that action can be stopped. Research indicates that people with strong self-control have better outcomes than people with less self-control. Students with more self-control also earn higher grades, are better adjusted, have better relationships with others, and respond to others in more emotionally appropriate ways. Tangney, Baumeister, and Boone (2004) indicated that self-control can be more clearly conceptualized as self-regulation. These authors cited a series of studies indicating that students with good self-control:

- Respond more competently socially as preschoolers.
- Function better socially as reported by parents.
- Are more popular.
- Have higher social status.
- Earn better grades.

A high level of self-control has been related to low levels of anger and a lowered tendency to vent or "let off steam," with reduced outward aggression. Well-controlled students tend to use "talking" to deal with their anger and therefore manage anger in a more constructive manner than those with a low level of self-control. Students with more self-control also have higher self-esteem and less shame than students with less. The current data available on the benefits of self-control are correlational rather than causal, but nevertheless are quite promising as justification for interventions to improve students' functioning.

Effortful Control

Effortful control involves stopping action by refocusing attention. It involves attention regulation or attention control in addition to behavior regulation. Effortful control is a dimension of temperament and can be thought of as the self-regulation component of temperament. It is a central and an important component of emotion regulation (Eisenberg, Smith, Sadovsky, and Spinrad 2004) and can be used to regulate both behavior and emotion (Spinrad, Eisenberg, Cumberland, Fabes, Valiente, Shepard, Reiser, Losoya, and Guthrie 2006).

A student must be able to both initiate action and inhibit action that may result from an environmental trigger that ignites a strong emotion (reported in Buckley and Saarni 2006). In the midst of a heated discussion, a teacher might instruct a student to "sit down." The student must not only sit down but also inhibit an inappropriate remark in order to decrease the heat of the moment. Effortful control also includes regulating one's attention by shifting attention away from a trigger or by focusing attention on something else. Thus researchers feel that effortful control involves executive functions such as integrating information and planning (Eisenberg, Smith et al. 2004; Eisenberg and Spinrad 2004). A student who is ruminating or obsessing on failure in the midst of a testing situation must be able to stop this negative thinking and refocus on the test question in order to avoid failure.

Effortful control is involved in self-regulation and affords a prediction of positive social functioning. Students who have skills in effortful regulation can ameliorate negative feelings, handle their anger, are sympathetic, and get along well with others. A child who fails to hit the baseball in a game on the playground must be able to shift his attention away from thoughts of letting himself and the team down or from looking bad in front of his peers, so he can muster up the concentration and effort to try again. Strong effortful control is most likely associated with resiliency (Spinrad et al. 2006).

It is important to distinguish among these varied concepts when engaging in research to advance knowledge, but it may be less critical for practitioners. Given our focus on identifying strategies to help children deal with poorly controlled emotions, our interest in training approaches to develop competency in regulating emotion, and our desire to develop interventions by which parents and teachers can help students regulate their emotions, the distinctions that are important in research become less significant.

Domains of Emotion Regulation

Various researchers and theorists describe differing numbers of domains of emotion regulation. Menesini (1999) writes about three levels:

* Regulation of sensation (input regulation).
* Information processing (central regulation).
* Response selection (output regulation).

Menesini conceptualizes emotion regulation as a sequence of events or processes, so that a problem at any point in the sequence would result in failure to regulate emotion. Yet others suggest that although the factors are interrelated, no individual factor is responsible for failure (Behncke 2002).

In practically terms, we can isolate several skills or domains involved in regulating emotions, including: (a) interpreting the facial and bodily expressions of emotion (information processing); (b) how clearly a young person can express his or her own emotions; (c) how aware the young person is of his or her emotions (emotional knowledge); (d) to what degree a young person understands his or her emotional triggers and has knowledge of the consequences of expressing that emotion in the respective culture; and (e) the ability to manage the intensity to which an emotion is felt and expressed (Shipman, Schneider, and Brown, 2004; Zeidner, Matthews, and Roberts, 2006). These domains and skills interact with one another.

Gross (1998b) described five sets of processes or five points in emotion generation that are involved in emotional regulation:

- Situation selection.
- Situation modification.
- Attentional deployment.
- Cognitive change.
- Response modulation.

Situation selection is the ability to interpret the context in which one finds oneself. Situation modification is the ability to use one's thinking and problem-solving ability to change the emotional impact of the situation. Attention deployment is the ability to move one's focus away from the situation triggering the particular emotion. Cognitive change refers to reinterpreting the context so that the experience is not felt as intensely or as irrationally or inappropriately. Response modulation refers to using strategies to dissipate the emotions that are felt at the time. The first four processes can be thought of as *antecedent focused* and the fifth as *response focused* (Beauregard, Levesque, and Paquette 2004).

The components of emotion regulation that we must consider include: "the latency, rise time, magnitude, duration, and offset of responses in behavioral, experiential or physiological domains" (Gross 1998a, p. 288). A student must be able to experience emotions without being overwhelmed and must learn to express emotions in a manner that is socially appropriate. He or she must also be able to express emotions without interfering or disrupting the interaction that is going on at the time. The student must remain in control when:

- Striking out in a ballgame.
- Disagreeing about an issue during a conversation.
- Making a mistake on an academic task or in a competitive game.
- Being reprimanded by an authoritative adult.
- Getting back an assignment with a low grade.
- Being mistakenly accused of a behavior.
- Seeing someone stepping in front of him in line.

- Being disappointed about a gift or a grade.
- Not being chosen for a game or a team or for a prize.

There is increasing evidence that leads us to believe that young people who can at least make the effort to regulate negative emotions will be less vulnerable to reacting to stress with inappropriate behaviors (Pardini, Lochman, and Wells 2004). Salovey (2006) points out that an individual who has difficulty regulating negative emotions is more vulnerable to the pressures of the environment. It appears that even *believing* that one's skills or abilities are weak is enough to increase vulnerability to stress.

Importance of Emotion Regulation

Emotions can organize attention or interfere with attention, facilitate or disrupt problem solving, and build or damage relationships. These two-way interactions intensify the need to help children learn to regulate their emotions. We know that attentional controls, problem-solving, and healthy relationships are vital for school success and for personal satisfaction. Emotion regulation is vital for positive functioning. At the same time, emotion regulation can compromise functioning.

Emotion regulation is critically related to behavior in that it organizes it (Gross 1998b). Regulation of emotions allows children to control their own behaviors so that they can react flexibly to what is going on around them (Forbes 2003). When a child is very angry, hitting a peer is only one of several possible options. Emotion regulation appears to be a key component of resilience and competence (Shapiro 2000). It acts as a powerful social mediator (Smith 2002); predicts good health (Salovey 2006); is key to adaptive success (Richards and Gross 2000); and is considered by some to be the best predictor of adjustment (Matsumoto 2002). It has also been described as critically important for success and happiness (Baumeister, Heatherton, and Tice 1994) and as the basis for the connection between social and academic competence and success in elementary school (Blair 2003; Masten and Coatsworth, 1998).

Current Research on Emotion Regulation

Given how central emotion regulation is to the functioning of children and adolescents, it is interesting to be aware of the directions that are being taken by researchers to increase our knowledge. Eisenberg, Champion, et al. (2004) have delineated some of the topics that have been posed for researchers. The role of cognitive processing needs more attention. This is relevant to practitioners who need specific interventions to assist students in planning and prioritizing, learning to distract themselves when challenged or overwhelmed, learning to reframe situations and contexts to which they are highly reactive, and challenging biases about others that they have learned. There has been fewer studies concerning the processes of socialization that occur in school environments than research regarding socialization that is a result of parenting. More work needs to done to develop interventions to assist older students with emotion regulation.

Eisenberg, Champion, et al. (2004) further indicate that the influence of culture on emotion regulation has to be explored. This is crucial given the number of different cultures and subcultures represented in our schools today. We need good measures of emotion regulation applicable to school-aged children, and studies of evidence-based practices to strengthen emotion regulation that we can put in place are particularly important for school-based practitioners. We have to know more about the relative effectiveness of specific strategies that we can teach students to help them to modulate emotion. This would allow us to develop very specific programs to assist children at different ages, to assist children who are more vulnerable than their peers, and to support children who have experienced trauma and may be highly dysregulated. For-tunately, some there has already been some work done in this area, and we now have both strategies and programs that appear to be quite promising for use in schools as we wait for results of new research.

Importantly, most practitioners believe emotion regulation can be trained. They believe that a child can be taught strategies to improve self-regulation of emotions. Recent research suggests that there may be a way to improve self-regulation and self-control through exercise and relaxation (Muraven and Baumeister 2000). Goldstein and Brooks (2005) believe that "...every child capable of developing a resilient mini-set of strategies will be able to deal more effectively with stress and pressure, to cope with everyday challenges, to bounce back from disappointments, adversity and trauma, to develop clear and realistic goals, to solve problems, to relate comfortably with others, and to treat oneself and others with respect." (p. 4). This seems like a tall order, but it makes it quite clear that emotion regulation can be taught to and strengthened in students.

Relevance for School Psychologists and Other Practitioners

For purposes of intervention, we might think of emotion regulation as a series of controls or strategies through which we learn to cope successfully with the emotions we experience. This would involve:

- Coping with the triggers in our environment that give rise to a particular emotion.
- Managing the intensity with which we experience a particular emotion.
- Mastering the skills necessary to return to a neutral emotional state within a reasonable and culturally acceptable amount of time.

- Controlling any thoughts, actions, or behaviors that might be driven by a particular emotion.

This becomes critical when an emotion is experienced that may be inappropriate for a given situation or be too intensely felt to fit a particular context or even to fit the culture in which the student finds herself.

Forbes (2003) compares emotion regulation to "coping" and argues that the concepts of emotion regulation and coping are similar. A student with good emotion regulation abilities can control his or her behavior and will be more flexible in various contexts and in dealing with stressful events. Emotion regulation can also be thought of as a *tool* to understand how emotions affect other processes such as attention, problem solving, and behavior (Cole, Martin, et al. 2004).

Learning to regulate emotional expressions depends on the socialization of parents, siblings, teachers, and peers. In the first few years of life, a child learns a whole range of emotions, learns to modulate them to some degree, and learns to make quick shifts in emotion. Emotion self-regulation continues to develop during the preschool years as the child learns the appropriate expression of emotion in his culture and to use language to modulate emotional behavior. The child also learns that she can experience more than one emotion at one moment in time and that emotions can be conflicting (Fox 1998).

By the time a child begins first grade, he or she may be demonstrating age-appropriate competency in emotion regulation (Cole, Dennis, et al. 2004), but there are significant numbers of children who have not developed age-appropriate skills by this time. A number of factors contribute toward competency in emotion regulation: personal history, early development and training, the context in which an emotion is felt, and the culture or cultures in which the student must function.

Not all children have secure attachments with their parents, some have experienced considerable insecurity in their home environments, and some have experienced trauma. Some have enjoyed highly competent and sensitive parenting during their preschool years and beyond, whereas others live with anxious, depressed, or emotionally distant parents. Some parents talk about emotions, recognize them in their children, and both suggest and model ways to deal with strong emotions. Other children witness intense and poorly controlled emotions expressed or are trained not to express a particular emotion in their home environment, especially anger. Still others are raised in culturally expressive or culturally reserved families that may not fit the prevailing school culture or expectations for emotional control.

We must keep in mind that experiencing strong emotion per se is not a "disability," yet at the same time, poor regulation of emotions is involved in most of the disorders of childhood. Moreover, there are children who show *some* symptoms of one or more of the major disorders who would not be considered disabled, but they often have difficulty regulating their emotions and need support.

Temperament is a concept that is generally thought of as being related to personality. A child's temperament may be intense, which would make it challenging for him to control the speed with which emotion might escalate. Emotions would be expressed more vividly and to a greater extent in a young person with an intense temperament. Emotional intensity is observed in students who talk loudly in the classroom or on the playground, become overly emotionally involved in the play episode, argue with peers or passionately defend their friends, or appear to be having the best time of anyone in the group. They may also be very quick to anger or may express excitement more rapidly and to a greater degree than others.

Language is associated with the regulation of emotion. Some young people may have a broader vocabulary for describing emotions or more vivid memories of previous emotional experiences than others, which they can describe in detail. Some may have more difficulty dealing with and dissipating negative emotions than others. Some may have less capability in identifying the particular emotional triggers that make them so vulnerable to inappropriate responses in social situations. Some have more difficulty coping with particular interpersonal situations that trigger specific emotions, such as performing poorly in competitive situations, and when they are teased or feeling shame they react intensely.

This whole constellation is further complicated by the fact that there may be situations or times or contexts in which intense emotional expression will be acceptable and other contexts in which those same feelings, expressions of the feelings, and associated behaviors will not be tolerated (Zeidner et al. 2006). Think of the child who cheers the loudest watching the ballgame but finds that the same energy gets her into trouble in the cafeteria. Or consider the child who expresses tremendous excitement when opening a birthday gift that he desperately wanted and expresses intense disappointment or anger when the gift does not match his expectations.

There are varying degrees of tolerance for decreased levels of self-regulation among different teachers as well as in different situations, even quite similar situations such as adjoining classrooms. Some teachers have high tolerance for students who express intense emotions because although they may be difficult at times, they are the most vocally appreciative of perks that the teacher might give the class. Next year's teacher may value restraint and prefer quiet and reserved students. This variation in expectation and tolerance level makes it complex and challenging for students to learn emotion regulation and for practitioners and parents to teach it.

Whereas we all experience emotions, it is important to understand that children can differ significantly in regard to how they experience emotions, how they interpret those emotions and experiences, and the ways in which they utilize and manage them. Young people, as they get older, are learning to regulate their emotions and, although they may be the same age or at the same grade level, they may be at different stages in the process. Teachers may interpret expression of certain emotions as "immature," or may see intensity when expressing emotion as immature rather than as a temperamental quality or emotional style.

Individual students, and adults for that matter, have different cognitive abilities, capacities, knowledge, and abilities to use strategies to regulate emotions. This is complicated by the fact that some individuals, including parents and teachers, who have developed a strong capability to manage emotion have little tolerance for, or understanding of, others who are less able to do so.

Another reason for learning about emotion regulation is that it can be thought of as a way to understand the role of emotion in our lives and in the lives of children. It helps us understand how emotions affect our attention and behavior to foster or impede growth and functioning. Emotion serves as a motivator (Cole, Martin, et al. 2004). Some students who worry about performing poorly work harder so that failure is avoided. Others avoid doing their class work and assignments because in some way that helps them tolerate their anxiety. Both researchers and practitioners want to know more about how students regulate their thinking, their emotions, and their behavior. Beyond this, we need to know how we can help students develop, improve, and utilize this critical set of regulatory skills and abilities to deal with emotion.

In school settings and in educational psychology, understanding emotion regulation has a very practical goal. We want to be able to teach and/or facilitate the development of regulation skills and abilities in children and adolescents. The importance of appropriately regulating one's emotions cannot be overstated. Given its importance, it is time for school psychologists and other mental health professionals who are involved with children to become aware of what is known about the processes involved in regulating emotions.

We need to know how we might use that knowledge to help students who may lack experience or training in emotion regulation or for whom emotional control may be more challenging given their individual biology. We want to be able to help other school staff understand the connection between emotion regulation and general adjustment, healthy socialization, positive relationships with others, and academic success. School psychologists understand the connection between students' social and emotional needs and their academic performance, but others may not as yet appreciate that connection. School administrators and teachers may not yet fully appreciate the value of counseling or training services to help students learn to regulate emotion. Given the pressures for improving academic achievement, school staff may be reluctant to share their class time with mental health providers or to allot time in their already packed schedules for social-emotional learning in an atmosphere of high-stakes testing (Perry and Weinstein 1998). This, too, is a challenge we face.

Chapter 2
Emotional Dysregulation

Emotion Regulation Gone Wrong

Underdeveloped Emotion Regulation

Successful accomplishment of the developmental tasks of childhood and adolescence requires emotion regulation, and the ability to regulate their emotions translates into physical and mental health for students. Taking a look at what can happen when age-appropriate emotion regulation has not been achieved will clarify the importance of emotion regulation in work with children and adolescents.

The failure to regulate emotion is called dysregulation. When temporary, it can cause symptoms of anxiety, possibly even intense discomfort, poorly controlled behavior, and/or withdrawal. If poor regulation is fairly constant, it can be manifested in the disorders we observe in some children (Dodge and Garber 1991). Dysregulated emotion is entwined with many of the psychological disorders we identify in young people; in fact, according to Gross (1998b), it is implicated in many of the disorders described in the *Diagnostic and Statistical Manual of the American Psychiatric Association* (DSM). It is involved in *more than half* of the DSM-IV Axis I disorders and in all of the Axis II disorders, and it has been called a *hallmark* of psychopathology (Beauchaine, Gatzke-Kopp, and Mead 2006).

Patterns of emotion regulation that strongly interfere with competence can become symptoms of a disorder. They can also place a student at risk for developing a disorder or for having problematic interpersonal relationships (Shipman et al. 2004). For example, problems regulating negative emotions are related to internalizing disorders such as anxiety and/or depression, and difficulty with a negative emotion such as anger may be related to externalizing disorders or "acting out" (Gross, 1998b). Emotion dysregulation is actually related to both types of problems; i.e., internalizing and externalizing behaviors. Children who exhibit behaviors associated with internalizing and/or externalizing disorders generally exhibit *more extreme* and *more frequent* emotions.

Negative affect is more important than positive affect when considering psychopathology (Sim and Zeman 2006). Difficulty dissipating or decreasing negative emotions is associated with both internalizing and externalizing difficulties. This can be thought of as a problem of calming down or simply down regulating emotions (Silk, Shaw, Lane, Unikel, and Kovacs 2005). It is important to keep in mind that the exact etiology of self-regulatory problems is probably a function of many variables acting together (Behncke 2002). Difficulty with emotion regulation is problematic but is certainly not the only cause of identifiable disorders of childhood.

Emotion dysregulation plays a role in:

- Physiological disorders
- Biologically based disorders
- Disorders caused by stress
- Psychological disorders

One should keep in mind that many "psychological disorders" are strongly connected to biology. It is helpful to explore some of the cognitive variables such as negative emotionality, effortful control, and attention that complicate a child's ability to develop age-appropriate emotion regulation.

Physiological Symptoms and Disorders

There are multiple physiological symptoms and disorders associated with emotion dysregulation. Some of these include: (a) pain, (b) smoking, (c) cutting, (d) eating disorders, and (e) addiction. Researchers have demonstrated a connection between physiological complaints and negative emotionality (Hagekull and Bohlin 2004). Some children experience decreased ability to regulate pain. Recurrent abdominal pain is a common physical complaint, experienced by 10 to 30 percent of school-age children. Children who have poor pain regulation focus on pain, feel it to a greater extent than their peers, and do not cope well with it (Boyer, Compas, Stanger, Colletti, Konik, Morrow, and Thomsen 2005). The role of emotion dysregulation in the development of somatoform disorders, where the primary symptom is pain that is not part of any identifiable disorder, has been explored. Waller and Scheidt (2006) connect these disorders to a decreased ability to experience and differentiate emotions as well as to the inability to express emotions in a healthy manner.

Adolescents who do not cope well with anger may use cigarettes as way to manage emotion. Nicotine decreases the intensity and frequency of felt anger, and this is especially notable in adolescents with a high level of hostility (Audrain-McGovern, Rodgiguez, Tercyak, Neuner, and Moss 2006). Negative emotions cause adolescents to fail should they decide to try to stop smoking. Anxiety increases smoking behaviors, as smoking helps individuals who experience anxiety feel better (Tice, Bratslavsky, and Baumeister 2001). These relationships help explain at least in part why some adolescents are more inclined to start smoking and why it is difficult for others to quit. As soon as the adolescent who has given up cigarettes is faced with a stressful situation, the old habit of using smoking to feel better may prevail.

Negative affect is tightly connected to clinical and subclinical eating disorders. Chronic negative feelings and negative mood along with difficulty identifying and naming one's emotional states places young people at risk for using eating behaviors to regulate negative emotions (Sim and Zeman 2006). Children and adolescents with eating disorders experience a cycle involving emotion and food so that emotional distress results in eating, which in turn, leads to increased distress, which triggers even more eating.

Behavioral control of many types breaks down when moods are negative. Negative moods result in regulatory failure before, during, and after treatment. For example, during treatment, efforts to stop drinking alcohol are more successful when negative emotions can be kept under control. Inability to tolerate certain emotional states has been associated with several other disorders and behaviors including cutting, binging, and excessive exercise with vomiting (Whiteside, Hunter, Dunn, Palmquist, and Naputi 2003). When associated with eating disorders, this model ties eating disorders in particular with difficulty in emotion regulation once an adolescent becomes upset. Fresco, Wolfson, Crowther, and Docherty (2002) describe problems with eating disorders caused by worry, and indicate that binging and purging are used to reduce intense emotion. The same research group reports a connection between generalized anxiety disorders and deficits in adaptive emotion regulation.

Role of Emotional Dysregulation in Many Childhood Disorders

Many childhood disorders involve difficulties with emotion regulation, and a quick review of the list will make that clear. Emotional dysregulation is a significant marker for both externalizing and internalizing disorders. The concept of externalizing disorders refers to conduct or disruptive disorders, whereas internalizing disorders refers to emotional problems or any mood disorder (Gjone and Stevenson 1997; Martin 2003). Figure 2.1 lists a number of specific emotion regulation weaknesses associated with both internalizing and externalizing disorders.

Of course, it is important to keep in mind that the distinction between internalizing and externalizing disorders is complicated. Several disorders can be present at once; moreover, it has been determined that all externalizing disorders are related to anxiety disorders (Marmorstein 2007). The association between externalizing disorders is stronger for boys than for girls and at younger ages. For example, according to Marmorstein (2007), there is a strong association between social phobia and all the externalizing disorders as well as between oppositional defiant disorder and overanxious disorder.

Students with Internalizing Disorders

Exhibit more extreme emotions, too intense for the situation.
Exhibit emotion more frequently.
Have difficulty decreasing negative emotions.
Have difficulty down-regulating emotion (Silk, Shaw, et al. 2005).
Have difficulty inhibiting emotional expression.
Have difficulty understanding emotional experiences.
Experience more negative emotions.
Are less able to calm themselves.
Are biased toward negative or threatening cues.
Choose irrelevant, avoidant, or aggressive strategies to deal with negative emotions.
Do not appreciate that it is possible to change emotional experiences.

Students with Externalizing Disorders

Exhibit more extreme emotions.
Exhibit emotion more frequently.
Have difficulty decreasing negative emotions.
Have difficulty down-regulating emotion (Silk et al. 2005).
Have difficulty identifying emotional cues.
Have weak emotional understanding and expression.
Do not easily recognize their own emotions.
Tend to focus on the negative aspects of situations.
Have difficulty with attentional control.
Have difficulty inhibiting behavior.
Use aggressive strategies to deal with negative emotions.

(Individual students may exhibit some or many of these symptoms.)

Fig. 2.1 Emotion Regulation Weaknesses Associated with Internalizing and Externalizing Disorders

Borderline Personality Disorder

The most extreme example of emotion dysregulation may well be borderline personality disorder; in fact, "emotional regulation disorder" has been proposed as a more clearly descriptive label (Fleener 1999). Finley-Belgrad and Davies (2006) note that if symptoms are observed over time and a student meets the criteria for borderline personality disorder, it is appropriate to make the diagnosis in children and adolescents. Personality disorders that begin in childhood may be diagnosed if symptoms have been present for at least a year (Ellett, n.d.). Today, borderline personality disorder is thought to be either genetic or caused by both genes and environmental triggers (TARA-APD 2004).

The child or adolescent with borderline personality disorder is primarily unable to regulate his or her emotions. Given that the central issue is emotion dysregulation, children at risk for it and adolescents with the disorder react more intensely and have a particularly hard time returning to a neutral state after upset. These boys and girls are demanding, unpredictable in relationships, immature, and suspicious (Kernberg, Weiner, and Bardenstrein 2000, p. 139). Symptoms of borderline personality disorder have been identified in children as early as fourth to sixth grade (Crick, Murray-Close, and Woods 2005), and such students can be expected to display a combination of externalizing, internalizing, and cognitive symptoms such as executive dysfunctions (Finley-Belgrad and Davies 2006).

Autism Spectrum Disorders

Some researchers have concluded that the problems of children with autism spectrum disorders stem from disorganization and dysregulation, and clearly, the regulation of play is particularly affected in this group. Children with autism may suddenly stop interacting and appear to lose focus. They change behaviors as the action continues, which is disconcerting for peers. They present better and are more successful in interaction with their peers if an adult structures the play (Blanc, Adrien, Roux, and Barthelemy 2005).

Bipolar Disorder

Children with bipolar disorder appear to have poorly regulated arousal systems, and they exhibit pronounced failures of emotion regulation. The complications that may arise from a poorly regulated arousal system include: (a) difficulty managing aggressive impulses, (b) problems with sleep arousal, (c) elevated anxiety and sensitivity, and (d) difficulty managing anger (Papolos and Papolos 2005).

Attention-Deficit Hyperactivity Disorder

From a behavioral point of view, attention-deficit hyperactivity disorder (ADHD) is primarily a disorder of self-regulation. Certainly, children with the combined type of ADHD exhibit emotional dysregulation to a pronounced degree and demonstrate intense negative and positive behaviors as well as impaired self-control (Casey and Durston 2006; Chen and Taylor 2005; Maedgen and Carlson 2000; Voeller 2004; Walcott and Landau 2004).

Young people with ADHD are not as skilled as their peers in identifying and regulating emotions and often feel frustrated. Although they understand a good deal about emotions they are less able to identify how to respond to frustration and do not seem to be able to use coping strategies *while* embroiled in emotional situations. It is important to teach them behavioral skills, but they also must learn strategies for regulating emotions (Scime and Norvilitis 2006). Some students with ADHD also exhibit oppositional behaviors and are particularly reactive to the negative emotions of anger and hostility.

Aggressive Students

Aggressive students have been found to have problems identifying emotional cues in those with whom they are interacting (Bear, Manning, and Izard 2003). Conduct disordered students with poor control or poor self-regulation, as reported by their teachers, exhibit more behavior problems, have more angry interactions with their peers, and exhibit both anger problems and aggression (Tangney 2004). Students identified as having conduct problems have poor emotion regulation along with weak emotional understanding and expression.

A series of studies reported by several researchers indicates that students with conduct problems experience emotion more intensely than their peers, have more difficulty matching emotions to social cues, are more likely than their peers to feel angry when shown videos that might trigger anger, do not respond as well as their peers to cues used to recognize their own feelings, and tend to not only focus on the negative aspects of situations but to vent emotionally (Fainsilber and Windecker-Nelson 2004; Katz and Windecker-Nelson 2004). Interestingly, girls with conduct disorders may be aware of the power that their intense behavior has over others. Many of them seem to understand that dysregulated behavior provides rewards in both attention from and power over others because their behavior is so intimidating (Kostiuk and Fouts 2002).

Often girls and boys who are at risk for conduct disorders and aggression but have not yet been identified as having these disorders have difficulty with emotion regulation. Those at risk for externalizing problems exhibit more negative emotions, less regulated emotions, and less regulated behaviors than children at low risk (Calkins and Dedmon, 2000). Dennis and Brotman (2003b) indicate that attention and inhibition make independent contributions to whether or not a child will respond with aggression. It is important to identify individual differences in ability to regulate emotion in order to understand a child's risk for psychopathology (Smith 2002).

Internalizing Disorders

Children with externalizing disorders, including ADHD, substance abuse, oppositional disorders, conduct problems, aggression, and even Tourette syndrome evidence problems with emotion regulation and self-control in general (Chen and Taylor 2005). But, it is not only children with externalizing disorders who have difficulty with emotion regulation; those with internalizing disorders also have difficulty managing their emotions. Young people with anxie orders have little understanding that it is possible to change their emotional experience and very little idea of how to inhibit emotional expression (Shipman et al. 2004). Young people with depressive disorders have difficulty regulating negative emotions.

Anxiety and depression appear to be related: in children, anxiety precedes depression. Children and adolescents with internalizing disorders seem to process emotional information differently than their peers, focusing attention on negative or threatening information. Youngsters who develop anxiety disorders focus on *threatening* cues in their environment, whereas children who become depressed are *biased toward negative emotional information* and cannot seem to suppress negative emotion (Beauregard et al. 2004: Ladouceur, Dahl, Williamson, Birmaher, Ryan, and Casey 2005).

Generalized Anxiety Disorder

Emotion dysregulation has been proposed as a central feature in generalized anxiety disorder (GAD). Youngsters with generalized anxiety have difficulty understanding emotional experiences and have little skill or ability to modulate their intense emotions (Mennin, 2006). Not only do they experience more intense emotions than their peers, they are more negative, are less able to calm themselves, and have more physiological symptoms after an anxiety-producing experience (Mennin, Heimberg, Turk, and Fresco 2005). Anxious ambivalent children have difficulty regulating emotions so that their arousal is too intense for the situation, and they both misidentify and misdirect their emotions (Kostiuk and Fouts 2002).

Children and adolescents with anxiety disorders have difficulty handling worries, sadness, and anger. This may be due to the intense degree to which they experience negative emotions. They generally have little confidence in their ability to deal with intensely aroused negative emotions (Suveg and Zeman 2004).

Depressive Disorders

Depressive disorders are very common, with one in five adolescents showing symptoms of unipolar depression before they complete secondary school and one in eleven evidencing depression by the end of middle school. Depressive *symptoms* are even more common, with 10–19 percent of adolescents reporting symptoms at moderate to high levels. It is important to note that young people with significant symptoms of depression appear very much as clinically depressed individuals in regard to social interactions (Gillham, Reivich, Freres, Lascher, Litzinger, Shatté, et al. 2006). Low self-esteem appears to be a clear risk factor for depression in early adolescence, with girls who act out and girls brought up in families who live in lower socioeconomic areas being particularly vulnerable (MacPhee and Andrews 2006).

As difficult as negative emotions may be for children with internalizing disorders, depressed juveniles do not process *positive* emotional information in the same way as their peers. Moreover, they avoid approach-related behavior (Ladouceur et al. 2005). Rottenberg and Gross (2003) remind us that emotional numbing occurs in individuals who are depressed. A study of depressed adolescents (Silk, Steinberg, and Morris 2003) showed that these young people experienced more intense and variable emotions than their typically developing peers. They were not as competent in regulating their emotions, self-reported more depressive symptoms, and exhibited difficult behaviors. There appear to be differences in girls who are depressed as compared to boys. It is well known that adolescent females report more depressive symptoms and have more difficulty controlling ruminating behaviors than boys. When ruminating, girls think negative thoughts over and over and have significant difficulty thinking in healthier ways (Thayer, Rossy, Ruiz-Padial, and Johnsen 2003).

In general, depressed young people use different and less effective methods for dealing with negative emotions. The strategies they choose to deal with issues and feelings are usually irrelevant or more physically aggressive. They tend to prefer avoidance strategies, such as sleeping or doing nothing, when they do not choose aggressive ones. These children do not believe that what they might think of to do to help themselves will work, nor do they think that the strategies that adults might suggest will work for them. This negative self-efficacy belief, combined with a lack of strategic knowledge, makes it very difficult for depressed juveniles to reduce negative emotions.

A key challenge for these young people is recovering from negative moods. Although they do experience some positive moods, the negative moods cause extensive problems (Garber, Braafladt, and Zeman 1991). Pessimism is associated with efforts to reduce unpleasant feelings when a child is stressed rather than problem solving. In fact, pessimistic students disengage from their goals when they are stressed. Optimism, on the other hand, appears to be a buffer for school stress. Students with optimistic mindsets cope better and report less academic stress (Huan, Yeo, Ang, and Chong 2006).

Negative Emotionality, Effortful Control, and Attention

Negative emotions can be a primary cause of pain and dysfunction among children and adolescents (Beauregard 2004). Negative affect is a mix of moods and emotions such as anger, distress, and agitation, and is prevalent in both externalizing and internalizing disorders. In fact, negative emotionality is a key component of both types of disorders. Students with either type of disorder, or both, experience considerably more anger than their peers, and their negative emotionality is extreme. Externalizing children have difficulty expressing emotion in appropriate ways, particularly negative emotion, which they in turn manage poorly. They experience intense anger and irritability.

Students who internalize tend to experience more intense sadness, depression, anxiety, and fear. They act out when they cannot meet their needs in any other way. They are angrier, sadder, and more fearful than their typical classmates. They deal with even more negative emotion as they get older and become even less well adjusted over time. Their difficulties with negative emotionality as they grow older has been (at least in part) linked to experiences in which they have not been successful in regulating emotions (Eisenberg, Sadovsky, et al. 2005). Ability to suppress negative emotion determines a student's tendency toward aggression (Davidson, Putnam, and Larson 2000).

Fox and Calkins (2003) suggest that three variables are related to emotion regulation:

- Executive functions
- Effortful control
- Attention

These three general cognitive processes affect an individual's ability to control emotion.

First, two types of executive functioning are particularly important: self-directedness or drive and performance control. The latter must be brought to bear before initiating behavior; it must be utilized while the behavior is being carried out and then brought to bear later, after the behavior or task has been terminated. Fox (1998) indicates that other executive functions, including switching set (changing behavior or thinking midstream), planning, generating alternative responses, or strategies to reach goals, may be involved as well.

Second, effortful control is involved as the child's ability to inhibit responding or not to respond to environmental triggers comes into play. It is also related to the ability to remain vigilant. These control processes regulate behavioral tendencies to approach or avoid situations. They also relate to whether or not a child will react to positive or negative emotions. Effortful control is required so that the child can act against a tendency to react in a particular manner, so that his or her behavior in a given context is appropriate. Regulating an emotional response requires effort, just as controlling impulses requires it (Fox and Calkins 2003).

Conduct problems in students are associated with poor skills in effortful control, weak inhibition, and difficulties sustaining attention (Dennis and Brotman 2003b). Students with externalizing disorders are low in all kinds of effortful control (Eisenberg, Sadovsky, et al. 2005). Studies indicate that effortful control in typically developing children rises sharply at around four years of age. This rise is related to a developing ability to modulate impulsivity, in which the child is becoming more competent through the use of strategies taught by the parents. At this age children work to control all behavior, but as they get older they tend to exert effortful control when anxious. There are clear age and individual differences in self-regulation. Young people who internalize exert efforts in anticipation, ahead of encountering a stressor (Lewis and Stieben 2004). Those who externalize act first and think afterward.

Third, studies show that attentional processes are involved when emotional information is processed. The ability to focus attention is related to emotional self-control. Attention used in this context refers to executive attention control. Children with stronger ability to focus attention and thus have lower distractibility are more likely to experience positive rather than negative emotions. They are also more likely to approach their peers in a positive way and remain engaged once they are interacting with others. They are comfortable asking others to play and can follow the action of the game. Young people with better ability to control their attention are also better at controlling their emotions. They remain in control when the play action does not go their way. In order to shift attention away from stressful negative triggers toward something positive, executive attention must be under conscious control (Fox and Calkins 2003; Ladouceur et al. 2005).

Externalizing juveniles have difficulties with attentional processes that relate to dealing with negative emotions. Children who internalize have difficulty shifting their attention away from cues or triggers in the environment that cause them distress. The ability to shift attention is involved not only in social interactions but in academic contexts as well (Eisenberg et al. 2005). A weak ability to control attention by shifting it or refocusing predicts behavioral difficulties in both early and middle childhood. When a child can focus on something positive and can draw his or her attention away from negative stimuli or away from something threatening, he or she will function better. Young people who have stronger tendencies to be drawn to negative emotions are most in need of attention control in order to deal with feelings of anger and tendencies to act out (Shipman et al. 2004). The ability to shift attention from negative toward neutral or positive stimuli appears to be especially important in *shutting down* negative emotion (Eisenberg, Sadovsky, Spinrad, Fabes, et al. 2005).

Attention may be the key connection between emotion regulation and processing social situations. Attention is required in order to organize thoughts and feelings to fit a given context. Students with poor attention regulation are at a disadvantage in social situations and demonstrate problems in social competence. They are less well liked by their peers and less well accepted (Gross, 1998b; Parke, Simpkins, McDowell, Kim, Killian, Dennis, Flyr, Wild, and Rah 2002). It has been demonstrated at several different ages that children who lack social competence and children who experience high negative emotionality have low attentional persistence in common (Huizinga, Dolan, and van der Molen 2006). Behavioral inhibition is also linked to executive functions (Davis, A. 2006).

Implications for Helping Students in Schools

Understanding the pervasiveness of difficulties in emotion regulation among students with social and emotional problems and disorders, as well as among children at risk, leads to an awareness of the need to develop interventions to ameliorate some of the stresses that these vulnerable young people have to deal with. Before taking an in-depth look at specific strategies and approaches, it may be helpful to review suggestions made by researchers studying the role that emotional regulation plays in the various disorders described here.

Researchers suggest that students of elementary and middle school age have to be exposed to one of the several evidence-based curricula that directly teach social and emotional competence (Blair 2002). Successful preschool programs have been developed that increase children's knowledge about emotions and help them become more aware of their own and others' emotions (Smith 2002), and there are many social-emotional learning curricula from which to choose. It is important to research the effectiveness of a program and to match the curriculum to local needs.

For elementary school-aged students, specific skills such as how to distract and soothe or calm oneself are important. Listing the positives and negatives of stressful or potentially stressful events and situations, learning to act differently from the way one has acted in the past, and "negotiating" are skills that have to be taught (Miller 2002). Since anger is often the result of blocked goals, it is important to teach children to think of more appropriate ways to get what they want or need (Fox 1998). It is vitally important for aggressive children to master the ability to inhibit behavior, as children with externalizing disorders have specific deficits in this area and their anger will fluctuate more when they cannot inhibit behavior (Dennis and Brotman 2003a; Hoeksma, Oosterlaan, and Shipper 2004). A program that improves parents' awareness of emotion may be particularly important for families that include younger children with behavior problems (Fainsilber and Windecker-Nelson 2004).

Cognitive-behavioral interventions and cognitive restructuring (thinking about stressors in a different, more positive way) are frequently recommended for decreasing negative affect for late-elementary, middle school, and high school students (Chen and Taylor 2005; Dodge and Garber 1991; Miller, Williams, and McCoy 2004). More specific skills such as shifting attention toward positive moods, activities, and events are important, as are engaging in pleasant activities, problem solving, utilizing available resources, and techniques for questioning one's negative thinking (Garber et al. 1991; Ladouceur et al. 2005; Woller 2006).

Group interventions that teach stress tolerance, improve interpersonal skills, and help students become more aware have been recommended, along with improving emotion perception and interpretation, goal setting, generating alternative responses, and evaluating behavioral responses (Garber et al. 1991; TARA-APD 2004). Prevention programs developed for adolescents that may be helpful include problem solving, coping with anger, examining the consequences of behavior before acting upon emotions, and refusal skills training (Audrain-McGovern et al. 2006).

More specific interventions may be needed for the most involved students and those identified with disorders. For example, teaching adults to model facial expressions when interacting with children who have autistic spectrum disorders is important because these students do not spontaneously display the emotions they are experiencing. They do not always understand tone of voice or read body language well. Teaching children with autism to distract themselves by engaging in motorically active behaviors is likely to be an effective strategy and can sometimes be taught easily (Bryson, Landry, Czapinski, McConnell, Rombough, and Wainwright 2004).

Specific strategies will be needed to help all children cope with stress and negative emotions. Research with individuals who have serious illnesses provides some information about the strategies that may be helpful. The literature on coping with cancer in childhood, for instance, has identified some specific strategies that are important:

- An optimistic outlook
- A minimizing perspective
- Problem solving
- Positively reinterpreting situations
- Self-restraint
- Finding social support

These have been demonstrated to be helpful, along with a belief that one is capable of coping successfully (Livneh 2000).

There are several considerations in regard to interventions and teaching approaches. First, a universal intervention designed for all students with the goal of teaching them about emotions and their regulation could not only serve as a prevention tool for typically developing children, but would also be helpful for students who are already exhibiting difficulties with emotion regulation. Second, more focused and targeted interventions may be needed for students with identified difficulties. Third, the intervention must be matched with specific needs. For some children, control of behavior or training inhibition must be added to emotion regulation strategies. For others, the appropriate ways to express emotion must be taught. For still others, enlisting a parent will greatly enhance the power of the intervention.

Chapter 3
Understanding the Biology of Emotion and Using this Knowledge to Develop Interventions

Brain-Body Connections

David Servan-Schreiber of the University of Pittsburgh School of Medicine (Center for Educational Research and Innovation 2003) reminds us that there are three influences on the human brain. The first is physical, a function of the effect of nutrition and exercise on the brain's ability to act, learn, and attend to the environment; the second is made up of social interaction and social learning; and the third is emotional and involves the management of stress and conflict as well as general emotional control. He contends that our schools could make improvements in all three areas that would enhance the brain's ability to function well in a learning environment.

Researchers and educators are increasingly interested in the relationship of emotion and emotion regulation to the learning environment and to mental health in general. In order to increase understanding of emotion, at least a cursory exploration of the biology of emotion may be helpful. First, some understanding of the connection between brain and body makes emotion less mysterious and possibly more controllable. Second, it may help us understand some child behaviors that we may not immediately connect to emotion. Third, an age-appropriate understanding of the connections among emotion, bodily sensations, and behavior is helpful to the students we work with, as well as to the teachers and parents who work with them in turn.

Affective Style

Davidson, Putnam, et al. (2000) coined the concept of "affective style" to help clarify individual differences in regard to emotion, emotion regulation, and behavior: "Affective style is a term that refers to consistent individual differences in the various parameters that govern emotional reactivity" (Davidson, Putnam, et al. 2000, p. 591). Young people are not all the same. They can feel and respond very differently when exposed to the same situations. Students participating in team sports react differently to the loss of an important game. One might experience intense anger, blaming the referee and coaches for 'bad' calls or the other team for cheating. Another may feel very disappointed but have sufficient emotion control to congratulate members of the other team and to reassure his teammates that they played their best. When a student exhibits similar emotions in specific contexts, Davidson identifies these differences as affective style.

Think of a positive or negative stimulus such as an exciting point in a game, opening a gift, being yelled at by peers, taking a test, or walking along a dangerous road to or from school. Different children will begin to experience emotion at different points during these episodes. Some may react by experiencing an emotion such as anger or fear or excitement well before others experience a similar emotion. In the same way, some youngsters experience emotion arising slowly in regard to events or situations, whereas others experience intense feelings very quickly. Some children when provoked may react with aggression immediately. Others, who have been taught by parents not to express anger, may not even feel angry for some time after the provocation.

Some children reach emotions of much greater intensity than others, whether or not their emotions arise quickly or at a more moderate pace. For some young people, the rise time and the peak of intensity are related for some emotions, but perhaps not for all of them. Children may experience anger and sadness differently in regard to rise time and peak of intensity. Some return to a neutral state faster than others. Some students, for example, do not calm down after being upset for an unusually long time, stressing and frustrating their teachers and parents who may consider them immature, stubborn, or unreasonable. For others, recovery is fast. Finally, some children may be able to get their behavioral reactions under control well before their heart rate slows or their facial muscles relax (Davidson, 1998).

We know that some of the students we work with are far more vulnerable than others when reacting to what happens to them, what they anticipate happening to them, or what has already occurred. An individual's affective style includes: (a) threshold, (b) peak, (c) rise time to peak, and (d) recovery (Davidson, 1998).

Differences in affective style also help us understand differences in a student's susceptibility to rewards versus punishments (Davidson 2000). For example, school-aged children with conduct problems appear to have reward insensitivity, also called "weak approach motivation" (Beauchaine, Gatzke-Kopp, et al. 2006). A tendency toward conduct-disordered behavior is related to poor emotion regulations skills (Buckley et al., 2003).

Developmental Changes in the Brain

Affective style implies stable individual differences, yet there is significant brain plasticity such that the environment can affect brain functioning. In fact, environmental influences can be very powerful and, if they last long enough, can produce permanent changes in the brain. Studies of children between the ages of three and eleven showed that identifiable changes had taken place in their brains; their baseline prefrontal activation asymmetry was not stable (Davidson and Rickman 1999). The central brain circuitry of emotion continues to change until puberty, and the prefrontal cortex undergoes significant developmental changes during this period (Davidson, 2001; Huttenlocher 1990).

Adolescence is the period during which affect regulation becomes functionally mature. Changes at this time also help clarify some of the ways in which behavioral health problems occur. The fact that emotions influence decision making during adolescence helps us understand alcohol use and drug dependence. Clinical disorders of emotion dysregulation increase at this time and gender differences in disorders such as depression first become evident (Dahl, 2001).

Brain Structures

We have a much better idea about the areas of the brain that are involved in emotional learning and emotion circuitry than we did even a relatively short time ago. Researchers have identified some of the brain structures connected to the various aspects of affective style. These include the amygdala and the prefrontal cortex, which are the two primary neural brain areas involved in the circuitry of emotion (Davidson, Jackson, and Kalin 2000), and the hippocampus. More and more research points to the link between the prefrontal cortex and the amygdala in controlling emotion (Hariri and Holmes 2006). Any abnormality in the complex circuits of the brain that regulate emotion can cause problems (Davidson, Jackson, et al. 2000). The three brain structures of interest and their various roles in emotional learning are represented in Fig. 3.1.

The Amygdala

The amygdala, a small almond-shaped structure, is located in the anterior part of the temporal lobe. It is triggered when we feel threatened by another's

Areas of the Brain Involved in Emotional Learning	
Amygdala	Generates fear and arousal Aversive learning Influences attention & perception
Prefrontal Cortex	Controls emotion recovery time Includes executive functions
Hippocampus	Context-dependent emotional learning Factual learning Long-term memory

Fig. 3.1 Areas of the brain involved in emotional learning

comments, we become aware someone moving toward us, or someone stares at us with a stern expression. The amygdala is an important piece of the circuitry that regulates emotion, particularly negative emotions, and generates feelings of fear and arousal (Davis, A. 2006). Several different external and internal signals cause it to activate: (a) fear conditioning, (b) someone's frightened facial expression, or (c) negative emotions that result from observing something upsetting in the environment.

The amygdala is more responsive to fear than anger and is involved in learning to connect events that are punishing or rewarding. If it is activated too much or not enough, a person might experience extreme negative emotion or a decrease in sensitivity to social cues that might otherwise ameliorate emotion.

There are individual differences in the degree to which the amygdala is activated, and this is significant. Anxious individuals have been shown to have more activation in the amygdala when they sense fearful stimuli consciously and this same reaction occurs when they sense threat unconsciously. Symptoms of posttraumatic stress disorder—intense arousal, intrusive thoughts, and nightmares—are related to a hyperactivated amygdala. There are some individual and gender differences as well. Girls who have been traumatized tend to feel that they are in more danger than boys, blame themselves, and experience more intense symptoms of distress (Kruczek and Salsman 2006). The amygdala sends a signal when conflict is detected that interferes with the person's ability to perform a task until that activity is dampened (Etkin, Egner, Peraza, Kandel, and Hirsch 2006).

The baseline rate of activation is important because the resting level is associated with negative disposition structure. The amygdala is active even during sleep (Davidson 1998). Activation at baseline (or rest) and in reaction to negative feelings in response to the environment explains how fast aversive learning takes place, how readily contexts are recalled in which negative affect occurred, and how negative individuals say they feel. Young people who are more sensitive to negative feelings or environmental threats quickly learn to avoid situations. When youngsters highly sensitive to threat sense danger, they readily distrust situations or individuals and experience heightened anxiety.

The amygdala protects us as it recognizes cues of danger such as vocal expressions of fear and anger. It is also involved in new learning of stimulus–punishment contingencies. When a teacher looks at a student with an angry or exasperated expression, that student needs to understand that his or her behavior must stop. The amygdala is involved in expressing cue-specific fears as in when a child reacts with fear to the sight of a large dog approaching and barking loudly (Davidson, Putnam, et al. 2000). If the amygdala was not functioning well, an individual would not react with appropriate fear, nor would he remember the fear previously associated with an event as well as others.

Reactivity and the ability to regulate emotions appear to have a genetic basis. When under stress, heritable differences in reactivity would make a person more vulnerable to negative emotions that could over time result in emotional disorders (Hariri and Holmes 2006). When students with behavioral inhibition have been studied, researchers have found that there is heightened activity in the amygdalae, in reaction to situations that they perceive as threatening. Behavior inhibition causes persistent fearful emotions that are also fairly predictable and constant. These anxious students have difficulty adapting socially, are hypervigilant, and tend to hesitate in some situations and to react strongly when encountering something new (Guyer, Nelson, Perez-Edgar, Hardin, Roberson-Nay, Monk, et al. 2006).

Depressed children attend more closely to negative events and thoughts. They become sensitized to attend to the negative situations, events, and interpersonal encounters they meet in their experiences. Researchers suggest that youngsters who show symptoms of disorders that we know often co-occur with depression should be watched for a pattern of behavior in which they pay particular attention to negative indicators in their environment. Some research indicates that a severely depressed child has a smaller amygdala (Davis, A. 2006).

An interesting example of the effect of the environment on the brain is the social fear experience by children with autism. When social fear is intense and experienced over time it can stimulate the amygdala to become hyperactive and grow in size. However, such constant activation kills amygdala cells and shrinks the structure. Adolescents with autism, who have particular difficulty distinguishing emotional expressions in others and seldom look at the eyes of others, have smaller amygdala. The brain structure has changed in response to long-term activation, and researchers have associated shrinkage of this structure with impaired nonverbal social behavior (Nacewicz, Dalton, Johnstone, Long, McAuliff, Oakes, et al. 2006).

The Prefrontal Cortex

There is extensive two-way communication between the amygdala and the second brain structure of interest in the brain's emotional circuitry (Davidson 1998). Davidson, Jackson, et al. (2000) indicate that the second structure, the prefrontal cortex, controls emotional *recovery time*. The prefrontal areas of the brain are involved in "reversal learning," so that the negative emotional feelings and reactions that had activated strong emotion can be changed. Areas in the prefrontal cortex can inhibit activity of the amygdala. Inhibitory actions dampen emotion and prevent what may be inappropriate behavior as a result. Differences in the way in which individuals regulate negative emotion can explain someone's vulnerability to act aggressively (Davidson, Putnam, et al. 2000). It is clear that the prefrontal cortex along with connected brain areas are involved in emotion regulation, most particularly in a child's ability to regulate negative emotion.

The prefrontal cortex allows us to anticipate future outcomes in terms of our emotional response, which may be a type of *affective working memory*. The prefrontal cortex is related to differences in affective style as well. If the amygdala is not checked or inhibited, its high level of activation will fuel the learned negative emotion in response to the perceived threat (Davidson, Jackson, et al. 2000). Children who are sensitive to threat experience anxiety in particular situations and react by freezing, escaping the situation, or fighting. Over time they may become so sensitized that they react without thinking. Once anxious, they may remain anxious for some time. There are clear differences among individuals in their ability to 'turn off' negative emotions after they have been activated. This is evident in students experiencing generalized anxiety and in students who cannot calm down once emotionally triggered for an inordinate amount of time, causing considerable difficulty for school staff as well as for themselves.

Asymmetries in the prefrontal cortex are connected to approach and withdrawal, which are only partially separate self-regulatory systems (Carver 2006). The approach system fosters good feelings, such as those involved when winning a game or getting a high score on a test. The withdrawal system assists a person in getting away from threatening situations by organizing appropriate behavioral responses, such as when a stranger offers a child a ride on the way home from school. The withdrawal system also causes feelings of fear or disgust. Although it may seem that anger would come into play, anger is not grouped with withdrawal emotions because it can result in approach behavior such as striking out. The differences in prefrontal activation asymmetry explain the link between approach and withdrawal.

When the left side of the prefrontal cortex is activated to a greater degree, an individual appears to recover from negative emotion or stress more quickly. The left prefrontal cortex is connected with the approach system and the right one has to do with negative emotions and withdrawal. Interestingly, differences in prefrontal activation asymmetry are also related to immune function (Davidson, Jackson, et al. 2000). Meta-analyses of research studies show us that psychological challenges or threats as seemingly nontraumatizing as school tests can affect our immune response (Segerstrom and Miller 2004).

The prefrontal cortex includes the executive systems of the brain. Executive functions are a group of processes that control thinking and emotions related to goal-directed behaviors. They include initiating actions, inhibiting competing actions, and selecting goals, as well as planning and organizing (Gioia, Isquith, Guy, and Kenworthy 2000). The prefrontal cortex, including the executive functions, is negatively affected by trauma. Given this, trauma that occurs over time in young children can impair the development of emotion regulation and self-control of impulsive responding. Traumatized children have considerable trouble in identifying, labeling, and appropriately expressing feelings (Cole, O'Brien, Gadd, Ristuccia, Wallace, and Gregory 2005).

The Hippocampus

The hippocampus is involved in factual learning and long-term memory storage (Davis, A. 2006). If the hippocampus is not functioning, typically an individual would not make associations among concepts or between situations and sensory input learned in the past, and the person's level of anxiety might not increase appropriately in dangerous situations.

The hippocampus is responsible for context-dependent emotional learning. A child might be terrorized by a bully on the way to school but may not react with nearly the same intensity when a teacher is nearby. A child may respond with intense anger when a stranger makes a critical comment but not when a friend makes a negative comment. Environmental stress produces an increase in cortisol, which damages hippocampal cells. When children have been exposed to trauma over time, they may develop impaired ability to regulate emotions. Such children would tend to interpret a facial expression as angry when someone's face is simply 'hard to read' or appears ambiguous to others (Kruczek and Salsman 2006; Smith 2002).

Negative or traumatic life events can result in impaired context-dependent emotional responses (Davidson, Putnam, et al. 2000). Just as the amygdala can be affected by stress over time, some forms of depression have been shown to cause first hyperactivity of the hippocampus and then shrinkage (McEwen, 2003). Researchers are looking at the hippocampus as they try to determine whether or not interventions such as behavioral therapy or medication influence brain functioning.

Response to Stress

When children or adolescents perceive that they are being threatened in some way, a complex reaction occurs called the *stress response*. This brain-based reaction involving the brain structures already described along with other areas of the brain triggers the commonly called *fight, freeze, or flight* reaction. Unfortunately, very high levels of arousal in the brain's emotional circuits can decrease arousal in other parts such as language areas (Cole et al. 2005). Students who are chronically aroused do not perform well in school.

Stress interferes with coping ability of young people with inhibition-based disorders such as ADHD. When under stress, such children deteriorate and exhibit their worst behaviors. Impulsivity is the order of the day and they cannot utilize metacognitive strategies they may have learned previously or recall what they have learned in other situations or contexts to deal with the current situation. When under stress, they are unable to self-regulate their emotions and have difficulty with attention regulation and energy mobilization, so they may present as disinterested, off-task, uncaring, or unmotivated (Crundwell 2006).

When a child who already is exhibiting poor emotion regulation is placed under stress, it will be especially difficult for him or her to recover from that stress. Moreover, the student with poor emotion regulation will have difficulty coping with stress flexibly (Shore 1994) and will not be able to shift from a strategy that is not working to one that might be more appropriate. When intensely frustrated, such a student's response may be to tear up or scribble on his paper rather than to put down his pencil and think about something else for a few moments. When very stressed or when being teased, the student may strike out instead of dealing with the upset in a manner that will keep him out of trouble.

Emotion Regulation, Stress, and Impulse Control

There is some interesting research examining the relationship between affect regulation, stress, and impulsive behavior in well-controlled studies, which may be helpful in understanding real-life behaviors of some children and adolescents. A young person's ability to control his or her emotions and behavior tends to diminish or break down when stress is intense or acute. Theory suggests that there are several possible explanations for this. It may be that distress leads to self-destructive or risky behaviors, such as driving too fast or punishing oneself by taking too heavy a dose of drugs, legal or illegal. In this case, emotional distress interferes with logical thinking. Children and adolescents experiencing emotional distress may not think of the consequences of their behavior *or* may abandon goal-directed behavior. Under stress they may no longer regulate their behavior toward goals *at all*. Still another theory suggests that under stress they may use *all* of their resources to deal with emotions and will have none left to regulate behavior. Or, it may be that stress impairs motivation rather than capacity, or that stress engenders rebellion (Tice et al. 2001).

Many adults may describe a a stressed child's behavior as irrational. Tice et al. (2001) conducted a series of experiments to explore their contention that a juveniles's behavior when stressed may actually be strategic rather than irrational. They proposed that when stressed, normal behavioral self-regulation is overridden by a need to regulate emotion. They contend that this occurs because the need to 'feel better' takes precedence over other needs that would necessitate continuing to feel bad in the current situation in order to work toward longer-term goals. Reaching long-term goals depends on controlling impulsive behavior, and the appeal of feeling better in the present overcomes that of the longer-term goal.

Looking at impulsive and self-centered behaviors in this way suggests that negative behaviors do not indicate poor control, but rather are examples of strategic efforts to control emotions. From an interventionists point of view this suggests that when some children exhibit impulsive behavior, the underlying emotions need to be addressed in order to change the resultant behavior.

Several experiments were designed and implemented to explore this theory. Tice et al. (2001) looked at several impulsive behaviors in reaction to feeling bad:

- Eating to relieve depressed feelings.
- Seeking immediate gratification by earning a smaller reward now versus a bigger reward later.
- Procrastination instead of studying for a test.

The hope of immediately accessing good feelings makes it challenging to resist immediate gratification. The goal to feel better right now is urgent in some children. The greater the stress, the more they are pushed toward the immediate goal of feeling better. The need to relieve stress and to regulate emotions over-whelms any attempts at impulse control even when the possibility of feeling better is unlikely, at least for feeling better for very long. Students may think that eating junk food, obtaining an immediate reward, or distracting themselves with an interesting activity rather than studying will result in feeling better because they believe that these enjoyable distracting behaviors will change their moods.

Studies indicate that mood change does not happen beyond the immediate feeling as one engages in the desired behavior. Resorting to impulsive behavior to repair mood does not work very well. The worse students felt, the more likely they were to engage in impulsive, pleasure-seeking behaviors. However, when researchers convinced their subjects that impulsive behavior would only change their moods for a very short time, they were more able to regulate their behavior. Researchers convinced their student subjects that their moods would return to a depressed level immediately after they indulged in the desired behavior such as eating, taking a small immediate reward, or getting involved in a pleasant distracting activity instead of studying for a test (Tice et al. 2001).

Tice et al. (2001) have provided evidence that a common reaction to stress is to seek pleasurable experiences to feel better. The need for emotion regula-tion overrides the desire to control impulses. The need to regulate emotions conflicts with behavioral self-control under distress, which people resolve by acting impulsively even when it may not be in their long-term interests. The work of Tice and his colleagues shows impulsive behaviors to be less irrational and more logical, and it may be very helpful to practitioners attempting to understand and work with students with impulse disorders or issues with procrastination.

Implications

An improved understanding of the biology of emotion can help us in our search for interventions that will be helpful in several ways. Researchers at Ohio State University have demonstrated that something as simple as watching emotional parts of a movie can deplete some of the energy needed to cope with stress and can impact a viewer's ability to do so. It has also been pointed out that stressors can affect an individual's ability to think flexibly (Alexander, Hillier, Smith, Tivarus, and Beversdorf 2005). Students' thinking can be impaired by stress. Relaxation techniques should be taught to students to improve performance in anxiety-provoking school contexts such as during high-stakes testing. Figure 3.2 suggests several relaxation strategies that can be used with students and explains when they should not be used.

Understanding a very simplified version of the biology of fear can be very helpful in assisting students to gain enough time to be able to generate and use strategies to deal with anxiety and worry. Children need simple and concrete explanations of what happens to them when they are under acute emotional distress generated by negative environmental events or situations. These explanations may help them feel less out of control and give them a key to regaining emotional control. The concrete tool shown in Fig. 3.3 may be helpful in decreasing any guilt and/or feelings of helplessness. The tool is a simple diagram to help children understand that distress can shut down their ability to problem-solve. They can interfere with this automatic response by engaging 'thinking,' which gives them some control over their emotions.

This tool can also be used to help individuals understand that the body can react to a sense of threat before any 'thinking' takes place. Youngsters need to engage 'thinking' in order to calm down or *down regulate* the anxiety they are

---

Relaxation Training

The best methods for training children to relax are strategies that are easy to teach and easy to learn; i.e., the simple ones. There are several general methods for teaching relaxation: tensing and relaxing, meditation, exercise and music, autogenic training (becoming aware of bodily sensations while creating a feeling of warmth and heaviness), progressive relaxation, and cognitive therapies.

Tensing and relaxing is easier than mediation if focusing is challenging. Exercise is helpful but not as powerful as relaxation techniques. The suggestions of warmth and heaviness involve both cognitive and somatic components and are more helpful than progressive relaxation. Cognitive therapies are more effective when symptoms are assessed using cognitive measures. Adding cognitive therapy to relaxation has a very positive effect so that combinations of cognitive therapy and relaxation are more effective than either approach alone. When training for relaxation, it is important to apply skills to everyday challenges.

If autogenic training or meditation techniques are used with students, watch for the following:

• Increased tension
• Fear of losing control
• Dizziness
• Muscle twitches
• Certain types of medical disorders.

If students experience these behaviors, intensive relaxation techniques are not recommended. Progressive relation is easier to tolerate for students who do not react well to other methods of relaxation (Sultanoff and Zalaquette 2000).

Fig. 3.2 Relaxation training

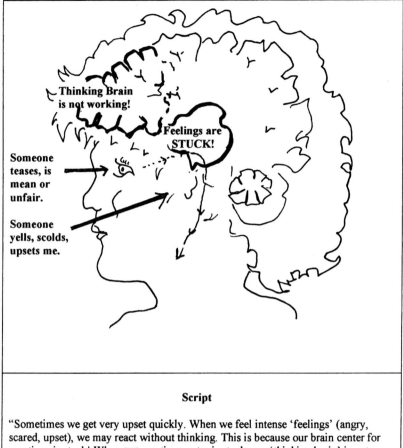

Script

"Sometimes we get very upset quickly. When we feel intense 'feelings' (angry, scared, upset), we may react without thinking. This is because our brain center for emotions is stuck! When our emotion center is stuck, our 'thinking brain' is not working. Messages come in and right away we react (we may act out, run away from the situation or shut down and not be able to move). One way to decrease the strong feelings is to think. If we use a thinking strategy, we can start to calm down."

Fig. 3.3 Emotional Pathways in the Brain (Children)

experiencing. This understanding is important for it helps them see the importance of, and the power of, using a strategy or problem solving.

A similar tool can be provided to parents of anxious students as shown in Fig. 3.4. Parents have to understand that their child may not have as much control over his or her anxious response as they might like to see. After the brain perceives a threatening or fear-inducing situation, there are two possible routes by which the signals can travel. One set of signals goes directly to the amygdala and the child will respond physiologically and possibly behaviorally without thinking. This occurs at a faster rate than the second route.

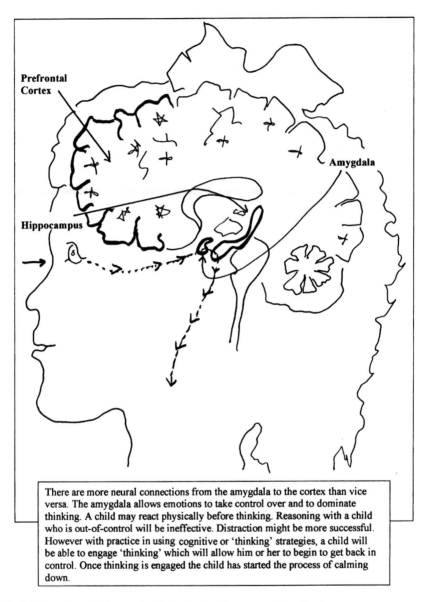

There are more neural connections from the amygdala to the cortex than vice versa. The amygdala allows emotions to take control over and to dominate thinking. A child may react physically before thinking. Reasoning with a child who is out-of-control will be ineffective. Distraction might be more successful. However with practice in using cognitive or 'thinking' strategies, a child will be able to engage 'thinking' which will allow him or her to begin to get back in control. Once thinking is engaged the child has started the process of calming down.

Fig. 3.4 Emotional Pathways in the Brain (for Parents and Teachers)

The other set of signals goes to the cerebral cortex, where the signal can be processed and the child can determine how serious the threat or frightening situation may be and to what degree he or she should respond (Pfaff 2007). Parents should suggest use of a strategy when their child responds with intense anxiety that may appear irrational. Engaging in problem solving (engaging thought) will help reduce the anxiety the child is experiencing.

The work of Tice et al. (2001) suggests that cognitive interventions, which address beliefs about how to change mood, may be very helpful for use with students. Such interventions should include work on students' beliefs about their ability to change negative moods. Tice et al. (2001) were able to improve impulse control when they taught a "mood-freezing manipulation." They convinced research participants that their moods were frozen and could not be improved by engaging in impulsive acts. In their research this was a deception because immediate gratification did lead to very short-term improved feelings, although it did not result in long-term mood improvement.

Clinically, it may also be helpful to work with youngsters so they will reconsider the strategies they use to control negative emotions. Rather than behaving impulsively, they have to learn to work to change their moods with more appropriate and effective strategies.

Chapter 4
Development of Emotion Regulation in Young Children

Influences on Emotion Development

Regulating emotions is an acquired set of skills and abilities (Dodge and Garber 1991). Emotion regulation develops early, and many important regulatory skills and strategies are developed during the first five years of life. Self-regulation is a critically important developmental task with outcomes that affect broad areas of functioning. Child factors including temperament and socialization by parents and caregivers all influence the development of emotion regulation (Cole, Dennis, et al. 2004; Dennis 2003). Moreover, the emotional environment in which children are raised can enhance or interfere with their ability to learn to regulate emotion and function with others (Beauregard et al. 2004; Cole, Michel, and Teli 1994). Children must develop a range of coping skills in order to successfully negotiate the social world. These skills and abilities, which they begin to learn during the preschool period, will allow them to control their emotions and behavior so that they fit successfully into their culture.

The development of emotion control or the self-control of emotions is influenced by forces within as well as external to the child: temperament and cognition, including the factors of attention and inhibition; parenting; the home environment; peer and sibling relationships; and the expectations of the culture in which the child is being raised all contribute to emotion regulation. All aspects of general self-control, including self-control of emotions, develop during the first few years of life and affect the child's current and subsequent behaviors. During this discussion emotion regulation should be thought of as the *self-control of emotion* (Fox and Calkins 2003), as this approach allows it to fit into the broader concept of self-control as it develops during the child's early years.

The Influence of Temperament

In his essay on *Eloquence* Ralph Waldo Emerson (1903) wrote, "Our temperaments differ in capacity of heat, or we boil at different degrees." Temperament has been of interest in describing individual differences for a long time. Kagan

(1994) described temperament as "stable behavioral and emotional reactions" (p. 40). Teglasi (1998a) wrote that temperament referred to the constant quality of a person's behavior, which was further delineated as:

- Activity level.
- Quality and intensity of emotional expression.
- Attention span and persistence.
- Whether or not the individual would approach or withdraw from novelty or from contexts in which the person was unfamiliar.

Fox (1998) considered temperament a "set point." The child's emotional reaction to novel, stressful, or unfamiliar stimuli occurred at a set point determined by temperament. Although temperament appears to be based in human biology, it is also quite likely that it can be modified through the influence of the environment.

Different theorists describe a larger or smaller number of distinguishable temperaments. Thomas and Chess (1977) identified seven temperamental dimensions in their model, whereas other writers have listed as many as fifteen dimensions of temperament (Goldsmith and Rothbart 1991). Teglasi (1998a) felt that four dimensions of temperament had solid support in the literature: (a) approach/avoidance, (b) fear, (c) irritability, and (d) attention/effortful control.

Attention/effortful control includes attentional persistence and activity level (Rothbart and Jones 1998). The models delineating a greater number of dimensions do not appear to separate the different temperaments clearly or uniquely. Some dimensions of temperament appear to cluster resulting in ways of describing children who are resilient and those who are not and children who are tightly controlled and those who are significantly less controlled than their peers (Holodynski and Friedlmeier 2006).

Temperament is not all positive or all negative, good, or bad. As described in the popular press it has been interpreted by people according to their own beliefs and their tolerance for various child behaviors and personality, as well as through cultural norms (Sanson, Hemphill, and Smart 2002). Temperament and behaviors resulting from temperament predict social competence and adjustment at least in young children (Smart and Sanson 2001). An *easygoing* temperament, which refers to a cluster of temperament factors, is one of several protective factors in life and contributes to a child's resilience (Ochiltree and Moore 2001). Moreover, it appears that differences in affective style and vulnerability are associated with temperament (Davidson 1998).

On the one hand, infant and child temperament plays an important role in the development of emotional regulation and, on the other hand, emotional regulation is central to temperament. Feelings and internal states must be controlled to some degree depending on a child's age, and this is easier for some children than others. Children have to be able to shift attention and cope with daily-to-significant stress, and depending on their temperaments, they have differing capacities to do it. Coping strategies are also involved and these improve throughout childhood (Eisenberg, Wentzel, and Harris 1998; Fox and Calkins 2003). More recently effortful control has been considered a dimension of temperament. Eisenberg, Smith, et al. (2004) consider effortful control the self-regulation component of temperament.

Emotion Regulatory Aspects of Temperament

Reactivity is a dimension of temperament that has to do with the activation of behavior and emotions and the physiological changes that accompany activation. Regulation is the set of processes that ameliorates reactivity including: (a) attention, (b) approach or withdrawal, (c) inhibition, and (d) ability to calm oneself (Teglasi 1995).

Reactivity, which involves the time to respond to a stimulus, the threshold at which the child reacts, and the intensity of the resulting response, is a very important aspect or dimension of temperament when considering emotion regulation. Highly reactive children are more likely to become inhibited, whereas less reactive children are more likely to be bold and social (Kagan and Snidman 2004). Anxious children have high reactivity, whereas socially popular children are often described has showing low reactivity.

Children with different temperaments can be distinguished by the ways in which they regulate their emotions. Inhibited children not only react fearfully to novelty, but also have trouble controlling fear, which exacerbates their inhibited reaction to the environment. As infants, children who are inhibited are more likely to turn away from strangers and avoid them than their less fearful peers. When placed in a novel situation, they are more likely to search for their mothers and are slow to vocalize or to reach out (Cole, Martin, et al. 2004). As preschoolers, they are not eager to attend until they get used to the new environment and are less likely to seek out children they have not yet met on the playground. Once they are of school age, the transition to kindergarten may be challenging for them, and it may take some time before they are comfortable with their new classmates and their teachers.

Researchers trying to determine the relationship between a child's temperament and the growing ability to regulate emotions have explored how behaviors that reflect temperament influence styles of emotional control. Studies demonstrate that there is a relationship between negative reactivity to frustration and the control of emotions. Infants and toddlers who are easily frustrated tend to act out instead of distracting themselves or redirecting their attention. They have difficulty regulating emotions (Cole, Martin, et al. 2004; Fox and Calkins 2003).

Children who can regulate emotions can increase or inhibit their reactivity. They can control their attention as well as their tendencies to approach or withdraw. They can and do use strategies to calm themselves (Kagan and Snidman 2004). A child who can more easily regulate his or her emotions is more likely to approach a novel situation. If he or she feels any temporary distress, the child who tends to approach would be more likely to make self-reassuring comments. A child who has fewer skills in emotion regulation might withdraw from interaction or just watch the other children, and comments to self would be neutral instead of helpful (Forbes 2003).

Children who can clearly distinguish among many different positive and negative emotions are better able to regulate emotions than their peers who experience emotion in an undifferentiated way. Children who can *label* negative experiences that affect them emotionally can regulate these emotions more easily. They also exhibit a wider range of strategies to deal with emotional experiences and experience emotions with less intensity than their less competent peers (Barrett, Gross, Christensen, and Benvenuto 2001).

A recent study shows that extremely shy children react to the most prominent events or situations in which they find themselves, and it is interesting to note that they react in the same way to positive or negative situations. When stressed these children will withdraw if they can, become frozen if they cannot withdraw, and stop talking. They may inhibit positive expressions of emotion as well and refrain from smiling or look away from the other person in a stressful encounter. Such children should not be 'forced' to interact in new groups, but rather they should be given an opportunity to watch from afar for awhile. They may overreact to criticism, to losing a game, or to small inconsequential injuries. Temperamental behavioral inhibition persists over time, even into adolescence (Guyer et al. 2006).

Fearful children who are frequently and easily frustrated by events are more likely to associate negative emotions with things that happen to them. Children who experience intense negative feelings and arousal interpret stressful occurrences more negatively than their peers. They cope less well. Both temperament and a tendency to interpret situations as threatening predict poor adjustment to stressful events such as divorce (Lengua, Sandler, West, Wolchik, and Curran 1999; Rothbart and Jones, 1998). School psychologists and teachers have to be aware of the fact that temperament is one more reason that children will react differently to stressful life events.

In predicting social competence, the Australian Temperament Project identified three aspects of temperament particularly strongly related to social competence: (a) reactivity, (b) attention regulation, and (c) emotion regulation. In this project reactivity referred to intensity of reaction as well as to irritability and negativity and attention regulation to the ability to sustain attention so that a task could be completed (Smart and Sanson 2001). The social consequences of poor regulation can be serious. Children who cannot remain engaged in play sequences or in peer interactions of any type, owing to difficulty regulating attention, and those who cannot control their emotional reactions to typical play events may be excluded or rejected. Peer group rejection in turn is related to adjustment difficulties, academic readiness, and school achievement, as students who are rejected reduce their classroom participation over time (Buhs, Ladd, and Herald 2006).

One reason that controlling the intensity of reaction to a situation may be challenging for some children is that they cannot fluidly transition between one feeling state and another. The child who has difficulty transitioning to a calmer state may be predisposed to interpreting situations negatively and experiencing more negative emotions (Fox 1998).

Development during the Infant and Toddler Period

Holodynski and Friedlmeier (2006) have presented a model of emotional development with several phases. They posit that during the first two years of life the child develops a repertoire of different emotions. These develop through the child's relationship with parents and caregivers who are modeling or directly teaching the signals of expression and some early coping strategies. During a second phase from three to six years of age, children acquire internal and external strategies for regulating emotions as they are learning to become more independent. They become more and more aware of and are better able to adjust to the cultural rules that are being modeled and taught directly during the preschool period. These phases describe the period of time that encompasses the focus of this chapter.

Infants calm themselves by sucking and looking away from whatever overstimulates them. They can do this at birth. As infants cry, express upset, fear, happiness, satisfaction, and/or sadness, parents or guardians respond to their expressions and the infants make the connection, so they not only learn something about their own expressions but also learn to understand the parent's behavior in response. By ten months of age, typically developing young children have learned that facial expressions provide information and that they can use them to attract the attention of the caregiver (Holodynski and Friedlmeier 2006). During the second half of the first year, regulatory abilities develop rapidly as the child develops self-consciousness. Regulatory skills help the young child monitor and manage emotions (Beauregard et al. 2004).

From about ten to eighteen months of age, changes in the prefrontal cortex make the process of regulating emotion more feasible, although exactly when a child might be able to regulate emotional expression may be different for different emotions (Shore 1994). During the second year of life, toddlers become able to differentiate between themselves and others; by the end of that year, they have learned rudimentary skills of self-comforting and self-distraction and can very actively recruit support from others (Holodynski and Friedlmeier 2006).

It is important to keep in mind the reciprocal nature of child temperament and parent response. Just as a parent is influenced by the child's temperament, parenting can ameliorate or exacerbate temperamental characteristics. Difficult, irritable infants and toddlers can trigger coercive discipline from parents. When these temperamental features are strong, they can evoke anger, hostility, criticism, or even avoidance in exhausted parents. Parents' style of interacting in turn affects children. When parents react to fearful children with subtle socialization practices, their children benefit. In like manner close and sometimes restrictive control predicts better outcomes when children are bold and fearless (Knox, McHale, and Windon 2004).

Emergence of Language

The emergence of language and communication skills is strongly associated with the child's ability to self-regulate, and language becomes a vehicle for developing self-regulation. Young children use language to get a response from others, to learn in this case about how to manage emotions, and to influence others (Bronson 2000; Dodge and Garber 1991; Eisenberg, Sadovsky, and Spinrad 2005). An infant's attention span and attentional persistence—important aspects of self-regulation—predict language ability eight to nine months later. This suggests that language development and regulation affect one another reciprocally.

Not only is parent language critically important to the child's development, but children with more ability to self-regulate are able to elicit more complex language from caretakers and others (Dixon and Smith 2000). Verbal labeling of feelings and moods along with knowing the causes and consequences of emotional expression are related to emotional understanding. Young children use their emotional knowledge and understanding to generate and use strategies for emotion regulation when they are stressed (Eisenberg, Sadovsky, Spinrad, Fabes et al. 2005). When a child can talk about emotions, he or she is better able to understand them and to learn and recall strategies to mange them. The child will be better able to regulate him or herself in an age-appropriate manner (Denham and Burton 2003). Of course, thinking and learning skills are developing in conjunction with emotional control (Bell and Wolfe 2004).

Preschool Period

School psychologists are responsible for evaluating children during the preschool period, as well as for consulting with parents and teachers concerning a child's development and behavior. Some school psychologists specialize in this developmental period, but even though these professionals are apt to think more broadly about child development than specifically about childhood problems, emotional development has not been widely addressed in the school psychology literature.

Dennis and Gonzalwez (2005) remind us that emotion regulation is a key developmental task of the early childhood period. Youngsters who do not develop age- and culturally appropriate emotion regulation become vulnerable on several fronts. However, it is important to keep in mind that regulating emotion voluntarily is challenging for young children, who still need adult coaching and modeling.

One situation in which children need emotion and behavior regulation strategies is when they must comply with a rule that interferes with an anticipated pleasurable activity such as play, and the resulting stress can cause them to experience negative emotions. Kalpidou, Power, Cherry, and Gottfried (2004) designed a study in which preschool children were placed in situations with either a low or a high demand for emotion regulation to determine the relationship between emotion regulation and behavior. The children were given a task to accomplish in the presence of attractive toys that were either visible or not visible, although in both cases they knew that the toys were available. Children who were better able to regulate their emotions worked longer at the task. In general, the demand for emotion regulation interfered with their ability to comply with adult requests.

The five-year-old children were more likely to use problem-solving strategies to deal with the challenging situation, as opposed to avoidance or aggression, exhibiting more emotion regulation than the three-year-olds, and the relationship between emotion regulation and behavior was stronger. The National Scientific Council on the Developing Child (2004) indicated that young children have limited ability to regulate emotion in order to focus and sustain attention in the face of overwhelming feelings. When anxious, angry, or frustrated, a preschooler is not going to easily down regulate these emotions. Several core features of the development of emotion in children in terms of various abilities have been identified, including:

- Identifying various emotions
- Understanding emotions
- Regulating strong emotions
- Expressing emotions appropriately

These core abilities lead to better behavioral regulation, the ability to feel and express empathy, and the capacity to form lasting relationships.

Cole, Martin, et al. (2004) have reported a series of experiments that clearly demonstrate that young children are capable of attempting to regulate negative emotions in conjunction with progress in the cognitive, motor, and language domains. These studies demonstrate that young children attempt to regulate emotion when they are placed in difficult situations and that their efforts to regulate are associated with negative emotion (p. 326). Early regulating efforts include distracting oneself, making an effort to soothe oneself, and seeking attention from adults. Even toddlers are able to regulate their emotions in a satisfactory way if social support is available.

When preschool-aged boys were frustrated, they were able to use strategies to control anger. However, some types of strategies are not as successful as others. Obsessing about what one wants, for example, can result in increased anger. Although the children in these studies said that they still felt bad, they hid their negative emotions when experimenters were present. Preschoolers who have not been taught this skill can learn to hide their feelings of disappointment if parents and teachers work with them to develop the skill.

Children as young as two years of age seem to be aware not only of their own emotions but also of the emotions of others. They are able to use strategies such as thinking about something else and doing something else after they reach three years of age (Cole, Dennis, and Cohen 2001). Three-year-olds appear to understand the intentional aspect of emotion but not how to control emotions. Four-year olds have a better understanding of effective strategies for emotional control (Dennis and Kelemen 1999). However, not all preschool children are equal in their emotional understanding. Differences emerge early and have been studied because they are correlated with social competency, which is a key interest of child development researchers (Pons and Harris 2005).

There appear to be gender differences in strategies used for emotion regulation. A study by Dennis and Kelemen (1999) found that young girls more often tended to endorse distraction and boys more often tended to endorse problem solving. These differences were interpreted as relating to differences in socialization.

The specific strategies that preschoolers learn to use to deal with strong emotions include redirecting attention away from whatever is stressing them. They learn to comfort themselves, approach or withdraw from situations, and use play to deal with difficult challenges. They become aware to some extent of the necessity of using regulation strategies and they appear to be less disorganized than toddlers when faced with strong emotional events and situations (Denham, von Salisch, Olthof, Kochanoff, and Caverly 2002). Preschool children can connect specific and appropriate feelings with events, understanding 'happy' and 'fear' earlier than they understand 'mad' or 'sad' (Hubbard and Coie 1994). Children high in negative emotion intensity increasingly play alone, and they try to hide the expression of negative emotions (Fabes, Hanish, Martin, and Eisenberg 2002). Figure 4.1 shows the range of emotion regulatory skills mastered by the end of the preschool period by the typically developing child.

A child's temperament is fully evident by five or six years of age (Turecki 2003). Furthermore, by the end of the preschool period, according to the National Scientific Council on the Developing Child (2004), the brain circuits for emotional regulation are interacting closely with brain areas

---

Emotion Regulatory Skills Mastered

By the end of the preschool period, a child can:

- Direct attention away from stressful triggers
- Anticipate another person's emotions
- Talk comfortably about emotions
- Use emotions to negotiate social interactions
- Use language to communicate feelings
- Use strategies to prevent being overwhelmed
- Stop from expressing inappropriate emotions
- Stop from exhibiting inappropriate emotional behavior, comfort her or himself
- Approach or withdraw from situations
- Use play to deal with difficult challenges
- Understand the need to use regulation strategies
- Remain somewhat organized when faced with strong emotional events and situations
- Connect specific and appropriate feelings with events

Fig. 4.1 Emotion regulatory skills mastered by the end of the preschool period

involved with executive functioning. Emotions can facilitate or depress attentional capacity and functions as well as cognitive decision making, depending on the child's strength in regulating emotions.

When they are ready for school, typically developing children can anticipate another's emotions, talk about emotions, and use emotions to negotiate social interactions. They can use language to communicate feelings and can use strategies to prevent being overwhelmed. They can stop themselves from expressing inappropriate emotions and emotional behavior that does not fit the culture. Of course, this is not true for all children. There are considerable differences from one child to another and significant numbers of children evidence continuing difficulties regulating emotions at this age.

Implications

School psychologists working at the preschool and early elementary levels are particularly interested in understanding typical emotional development in young children so that they can assist children who are not mastering important regulatory strategies, skills, and abilities. Studies that demonstrate the strategies that children at particular ages can use effectively are particularly helpful. Figure 4.2 depicts the range of coping strategies that preschoolers use. The major categories include: (a) instrumental coping, (b) seeking help, (c) venting, (d) aggression, and (e) avoidance (Kalpidou et al. 2004).

Coping Strategies of Preschoolers

Instrumental Coping

Taking action to solve the problem
Trying different approaches
Trying to think positively

Seeking Help

Telling others about the problem (goal of obtaining help)
Talking with adult or another child about the problem (goal to solve the problem)
Asking an adult or another child to solve the problem
Asking an adult or another child *to help* solve the problem

Venting

Crying (with goal of releasing tension)
Crying (with goal of obtaining help)
Stamping feet (or clenching fists or gritting teeth)
Yelling
Complaining or fussing
Sighing

Aggression

Using physical or verbal aggression to solve the problem
Using physical or verbal aggression (with goal of releasing tension)

Avoidance

Avoiding thinking about the problem by engaging in another activity
Trying to ignore the problem or situation
Denying that there is a problem
Leaving the situation or avoiding the problem
Doing nothing and sucking thumb
Doing nothing

Fig. 4.2 Coping strategies of preschoolers (Adapted and expanded from Kalpidou, Power, Cherry, and Gottfried 2004)

Within each of these larger categories are a number of strategies. Different children will rely on the strategies found in some categories more than others, with more mature preschoolers using more active and less negative strategies. These differences enable practitioners to develop age-appropriate goals for children and develop or select a curriculum that is designed to teach the important strategies.

Chapter 5
Parenting and Emotion Regulation

The Effect of Parenting on Children's Emotional Development

Researchers are exploring the connection between parenting practices and children's ability to express and regulate their emotions (Jones, Eisenberg, Fabes, and MacKinnon 2002). This work is important for school-based practitioners who are designing interventions for younger children. There is often better progress in helping students when the school psychologist offers consultation or direct training for parents rather than, or in addition to, working directly with a given student. Group interventions must be considered as well, as they make it possible to help a greater number of students and families. Practitioners are also involved in designing and delivering prevention programs with the goal of reducing academic-related risks and improving social-emotional functioning (Ysseldyke, Burns, Dawson, Kelley, Morrison, Ortiz, et al. 2006).

The ways in which parents and guardians interact with their children are socially constructed and influenced by the degree of stress and resiliency exhibited by any particular family (Family and Community Services 2004). Parents directly teach, selectively reinforce, and clearly demonstrate emotion regulation as they interact with their children. They influence the development of emotion regulation through affective induction and modeling, control the child's environment in order to limit or extend his or her opportunity to experience strong emotion and to control its expression, and teach the child strategies to control emotion (Thompson 1991).

The affective environment that the parents provide during early childhood is very important in influencing the development of emotion regulation in regard to a youngster's competency in interpersonal interactions. Over time these emotional experiences can become part of a child's emotional repertoire and affective style (Cole et al.; Teli 1994). Diamond and Aspinwall (2003) describe the optimal developmental outcomes for a student and indicate that *breadth and flexibility* are the best descriptors of healthy emotional reactions, along with the ability to *utilize emotion* in order to reach goals in the various contexts in which a student operates (Cole et al. 1994; Diamond and Aspinwall 2003).

Parenting Styles

Parenting styles have been described in a variety of ways. As conceived by Maccoby and Martin (1983), they involve two important elements of parenting—parental demands or behavioral control and parental responsiveness. Parental responsiveness (or parental warmth and support) refers to the parents' efforts to help children assert themselves as well as to help them learn to self-regulate (Baumrind 1991, p. 62). Various combinations of these variables resulted in the delineation of four well-known parenting styles: (a) permissive or indulgent, (b) authoritative, (c) authoritarian, and (d) uninvolved. Of these, the authoritarian style has been considered the most effective (Maccoby and Martin 1983). The several parenting styles are described in Fig. 5.1.

A recent study using these descriptors looked at those aspects of parenting style that might influence a child's self-concept, locus of control, and academic achievement (Lee, Daniels, and Kissinger 2006). Locus of control refers to the extent to which individuals believe what happens to them is under their own control (Moorhead and Griffin 2004). There appear to be different effects of parenting styles as used by mothers and fathers. For example, authoritative parenting by mothers, but not fathers, helps establish an internal locus of control (Marsiglia, Walczyk, Buboltz, and Griffith-Ross 2006).

Fathers who utilize an authoritative parenting style characterized by high demand and high responsiveness appear to increase the risk of delinquency and substance abuse in their children. This effect is ameliorated if fathers also have positive relationships with their adolescents. In like manner, a positive relationship between fathers and their children reduces behavioral risks when

---

Parenting Styles

Permissive parenting is an indulgent style of interaction in which parents are not very demanding but are quite responsive.

Authoritative parenting has been described as an interactional style in which parents are both demanding and responsive.

Authoritarian parenting has been described as an interactional style that is demanding but not particularly responsive.

Uninvolved parenting is neither demanding nor responsive and has been described as indifferent.

Research suggests that the authoritative style involving firm controls but where parents are also quite warm and child centered has more positive results for students in middle childhood. Yet, it is important to keep in mind that differences in parenting style vary according to ethnic group, culture, single-parent versus two-parent families, and the stresses and circumstances of the family (Keith and Christensen 1997).

Flexibility may be more important than one style versus another, and a parent's ability to match the child's needs is very important. Parent-child relationships are bidirectional.

Fig. 5.1 Parenting styles (Maccoby and Martin 1983)

permissive parenting is the manner of interaction in the family. In the adolescent years these relationships are stronger for boys than for girls (Bronte-Tinkew, Moore, and Carrano 2006).

We have to look carefully at parenting style when trying to help children with emotional regulation. There are several styles of parent interaction that are particularly helpful in strengthening the required skills.

Positive Parenting

"Positive parenting" is a term that is used to describe parent-child interactions that have importance for studying the development of emotional regulation. It involves several features, including:

- Parental responsiveness to a child's distress
- Warmth
- Cooperating with the child
- Cognitive scaffolding

Davidov and Grusec (2006) found that parents' responsiveness to their children's distress strongly determined how well their children learned to regulate negative emotions, although less strongly in the case of mothers' effect on their daughters. A mother's responsiveness to her child's distress additionally predicted whether or not the child would respond positively and empathetically to others. Mothers' warmth, another feature of positive parenting, was determined to be associated with better regulation of positive emotions in children and to greater acceptance by friends and classmates in the case of sons but not daughters.

Parental warmth and parental responsiveness make unique contributions to different outcomes and are not interchangeable in Western cultures. A parent's responsiveness to a child's distress can engender concern for others in terms of developing a more *flexible* way of regulating negative emotions. The child can then react helpfully toward a peer without becoming overwhelmed by the other's emotions. However, warmth alone does not teach coping strategies. Davidov and Grusec (2006) hypothesize that boys may be more influenced by their mother's regulation of negative emotion than girls. Boys are more easily dysregulated by stressors or possibly because they tend to externalize rather than internalize emotion. Responsiveness to distress includes behaviors such as giving comfort and helping a distressed or frightened child problem-solve.

Parents who use positive parenting create a positive mood in the home that facilitates the development of flexible thinking and problem solving. They promote regulated behavior by providing a predictable and secure home climate. A positive environment encourages children to attend to and learn from parents. Positive parents model emotional control, dealing with stress, and

ne's behavior. When children can keep negative emotions under
/ tend to get less emotionally aroused and express emotion more
ly. Positive parenting is particularly important during the early
parents are the primary socializers and peer influences are minimal,
and _____ ects are very strong during this period (Eisenberg, Zhou, Spinrad,
Valiente, Fabes, and Liew 2005). Figure 5.2 lists the elements of positive
parenting that effect emotion regulation.

Students who are more vulnerable to emotional dysregulation are at risk
when they have parents who are punishing and not supportive. Less positive
parenting of boys sensitive to negative emotions when they are two to three
years old is associated with acting out (Jones et al. 2002). Parents tend to use less
positive parenting with children who exhibit mild or subclinical difficulties with
attention, and these children in turn tend to have more social difficulties than
their peers (Rielly, Craig, and Parker 2006). Failure to comfort children affects
their development of emotion regulation (Shore 1994).

In the extreme case, students who are mistreated learn that they cannot
expect support when they experience intense emotions. Moreover, they learn
that it is not wise to exhibit strong emotions in front of their mothers. This has a
serious effect on their ability to learn how to cope with anger effectively
(Shipman and Zeman 2001). Exposure to trauma decreases the likelihood that

---

Elements of Positive Parenting that Effect Emotional Regulation

- Responsiveness to a child's distress
- Warmth
- Cooperating with the child
- Cognitive scaffolding
- Regulation of negative affect
- Expression of positive mood in the home
- Emotional support and comforting
- Encouraging the appropriate expression of emotion
- Reacting to situations with a problem-solving orientation
- Talking with interest about emotions (causes, consequences)
- Using open-ended questions
- Using broad 'emotion' vocabulary (depending on the child's age and verbal ability)
- Explaining negative situations
- Answering questions about emotion
- Avoiding angry exchanges yet acknowledge negative feelings
- Teaching children to tolerate negative feelings
- Teaching children to respond to anger neutrally
- Model emotional regulation (self-calming and self-soothing)

Fig. 5.2 Elements of positive parenting that influence emotional regulation in children

a child will develop adequate emotion regulation (Lubit, Rovine, Defrar and Spencer 2003).

Family Expressiveness

Family expressiveness of positive emotion has been connected to emotion regulation. Parents who express more positive emotions have a facilitating effect on their children's social interactions (Denham and Grout 1993). When parents express positive emotions, children generally exhibit low levels of acting out behaviors, are less likely to feel angry or frustrated as often as their peers, and are less likely to act out aggressively, even if comments are not directed to them (Eisenberg, Zhou, et al. 2005).

Children whose parents who are warm, positive, and expressive in their interactions become more capable of emotional control (Eisenberg, Zhou, et al. 2005), and tend not to internalize negative emotions even in adolescence. Encouraging the appropriate expression of emotion along with other parent behaviors, such as mothers' problem-focused reactions to events, helps sons learn to comfort others (Eisenberg, Fabes, and Murphy 1996). When mothers express positive emotion in the home, they can ameliorate some of a given child's tendencies toward temperamental negativity (Cumberland-Li, Eisenberg, Champion, Gershoff, and Fabes 2003).

Parents react to their children's expressions of emotion and behavior, and children in turn react to parents' attempts to initiate interaction with them. They try to regulate their child's moods and to influence his or her reactions. This process of reciprocal responsiveness is driven and controlled by the parents, at least when children are young (Kochanska and Aksan 2004).

Unfortunately, mothers of children with conduct problems tend to minimize their children's emotional outbursts. It may be that these children have such poor emotional regulation that their mothers feel that minimizing is necessary. However, these mothers appear to have less knowledge about their own emotions, as well as knowing less about those of their children. This suggests that it is the parents who have the most influence (Katz and Windecker-Nelson 2004).

Parent 'Talk' about Emotions

Lagattuta and Wellman (2002) examined the quality and content of parent 'talk' with preschool children. They found that parents talked with their children in different ways depending on whether they were talking about positive or negative emotions. When relating to negative emotions, they talked more about past feelings, causes of emotions, and connections between emotions and thinking than they did when discussing positive emotions. Moreover, they had a more extensive vocabulary in regard to negative emotions, there were more open-ended questions, and they, and they also talked more about other people. Eisenberg, Zhou, et al. (2005) determined that parents who encourage their children to talk about emotions are actually teaching them to down regulate intense emotions.

Garner (1999) was interested in preschoolers' abilities to interpret facial expressions, their knowledge about situations that might elicit emotion, and their ability to act out emotional roles in play acting. Mothers' explanations about emotions to their preschool children were found to positively connect to children's emotion knowledge as well as their cultural knowledge about how to exhibit emotions appropriately four years later.

The conversations that mothers have with children when they misbehave are particular important in regard to emotion regulation. When parents elaborate around negative situations and explain them clearly, children's understanding about emotion and emotional contexts improves. This effect was still evident six months later (Laible 2004).

Parents can affect their children's emotion regulation to a great degree positively or negatively, depending on whether or not they discuss emotions and emotional experiences with them. Researchers have found that mothers of children with anxiety disorders may not be assisting their children to develop "emotion language." These mothers discourage discussion of negative emotional events and use fewer positive emotion vocabulary words when talking with them. In fact, they used fewer words in general when talking with their children, changed the topic when negative emotional experiences were introduced, and even in some cases ignored the child. Researchers hypothesize that anxious children may expect a negative reaction from mothers when they express emotion or try to talk about negative feelings. This is problematic in that reactive children who cannot, or do not, use detailed or descriptive labels for negative emotional experiences tend to handle negative emotions less well than their peers (Barrett et al. 2001).

Barrett et al. (2001) demonstrated that emotion differentiation correlates with emotion regulation. The ability to distinguish among different negative emotions, events, and situations is related to adequate emotion regulation. When a parent's discussions with a child involve support and problem solving, they are thought to facilitate emotion regulation and expression (Jones et al. 2002). Mothers who can comfortably answer questions about emotions and talk of them with interest may be teaching their children about subtle changes in emotion. Their children become more aware and tend to engage in more imaginative play (Katz and Windecker-Nelson 2004).

When parents interact negatively with their children, there are costs in terms of the children's ability to regulate emotions. Parents' verbal aggression, for example, has particularly negative effects (Teichner, Samson, Polcari, and McGreenery 2006). Angry exchanges and emotional mismatches particularly between mothers and their children during the preschool period have been found to increase the likelihood that sons will act out. When both mothers' and sons' behaviors continue without change, conduct difficulties can be predicted by the time the boys are of school age (Cole, Teti, and Zahn-Waxler 2003).

Parents' Reactions to Negative Emotions

Parents' reactions to children's negative emotions are particularly influential in regard to the development of emotion regulation. Parents who react in a punitive manner or who minimized their children's expression of emotions have children with poor emotional competence. This effect is particularly damaging to children who have intense temperaments and experience emotion deeply. Punishing or minimizing a child's emotional expressions leads to poor social competence (Jones et al. 2002).

When children fail, the ensuing conversations with parents can affect negative emotionality. When mothers express anger toward their children and give negative feedback over time, those responses in combination with children's own reaction to the negative experience make them vulnerable to depression (Mezulis, Hyde, and Abramson 2006).

When parents work hard to regulate emotion in their homes and respond positively to children, their children's developmental outcomes tend to be positive (Cumberland-Li et al. 2003). Parents who acknowledge their children's negative feelings, try to teach them to tolerate those feelings, and instruct them in regard to problem solving help their children develop the important skills needed to regulate emotions. When parents accept both positive and negative emotions and talk about them, rather than punishing children by ignoring or distracting them, emotion understanding and regulation is facilitated. Few parents understand that distraction is not helpful as long as children are of school age and in at least some control. Dealing with high levels of distress, as in a temper tantrum, requires some skill, and parents have to remain in control themselves. Figure 5.3 suggests appropriate adult responses for each level of tantrum behavior.

Children who are punished when they exhibit negative feelings associate the emotion with negative consequences increasing their distress and the intensity of emotion, so that it is difficult for them to regulate their emotions. Minimizing negative emotions can be considered belittling by children. On the other hand, comforting preschoolers who express negative emotions has been associated with decreased anger intensity and expression (Jones et al. 2002). Mothers who acknowledge their children's emotions have children who exhibit more sophisticated play (Katz and Windecker-Nelson 2004).

Mothers' reactions to children's negative expressions have an effect on older children as well as on younger ones. First to fourth graders whose negative emotions are minimized by their parents are not as competent socially or emotionally as their peers (Jones et al. 2002). When parents react with upset or punishment in response to children's negative emotions at ages six to eight, it

Matching the Adult Response to the Child's Level of Distress	
Child's Behavior	**Adult's Response**
Pretantrum	
Frowning, sighing, pulling away, fussing	Respond with suggestions, label the feelings, explain the causes of the feelings, offer problem-solving strategies.
Whiny, complaining, demanding	Take a break, go for a walk with the child, encourage talking (just listen), offer to help find a solution, give an explanation, offer to help.
Irritable, agitated	Give choices, give close attention, help to relax if allowed, validate feelings, offer your help.
Tantrum	
Arguing, yelling	Stay calm, speak very softly if at all, remind you are nearby and understand why the child is upset, indicate you are standing by to help.
Kicking, throwing	Move away, out of sight if possible but make sure the child is safe, remain calm.
Post-tantrum	
Crying	Help to relax, give positive assurance.
Sad	Support and reassure, remind the child that he or she can try again.
Seeking out support	Help to save face, offer options, begin problem solving, talk about how to make things better and how to deal with the emotions in the future.
Keep a journal of the behaviors and the emotions you observe and the duration of the emotions. Make notes in regard to triggers and what worked at which stages of the upset.	

Fig. 5.3 Matching the adult's response to the child's level of distress

predicts the competency with which the children will regulate emotions two years later (Eisenberg, Fabes, Shepard, Guthrie, Murphy, and Reiser 1999). It appears that punishing negative emotions intensifies the children's experience and expression so that they may attempt to hide their emotions (Jones et al. 2002).

Emotion Coaching

Parents who use an interactive style around expression of emotion that is similar to 'coaching' have children who can regulate their emotions and tend not to behave aggressively. Emotion coaching refers to talking about emotions, showing children how to express emotion appropriately, modeling calming and soothing strategies, demonstrating interest in children's emotions, and interacting confidently with them when they are reacting emotionally.

Both aggressive and nonaggressive children do better socially when their mothers 'coach' emotion. The children of emotion-coaching mothers exhibit less negative interactions with one another, their play tends to breakdown less often, their conversation is less negative, and they show fewer negative emotions when interacting with their peers (Katz and Windecker-Nelson 2004).

Parents who coach their children's emotion help them express it appropriately, regulate them, and reduce their need to act aggressively (Jones et al. 2002). Parental emotional coaching of negative emotions has a protective effect (Lunkenheimer, Shields, and Cortina 2007). When mothers use emotion coaching it protects children from some of the negative effects of domestic violence, which would otherwise increase a child's aggressiveness and depression-anxiety. When fathers use emotion coaching it moderates the effect of domestic violence and the child's withdrawal (Katz and Windecker-Nelson 2006).

Mothers who act as emotion coaches teach their children how to work through conflict situations with other children. In this way, the intensity of their negative emotions does not interfere with play to such as the extent that it results in negative behavior or terminating the play, perhaps by walking away (Katz and Windecker-Nelson 2004). Mothers' coaching facilitates conversations about positive and negative emotions. These mothers may believe that expressing emotion whether or not it is negative is okay. Children with coaching mothers, even those with conduct problems, are generally able to remain in interactions with their peers when things go wrong. Emotion coaching appears to help children learn to 'repair' play that breaks down and to remain engaged when things go wrong, which could mitigate against future rejection by their peers.

In studies with elementary-age children, it was concluded that emotion discussion and problem solving, such as responding to anger neutrally, and teaching calming strategies continue to be important. Parental problem-solving discussions are linked with greater social competence for school-aged children. Parental skills in allowing a moderate expression of negative emotions along with problem solving help to prevent a negative reaction by the child. Children who feel overwhelmed and powerless when experiencing negative emotion do not function well.

Parental reaction to children who experience emotions intensely is particularly important. Parenting that is negative and controlling, when interacting with intense boys when they are young, can foster acting out particularly if these boys are likely to experience more negative emotions than their peers. Temperament plays a role here as well, so that the same parenting practice can have different effects depending on the child's temperament. Children who express more negative emotions than their peers can be challenging for parents. For example, juveniles who tend to be irritable paired with controlling mothers tend to internalize emotions, whereas good-natured children would not be so strongly affected. Children who are easygoing may tolerate some degree of negative parenting (Jones et al. 2002).

Positive parenting by itself may not have as strong an effect on some children as it would have on most others. Aggressive children may be less able to respond to their mother's teaching about emotions because their behavior is impulsive, and they are less likely to accept her suggestions to change their behavior during play. In comparison, nonaggressive children appear more skilled in play when they have mothers who engage in emotion coaching (Katz and Windecker-Nelson 2004).

Fathers have a major influence on children's emotional development (Parke 2004), but there has been very little research done on fathers' role in regard to emotion regulation. Fathers tend to play with their children in a highly active manner, and those with good parenting skills know when to stop the rough-housing and help their children return to a calm state. This behavior would be expected to have a positive effect in teaching children to down regulate emotion. Fathers who teach and encourage problem solving help their children with social development, particularly in the case of withdrawn boys (Miller, Murry, and Brody 2005). Downer and Mendez (2005) found that African American fathers who are more involved with caring for and educating their children had children with stronger ability to regulate their emotions. NICHD (2006) reports indicate that fathers who support their children emotionally and know what they are doing have fewer problems with their children, and step-fathers who have positive relationships with their stepchildren have children with fewer emotional issues.

Parental Approach and Avoidance

The literature on child development often refers to the interaction effects of parent and child behaviors and the mutual influence of behaviors. Dennis (2006) suggests that child regulatory behaviors are likely to 'pull' specific parent behaviors in reaction. The parent's reaction to those behaviors is likely to influence the child's behavior in return. Parent behaviors that attempt to control a child's emotions and emotional behavior may affect children with different temperaments differently. A specific parental approach may help or hinder emotion regulation depending on the child's temperament.

Dennis (2003) describes both parenting and child behavior in terms of approach and avoidance motivation. There are differences in how emotion regulation develops for children who are either high or low in approach motivation. A competent mother appears to use a range of strategies and vary her own behaviors according to the needs of her child, and this balancing act may be the most powerful predictor of outcomes.

Approach parenting can be thought of as promoting self-regulation and sensitivity to looked-for events. Avoidance parenting may involve prevention of negative events. Parents who use avoidance parenting are attempting to prevent negative events from occurring. Children with strong avoidance tendencies do better when their mothers use prevention. They exhibit social shyness, and parents' use of prevention decreases their need to use avoidance to tolerate situations. Such parents control their child's environments carefully so that his or her tendency to avoid situations does not intensify. Of course, it is also important that mildly stressful events be gradually introduced so that the child can learn strategies for managing emotional reactions to events.

Many mothers attempt to control young children by guiding them to react with competence and by reminding them about how to behave in certain situations. Children's sensitivities to threats and rewards are related to their ability to regulate themselves. Compliance requires both the ability to control impulses and a desire to approach others. Ability to persist when a task is extremely difficult or impossible and one is experiencing negative feedback requires a good deal more approach motivation than other situations. Children whose mothers use threats to control them experience more frustration, which affects their persistence (Dennis 2006).

A child who exhibits a high degree of persistence has stronger emotion regulation (Dennis and Gonzalez 2005). Children who are high in approach motivation react to mothers' warm encouragement when they have to wait during an emotional challenge, whereas children low in approach motivation become more frustrated and disengage when they experience the same parenting behavior. Children low in approach react with compliance when mothers interact warmly with them (Dennis 2006). Parents must work hard to first understand their child's temperament and then to respond appropriately even when they may prefer to respond in a manner that reflects their own temperament or desires.

Parent Training

A very effective way to deliver services to students who need them is to offer parent training during the school day. There has been moderate success with a number of interventions to help parents increase positive behaviors when they interact with their children. Programs have been developed that help parents set limits on negative behaviors and teach alternative less harsh ways of disciplining children with behavior problems.

Several limitations have been noted in the literature on parent training. First, one study found that some of the interventions that are appropriate for Caucasians are not as effective for African Americans. The Center for the Improvement of Child Caring has a special parenting program for African American families, which enjoys some support: *Effective Black Parenting* (http://www.ciccparenting.org/EffBlackParentingDesc.aspx). Parent training must be sensitive and respectful of cultural and racial patterns of communication and family values of obedience and achievement. Second, parent-training interventions may be too short to engender permanent change (Raver 2003). Targeted training aimed specifically at management strategies has been more successful. In fact, Keyes (2004) notes that teaching parents to manage non-compliant children has "...been the single most successful treatment approach for reducing problem behavior" (p. iv). Her work has demonstrated that the disciplinary approaches that parents use affect not only behavior but the child's emotion regulatory abilities as well. Thus, parent training can influence not only parenting disciplinary strategies but can indirectly improve children's emotion regulation.

Repair Strategies

Children who have difficulties with emotion regulation and handle situations emotionally tend to make mistakes, saying something in anger that they regret later on, crying in front of peers when extremely stressed, or acting out in some manner. These children have to be taught a way to repair the loss of control and any mistakes made during highly stressful situations. School psychologists can teach parents how to help their children repair their mistakes. One repair strategy involves a series of questions:

- What is the problem?
- How do you feel?
- How does the other person feel?
- How can the situation be made better?
- What is the best action to take?

Unless the child can label the problem it will be very difficult to fix, and he or she needs help in describing it clearly and succinctly. Talking about feelings distracts the child momentarily from the situation and helps him or her learn to see things from the other person's perspective. Finally, brainstorming or using a prepared list as in Fig. 5.4 can help direct the action that the child might take.

Cognitive-Behavioral Training

Clinic-based interventions involving parent training have been repeatedly demonstrated to be effective. Studies indicate that family cognitive behavioral treatment is more effective than child-focused treatment alone. Important skills for parents in this model include learning to give children choices instead of making choices for them and allowing children to struggle rather than taking over for them. Parents have to learn to recognize and reward children when they try to help themselves, as well as to ignore anxious behaviors and refrain from criticizing their child's behavior (Wood, Piacentini, Southam-Gerow, Chu, and Sigman 2006).

Possible Ways to 'Fix a Problem

Emotion-Focused Strategies for Preschoolers to use

1. Take a break.
2. Take a deep breath and let it out slowly.
3. Count to ten (backward).
4. Ask an adult for help.
5. Walk away until you feel better.
6. Give yourself a hug.
7. Say, "I can do this."
8. Say, "Today it's hard, soon I will do it."

Action-Focused Strategies for Preschoolers to use

1. Say, "I don't like that, please stop it."
2. Say, "I had this toy first, I will give it to you when I am finished."
3. Say, "You can have this one, I am using that one."
4. Say, "I need another minute please."
5. Offer the child a different toy to play with and say how great it is.
6. Say, "You can be first this time, but next time I will be first."
7. Say, "I have a great idea." (Share your idea.)
8. Ask, "What are you doing?" or "How do you play this game?"

Fig. 5.4 Repair strategies

Thienemann, Moore, and Tompkins (2006) have demonstrated that training parents to act *as if* they were cognitive behavioral therapists, rather than working directly with anxious children, can be successful. Researchers have found that school-based programs using cognitive behavioral interventions that include parent training provide additional benefits for children (Bernstein, Layne, Egan, and Tennison 2005). The ADHD parent training program has been demonstrated to be effective, and when teacher training was added to parent training, children's symptoms were reduced even further (Corkum, Mullane, and McKinnon, 2005).

School-based interventions are becoming more common because they are an efficient—and sometimes the only—way to provide services for children who have been identified with mental health needs, as parents cannot get to clinics for a variety of reasons such as lack of transportation, no insurance and no free clinic nearby, family upheaval, single-parent with no child care etc. Awareness of this fact is increasing and more and more programs are adding parent components. For example, a pilot parent component to accompany the Penn Resiliency Program for Children and Adolescents has been developed for middle school students and their parents. Through this program students are helped to: (a) understand pessimistic explanatory cognitive styles, (b) look for evidence for and dispute their negative thinking, (c) generate alternative thoughts, and (d) put thoughts into perspective.

Parents are taught core skills as well and are helped to use these skills in parenting activities by modeling them for their children and by supporting their children when they use the skills. The program proved to be quite effective in reducing anxiety symptoms in children, but the reduction in depressive symptoms was only small to moderate. Effects of the program increased over time (Gillham et al. 2006).

School psychologists who are interested in providing parenting skills workshops for parents have to enlist classroom teachers to help them identify specific parents and encourage them to attend. Goals must be established. It may be important to describe the group as teaching specific techniques or teaching advanced skills, so that parents feel comfortable in attending and their sense of competence is not challenged. Careful planning is necessary so that needs are met. Topics might include:

- Positive parenting
- Coaching
- Relationship building
- Compliance training
- Inductive discipline
- Emotion regulation

Inductive discipline involves asking questions so a child can understand how his or her behavior affects others. Questions might include asking children what happened, how they feel, how the other person felt, what effect their behavior had on others, and how they can prevent making mistakes in the future. Finally, both evaluation and follow-up are necessary components of a strong program (Macklem and Pluymert 1998).

Chapter 6
Emotion Regulation in the Classroom

Social-Emotional Adjustment and Academic Success

There are a number of reasons to explore the relationship between a child's ability to regulate emotion and his or her functioning in the classroom. Students must deal with all sorts of stressors in the school environment, and their adjustment to school depends on their ability to cope with these stressors. If a student has mastered a range of effective coping strategies, he or she can use them as protective factors.

Social-emotional adjustment and academic success are both influenced by several variables, including emotion regulation. There has been a great deal of research interest in all types of self-regulation in children, as it affects school adjustment and performance. The more specific interest here involves emotion regulation as it is manifested in a child's readiness for school, ability to deal with school-related stress, and academic performance. Emotions that relate to interpersonal relationships and academic functioning are important for a child's adjustment in school, but academic emotions have not received the same attention in educational psychology as emotions in other contexts. The one exception is test anxiety, which has been studied for some time (Pekrun, Goetz, Titz, and Perry 2002).

Academics and Emotions

Children actually experience a wide range of emotions in the school setting. Emotions are social and are based on students' appraisals of situations, which are in turn based on their beliefs. These emotions are influenced by personal histories with different subject matter, teachers, parents, peers, and situations, and they are changeable because contexts are changeable (Eynde and Turner 2006). Emotional events in the classroom setting are triggered by the beliefs and goals of both the teacher and the students. Feelings of shame, hope, pride, and anxiety are related to goals, and emotions connected to wishful thinking and self-blame are associated with increased anger and elevated anxiety (Schutz et al. 2006).

Anxiety may be the most frequently experienced academic emotion, although both positive and negative emotions are experienced in the school environment. Emotions are related to motivation and achievement, as well to broad aspects of self-regulation and learning strategies. Emotions can be predicted from classroom antecedents (Pekrun et al. 2002). Achievement goals influence a child's emotional reactions in school, while emotional reactions influence coping strategies that a child can generate and use (Uebuchi 2004). The positive and negative emotions that students experience trigger specific problem-solving strategies. Interestingly, healthy individuals who are experiencing negative emotions tend to be more focused on finding information and using it than those experiencing positive emotions (Spering, Wagener, and Funke 2005).

Buckley and Saarni (2006) point out that emotion regulation and attitudes toward academics connected with moods predict grade point averages for middle school students. These authors found that young teens who had more negative feelings toward academic routines did less well academically, whether or not they were brighter than their peers. The relationship is complex, however, in that emotion regulation, students' dispositions, and academic emotions each contributed separately to achievement as measured by grade point averages in middle school (Gumora and Arsenio 2002).

Self-Regulation of Attention

Self-regulation per se, which is a hot topic in education, appears to be a broad concept that is primarily cognitive and relates to academic achievement. Students are taught skills to self-regulate their thinking and behavior so that they can achieve at higher rates and not disrupt the learning environment. However, there is less focus on the regulation of emotion, which predicts social interactions and goal-directed actions. Regulation of attention and the use of strategies are important not only for academic success but for social success and general adjustment as well. Differences in emotional reactivity among students along with their emotion regulation abilities may be the connection between social competency and academic performance, at least in the early school years. Children who are extremely reactive emotionally and are not supported will have difficulty in school (Blair 2003).

The broad executive function system acts as a "supervisor" facilitating regulation of thoughts and actions (Waber, Gerber, Turcios, and Wagner 2006). Attention control is positively related to student achievement (Muris 2006), and teaching students to monitor their own behavior improves attention. Students can learn to check whether or not they are attending by asking themselves questions, e.g., "Am I paying attention?" If they can master a "self-checking" system, they are less disruptive and spend more time on-task. Learning to self-monitor is associated with increased productivity and more accurate schoolwork (Amato-Zech, Hoff, and Doepke 2006). Executive weaknesses are not unusual among students from urban low-income schools. Executive functions are closely related to achievement on tests, and these weaknesses place some children at a disadvantage. Students in low-income urban area schools often have difficulty with high-stakes tests partly because of weaker executive functions (Waber et al. 2006).

Attention and emotion processes are related. Attention shifting and focusing are considered to be strong indicators of self-regulation ability. These processes have overlapping neural circuitry and are closely linked. Students with good attention also tend to learn appropriate emotion display rules and emotion management skills. Attentional competence relates to how an individual will exhibit both positive and negative emotion and also determines how peers will regard a particular child. Students who have difficulty focusing in class may also have difficulty identifying and managing their emotions. Teachers have to be aware of the connection between attention and emotions in order to be able to anticipate a student's reactions to stress, and both have to be addressed in prevention programs. Importantly, interventions that improve attentional and emotional competence may also strengthen social functioning (Trentacosta, Izard, Mostow, and Fine 2006).

Academic Emotions

Academic emotions or the emotions experienced in academic situations constitute a new area of interest in educational psychology. Academic emotions appear to be specific for each subject area. Anxiety is the one emotion that seems to be somewhat less domain specific, and text anxiety is the only academic emotion that has been studied in depth (Goetz, Pekrun, Hall, and Haag 2006). Linnenbrink (2006) writes that "affect is critical to understanding students' and teachers' educational experiences, and that it has been ignored for far too long" (p. 313).

The importance of emotions in the school setting is of increasing interest as researchers continue to demonstrate their significance. School is a highly emotional place for both students and teachers. Students experience feelings associated with success and failure and of acceptance and rejection (Meyer and Turner 2006; Schutz et al. 2006). Emotions influence a student's interest in learning, engagement, achievement, and motivation, as well as the social climate of individual classrooms and the general school environment. A student's emotional development is an important educational outcome by itself, even if we do not take into account the effect of emotions on other aspects of his or her life.

Pekrun (2006) defines achievement emotions as "...emotions tied directly to achievement activities or achievement outcomes" (p. 317). Little is known about the functions of emotions in schools, and we do not *yet* know how to make classroom instruction and learning environments emotionally healthy (Pekrun 2006). However, it appears that there are bidirectional and reciprocal relationships among motivation, affect, and cognition, and all of these must be understood if we are to fully appreciate a student's educational experience (Linnenbrink 2006). We do know that matching the demands of academic tasks to each student's ability can enhance achievement motivation. Providing authentic learning tasks, engaging all students in classroom discussion, avoiding social comparisons, and minimizing competition are all important in enhancing the emotional climate of the classroom.

Test Anxiety

Anxiety is individual. For some students anxiety increases motivation and for others it decreases it (Pekrun 2006). A student who receives a failing grade on a test may become emotionally overwhelmed and burst into tears. Another may become very frustrated and angry, blaming the teacher for poor instruction. Another may react with intense anxiety and ruminate about the manner in which her parents will react, and will concentrate less well for the remainder of the school day. Still another student may become focused and more determined to be prepared for the next test.

Anxious children and adolescents focus inward and worry about what they should be doing differently *during* a test. In high-pressure testing situations they think about how they are doing rather than about taking the test, which may well affect their performance. Emotion regulation during test taking includes appraisal processes and task and emotion focusing. It also involves regaining focus once it is lost because of the anxiety that the situation has generated (Schutz et al. 2006).

According to the National Scientific Council on the Developing Child (2004), thinking can be impaired when a student does not manage feelings well, and there is a body of research that indicates that anxiety decreases children's test performance. Many children worry about tests, and anxiousness around testing may be increasing owing to the proliferation of testing associated with the standards movement in schools across the United States (McDonald 2001). High-achieving students often manage anxiety sufficiently well to perform in high-pressure situations, frequently using self-regulation strategies (Cleary 2006).

Although any high-stakes learning environment can stress some students, those with negative attitudes and those who perceive evaluations as threatening perform less well on tests (Wallace and Truelove 2006). Moreover, repeated or subtle disapproval is a form of punishment after failure and is a known precursor of test anxiety (Pekrun 2006). Figure 6.1 provides some additional information about test anxiety.

Test anxiety is related to weak study skills, poor organization, fear of failure, and difficulty understanding main ideas (Wallace and Truelove 2006). Furner and Berman (2003) posit a variety of possible causes of math anxiety, including:

Test Anxiety

Test anxiety is a form of performance anxiety associated with fear of being judged by others (Black, 2005, p. 42). The more students ruminate over tests, the more anxious they become. Students with true test anxiety are preoccupied with worry, deal with fear of failure, feel worthless when stressed, and are physically affected when worrying about testing (Zbornik 2001).

For students underachieving in general, the ability to tolerate stressful situations and to feel challenged by demands explains a great deal of the variability in performance. Teens perceive their academic ability or competence either positively or negatively. Negatively oriented students do not believe that they can do well, actually perform less well, and experience higher anxiety (Giota 2006).

Adolescents' belief about their cognitive ability affects performance. Good and Dweck (2003b) indicate when students believe that their intelligence is fixed and *not strong enough*, their goal becomes to avoid any indication that they lack ability. They look for easy, low-risk tasks that do not require much effort. These students' grades drop between the seventh and eighth grade. When seventh graders were placed in a study skills class that included information about how the brain forms new connections when students make concentrated efforts to learn, their academic motivation increased (Good and Dweck 2003a).

Finally, students given praise for effort rather than achievement learn to be more resilient when things do not go well. Praise for effort, or *process praise*, emphasizes the strategies that students use to master a challenge, and the choices made that result in success increased (Good and Dweck 2003a).

A student who already has difficulty with emotional regulation and often feels anxious will score lower when he or she is told that the exam will be difficult just before the exam begins (Weber and Bizer 2006).

Fig. 6.1 Test anxiety

- Lack of sufficient exposure to educational experiences that promote positive attitudes.
- Parents who pass on math anxiety.
- Poor teaching techniques.
- Too much repetition.
- Lack of application of math to everyday life.
- Particular cultural beliefs.

Reassuring self-talk such as "don't worry" or "try harder" are strategies that help some students control anxiety that is interfering with test taking (Meyer and Turner 2006). Interventions for test anxiety are listed in Fig. 6.2.

When a student has had a lot of experience with particular subject matter, situation-specific beliefs are developed that influence his or her expectations of performance. On the other hand, if there has not been a lot of experience with a particular content area, appraisals may be determined based on the student's general optimism or pessimism (Pekrun 2006). For example, students' beliefs about mathematics are determined by the immediate classroom context, as well as by prior experiences with mathematics, parents' beliefs about math, and their

> **Interventions for Test Anxiety**
>
> **(Skills and Positive Thinking)**
>
> - Practicing with sample questions.
> - Taking a study skills course and using the strategies.
> - Learning test-taking strategies and self-talk.
> - Using relaxation techniques and visualization.
> - Remembering to stop working momentarily during the test and thinking of something pleasant.
> - Changing negative worries to positive thoughts.
> - Believing that basic ability is changeable.

Fig. 6.2 Interventions for test anxiety (Black 2005; Good and Dweck 2003a)

home culture (Eynde and Turner 2006). Some students believe that boys are better at math, or that they themselves are not "mathematically inclined," or that they have a learning disability in mathematics. By late junior high or early high school, girls begin to demonstrate more math anxiety than boys. They do not enjoy math as much and experience more shame around math performance than boys (Pekrun 2006). Cates and Rhymer (2003) find that math anxiety affects *math fluency*, particularly for older students.

For the most part, students who believe that they can achieve perform well. Even those who overestimate their ability perform at a higher level than others who are more realistic. Overestimating ability can be described as a self-regulatory strategy (Lopez, Little, Oettingen, and Baltes 1998), and students who believe that they are capable downplay intrusive negative emotions when they are dealing with stress. Beliefs about one's competency to regulate one's emotions, attention, and behavior can make things worse or can facilitate school performance. If students do not believe that they are in control, they experience more negative emotion and more school-related stress as they enter middle school. Maladaptive self-regulatory beliefs make them vulnerable to both emotional and academic stresses during this normal school transition (Rudolph, Lambert, Clark, and Kurlakowsky 2001).

Student-Teacher Relationships

If students are to be engaged in their classes, their classroom environment or climate must provide positive emotional experiences, which are the bases for positive student-teacher relationships. If these variables are positive, motivation to learn is enhanced (Meyer and Turner 2006). According to the National Research Council and Institute of Medicine (2000), there is convincing evidence to indicate that not only are early relationships with parents important, but early relationships with teachers are also important in determining whether or not a child will learn self-regulation skills, emotion regulation, take others' perspectives, and develop relationships. Students who are attached to school and do not show signs of negative behaviors tend to be high in affiliative orientation (Hill and Werner 2006). Healthy school-aged children use more mature coping strategies to regulate emotion as they grow older and depend less on seeking support to control their emotions (Denham et al. 2002).

Emotion regulation is related to school performance and behaviors in complex ways. In demonstrating the effect of emotion regulation on cognitive performance. Pianta, Nimetz, and Bennett (1997) showed that the quality of the teacher-child and parent-child relationships predicted how well children managed a concept development task. Studies have shown that if teachers believe that a student is able to control his or her emotional expression and behavior, they are more likely to discipline the child coercively.

Teachers are clearly influential in children's lives, although this variable in relation to child performance and adjustment is complex. The teacher-student relationship is related to a child's emotional responses to the classroom environment. In the elementary school, at least, the teacher is the most powerful person in the classroom and the source of the strongest concentration of emotion (Goleman 2006).

Studies have shed some light on student-teacher relationships during the school years, particularly when that relationship is negative. Dependency in that relationship correlates with adjustment difficulties in school and is associated with depressed academic performance and more negative attitudes and feelings toward school. Moreover, students who have this type of relationship with their teachers are less engaged. A negative teacher-student relationship is particularly problematic. Teacher-rated conflict was associated with school avoidance, depressed self-directedness, and weaker cooperative participation, and affected how well the student 'liked' school. The importance of student-teacher relationships is discussed in Fig. 6.3. The closeness of the teacher and the student is linked to academic performance in that children with close relationships with their teachers do better and enjoy school more (Birch and Ladd 1997). Boys with low affiliative orientation tend to have poor school attachment (Hill and Werner 2006).

Early student-teacher relationships are particularly important. A longitudinal study showed that children who enjoyed a positive social-emotional classroom environment in preschool with a good teacher-child relationship interacted with a higher degree of competence with their peers in second grade (Howes 2000). In yet another study of preschool, kindergarten, and first-grade children, positive teacher-child relationships contributed toward the children's ability to learn skills that contributed toward success in school. At the same time, negativity in the relationships of boys with their teachers in kindergarten were associated with both academic and behavioral issues all the way through eighth grade, but only for boys who exhibited behavior problems in kindergarten (Hamre and Pianta 2005). The teacher-student relationship may be more important for some students than for others. Hughes and Cavell

---

Student-Teacher Relationships

The literature has demonstrated that student-teacher relationships are very important. Recent efforts to explore how students feel about their relationships with their teachers and what they feel might improve those relationships are interesting. These groups have looked at the issue from the students' point of view.

A recent 18-month project sponsored by MetLife and What Kids Can Do involved teams of students and teachers conducting surveys in Chicago, Houston, Oakland, Philadelphia, and St. Louis. More than 6,350 students and, in St. Louis and Chicago, 446 teachers completed surveys. The key finding was a call for open communication between teachers and students. Students feel that they need more real-world learning (47%), more one-on-one attention from *teachers* (37%) and more challenging classes (22%) (http://www.what-kidscando.org/specialcollections/student_as_allies/ pdfs/saa_keyfindings.pdf)

A second project, conducted by the New York State Center for School Safety, involved student-led focus groups. For more than five years data were collected to explore school safety. The students extended the original parameters of the discussions into dialogues about learning, relationships, risk prevention, and family and community concerns.

Early data determined that 86 percent of students wanted social-skill-building programs. When more detailed data were collected between 2000 and 2003, they indicated that a student's desire to achieve academically is often driven more by the student-teacher relationship than by interest in the class subject. Students see that relationship as coming before learning. All the schools in the study had large numbers of students who were not connected to any teachers or adults, and these students, particularly, wanted a more trusting and confidential relationship with the adults in the school. Many students had seen staff openly talking about information shared in confidence by other students in the hallways and other public areas of the school. Students reported that significant adults in the school gossip and break confidentiality. Teachers appear to be critical of students, who need more encouragement and respect.

Students are clearly asking for more personal attention, for a trusted adult in whom to confide, and for adults' time. Adults who work in schools can begin to work on these relationships by desisting from conversations in open school areas that include students.

Fig. 6.3 Student-teacher relationships

(1999) found that a positive relationship between students and their teachers was of most value to students whose mothers admitted to having a history of rejecting parenting in their own relationships with their children. Elementary school classrooms are often emotionally intense environments. Teacher warmth creates a strong basis for emotional understanding (Hargreaves 2000).

Teachers tend to explain poor relationships with students on the basis of a particular student's poor relationship with his or her parents. By middle school, however, student-teacher relationships are determined less by the parental relationship and more by the relationships that the student had with teachers in elementary school. Students who liked the subject matter in a class, felt that they would do well in the class, and were able to regulate their emotions and behavior had better relationships with their teachers. A student's motivation, confidence, and appreciation for the content in a course determine how well he or she will get along with the teacher, and this relationship is bidirectional. Students who get along better with their teachers feel more motivated to learn; those who are most motivated report that their teachers shared their own experiences when in school, their own struggles with learning, and something of themselves (Davis, H. 2006).

In studying student-teacher relationships in middle school and beyond, Goodenow (1993) looked at sixth, seventh, and eighth graders' sense of belonging, being valued, and being liked by the teacher. In this age group, teacher support was more powerful in relation to achievement motivation in girls than in boys; it also predicted types of interest and goal orientations (Wentzel 1998).

Teacher support may be critical in the transition to middle school, but it may not remain as important as other types of support as children continue through the school grades. Several researchers have found that the correlation between teacher support and student outcomes declines over the middle school period. Goodenow (1993) found that the strength of the relationship between teacher support and academic motivation decreased between the sixth and eighth grades. However, Reddy, Rhodes, and Mulhall (2003) determined that students' perception of teacher support declined as did students self-esteem along with increases in depressive symptoms over the same period. Those students who continued to view teacher-student relationships positively or as increasing showed a concomitant increase in self-esteem and decreased depressive symptoms. It is important to note that teachers and students do not always agree in their perceptions of the relationships they may have with each other (Hughes and Cavell 1999).

At the secondary level, teachers often consider emotions disturbing elements in the classroom. Secondary school teachers are more distant from their students, which may be due to the high school schedule. Shorter classes limit the amount of time that teachers spend with individual students, and this in turn affects the quality of student-teacher interactions. Personal knowledge and personal acknowledgment are more challenging for teachers at this level, and emotional understanding may be less likely (Hargreaves 2000).

To some extent, relationships with both teachers and peers are based on emotion regulation. Children must be able to regulate their emotions in acceptable ways so that the resulting healthy relationships can become a source of support in the classroom, thus affecting achievement. Longitudinal research clearly supports the critical nature of emotional and social adjustment as it relates to academic success and success in the school setting (Raver 2003). Children with poor emotional resilience and children who do not regulate their emotions and behavior are at risk academically (Ellis and Bernard 2006; Morrison, Brown, D'Incau, O'Farrell, and Furlong 2006).

Classroom Climate

A school's climate is the total of all of the interactions that take place in that environment among all the members of the community. The culture, norms, and traditions of a school influence those interactions. Students learn and achieve more in a positive emotional school climate (Goleman 2006). To some degree classroom climates are created through interpersonal interactions, and it is through these interactions that students and teachers establish expectations, routines, and class norms (Meyer and Turner 2006). Each classroom climate is distinguished by general affective states, which determine the actions that take place in that environment.

Positive teacher support in both academic and interpersonal matters is associated with student motivation. Positive emotions may be critical in developing a "mastery goal structure," and students who have developed such a structure understand that the purpose of schoolwork is to develop knowledge and master skills and strategies. Students who accept this prefer difficult tasks, like school, and feel good about taking part in academic work (Freeman and Anderman 2005). Engaging teachers demonstrate positive emotions with humor and enthusiasm. However, when the classroom climate is ambiguous or negative, avoidance behaviors, disruption, and cheating are more likely (Meyer and Turner 2006).

Certainly the emotions that students display to others influence the social environment of the classroom (Pekrun 2006), but teachers' emotions are also important. Teachers today have less influence over what is taught and when it is taught, which can result in feelings of powerlessness, and they, as well as their students, are emotionally vulnerable in today's schools (Schutz et al. 2006).

Social-Emotional Development and Schooling

The current focus on academic performance overshadows the importance of students' social and emotional development, even though we know that emotional adjustment makes a difference in both general adjustment and academic success. There is considerable evidence to indicate that emotional and social skills are closely connected to academic performance. Several longitudinal studies have given us data that indicate that emotional competence predicts academic outcomes (Trentacosta et al. 2006). The Attorney General's Safe School Initiative in Massachusetts found that most educators are not aware of the relationship between social-emotional curricula and academic performance as explained in Fig. 6.4.

Introducing a new curriculum into a school program that is already packed can meet with resistance. Sharing the research that supports the relationship between social-emotional learning and academic performance, as found in Fig. 6.5, may be helpful in breaking down that resistance.

Emotional knowledge and regulation are key aspects of social and emotional learning programs. Children use attention to regulate emotions, and emotional situations influence their ability to pay attention as emotional cues associated with the situation draw their focus away from academic tasks. Attention difficulties and expressions of sadness are connected to internalizing behavior,

---

**Implementing SEL (Social-Emotional Learning) Curricula Additionally Affects
Academic Performance**

Implementing social-emotional learning curricula not only has an effect on social and
emotional development as well as on academic achievement (Aber, Brown, Roderick, and
Lantieri 2001; Elias, Parker and Rosenblatt 2005; Joseph and Strain 2003). Better social
skills and social competency correlate with higher achievement scores and better grades
(Bloodworth, Weissberg, Zins, and Walberg 2001; Wentzel 1991).

Programs have been demonstrated to:

- Affect reading and math scores (Brigman and Campbell 2003).
- Improve learning skills when the general curricula is infused with social decision
  making (Elias 2001).
- Demonstrate a gain of from 8 to10 percentile points on standardized achievement test
  scores (Fonagy, Twemlow, Vernberg, Sacco, and Little 2005).
- Improve cognitive problem-solving as well as reading and planning skills (Greenberg,
  Kusché, and Riggs 2001).
- Result in greater commitment and bonding to school along with improved grades
  (Hawkins, Catalano, Morrison, O'Donnell, Abbott, and Day 1992; Hawkins, Smith,
  and Catalano 2001).

The most comprehensive collection of data indicated that integrating social-emotional
learning with academic curricula and teaching approaches is associated with improved
grades, improved standardized test scores and grade point averages, improved reading,
math, and writing skills and increased graduation rates (Zins, Bloodworth, Weissberg,
and Walberg 2004).

Other benefits of integrating social-emotional learning in the general school curricula
include: reduced dropout rates, improved attendance, fewer retentions, fewer out-of-
school suspensions, and lower rates of special education referrals (Zins et al. 2004).

Fig. 6.4 Implementing SEL (Social-Economical Learning) curricula additionally affects
academic performance

whereas attention and anger dysregulation are associated with externalizing
behavior (Trentacosta et al. 2006). Children who are having trouble attending
and are in difficulty with their peer relationships are not as sufficiently skilled in
controlling their negative emotions, particularly anger and distress, and need
help with these specific emotions (Raver 2003).

As children attend school daily, it is an appropriate place to address their
many emotional needs. Moreover, the most significant amount of federal and
state funding is tied to schools. It is easier to increase competencies than it is to
ameliorate deficits, so school-based prevention programs make good sense. To
date, school-based programs have had meaningful, albeit limited, effects on
students in their first few years of school, but the efficacy of prevention programs for children aged seven years and older is minimal, at least in regard to
reducing aggression.

Young children's emotional and social competence is tied to their academic
and cognitive competencies (Joseph and Strain 2003a; Taub and Pearrow 2005).
Classroom-based and schoolwide programming is currently the preferred way

Studies Supporting the Relationship between Social-Emotional Learning
and Academic Success

Aber, J. L., Brown, J. L., Roderick, T., and Lantieri, L. (2001). The Resolving Conflict Creatively Program: A school-based social and emotional learning program. *The CEIC Review, 10(6)*, 24–26.

Bloodworth, M. R., Weissberg, R. P., Zins, J. E., and Walberg, H. J. (2001). Implications of social and emotional research for education evidence linking social skills and academic outcomes. *The CEIC Review, 10(6)*, 4–5, 27.

Brigman, G., and Campbell, C. (2003). Helping students improve academic achievement and school success behavior. *Professional School Counseling, 7*, 91–98. Also reported in *Does Implementing a Research-Based School Counseling Curriculum Enhance Student Achievement?* School Counseling Research Brief 2.3, April 15, 2004, Center for School Counseling Outcome Research.

Elias, M. J. (2001). How social and emotional learning is infused into academics in the social decision making/social problem solving program. *The CEIC Review, 10(6)*, 16–17.

Elias, M. J., and Arnold, H. (Eds.). (2006). *The Educator's Guide to Emotional Intelligence and Academic Achievement.* Thousand Oaks, CA: Corwin Press, pp. 4–14.

Flook, L. R., Repetti, R., and Ullman, J. (2005). Classroom social experiences as predictors of academic performance. *Developmental Psychology, 41(2)*, 319–327.

Fonagy, P., Twemlow, S. W., Vernberg, E., Sacco, F. C., and Little. T. D. (2005). Creating a peaceful school learning environment: The impact of an antibullying program on educational attainment in elementary schools. *Medical Science Monitor, 11(7)*, 317–325.

Greenberg, M. T., Kusché, C. A., and Riggs, N. (2001). The P(romoting) A(lternative) TH(inking) S(trategies) Curriculum Theory and Research on Neurocognitive and Academic Development. *The CEIC Review, 10(6)*, 22–23, 26.

Greenberg, M. T., Weissberg, R. P., O'Brien, M. U., Zins, J. E., Fredericks, L., Resnik, H., and Elias, M. J. (2003). Enhancing school-based prevention and youth development through coordinated social, emotional and academic learning. *American Psychologist, 58(6/7)*, 466–474.

Hawkins, J. D., Smith, B. H., and Catalano, R. F. (2001). Social development and social and emotional learning. The Seattle Social Development Project. *The CEIC Review, 10(6)*, 18–19, 27.

Joseph, G., and Strain, P. (2003). Comprehensive evidence-based social–emotional curricula for young children: An analysis of efficacious adoption potential. *TECSE, 23(2)*, 65–76.

NASP CENTER (2002). *Social Skills: Promoting Positive Behavior, Academic Success, and School Safety.* Retrieved May 26, 2006 from *http://www.naspcenter.org/factsheets/socialskills_fs.html*

Simons-Morton, B.G., and Crump, A.D. (2003). Association of parental involvement and social competence with school adjustment and engagement among sixth graders. *Journal School Health, 73(3)*, 121–126.

Zins, J. E., Bloodworth, M. R., Weissberg, R. P., and Walberg, H. J. (2004). The scientific base linking social and emotional learning to school success. In J. E. Zins, M. R. Bloodworth, R. P Weissberg, and H. J. Walberg (Eds.), *Building Academic Success on Social and Emotional Learning: What Does the Research Say?* (pp. 3–22). Teachers College, Columbia University.

Fig. 6.5 Studies Supporting the Relationship between Social-Emotional Learning and Academic Success

to deliver social and emotional interventions, and the need is particularly acute in urban areas (Boxer, Musher-Eizenman, Dubow, Danner, and Heretick 2006). When prevention and intervention programs are delivered right in the classroom: (a) the cost is reasonable, (b) children remain in the room where teachers are involved with the new attitudes, behaviors, and competencies that are being taught, (c) skills generalize more easily, and (d) negative models are contained (Merrell 2002; Raver 2003).

Taking students who are having behavioral control difficulties and working with them together outside of the classroom may only exacerbate behavioral difficulties because children model negative behavior for one another and reinforce one another's inappropriate behaviors. School psychologists are aware of the fact that as early as fourth grade some aggressive students are perceived to be 'cool' by their classmates and their popularity increases (Boxer et al. 2006).

Some programs are designed to change the way students think about situations in which they find themselves. Through modeling, role-play, and group discussions, teachers and school psychologists assist children in identifying and labeling emotions in themselves and others, in communicating about emotions, in controlling their reactions to emotional events, and in problem solving. Some programs also teach children how to manage anger and to change their thinking. These social-emotional learning programs have added value in that they increase academic resilience and have been connected with higher test performance (Elias, Parker, and Rosenblatt 2005; Raver 2003; Winslow, Sandler, and Wolchik 2005).

Pincus and Friedman (2004) note that a number of school-based prevention and intervention programs are now on the market. Many of these teach problem-focused skills, which are expected to increase a child's ability to cope with stress. There are not nearly as many programs that teach emotion-focused skills that include emotion regulation and reframing one's thinking about an uncomfortable situation when that situation is not controllable. Shipman et al. (2004) advocate for prevention programs to help children acquire skills associated with emotion regulation and to strengthen emotion regulation in children who have fewer skills or abilities than their peers, so that psychopathology can be prevented.

Emotion Regulation Can Be Strengthened

Before exploring programs that might be implemented to strengthen students' skills of emotion regulation, it is important to know whether or not emotion regulation can really be changed or strengthened. There has been some very interesting recent research designed to address this question.

Lane and McRae (2004) indicate that emotions compete with one another for conscious processing. Thus, there are large individual differences in the extent to which students can pay attention to and use emotional information. This also explains differences in whether individuals attend to internal information, such as body signals and negative and repetitive thoughts, or to external information from their environments. It takes a good deal of energy to regulate emotions.

Baumeister, Gailliot, Dewall, and Oaten (2006) have proposed that self-regulation is a *limited resource*, which can be depleted when used. They liken all types of self-regulation to a single source of energy, which in turn is used to alter a person's behavior. This energy resource diminishes when it is used, and when it is worn down, the individual's ability to cope will be much less successful. When low-anxious people are energy depleted, they become just as passive when facing stress as high-anxious individuals. After resisting the desire to eat cookies, individuals who participated in a laboratory study gave up sooner than their peers on the next task, which required both effort and persistence, because their energy was theoretically diminished (Baumeister, Bratslavsky, Muraven, and Tice 1998).

Coping with stress and regulating negative emotions require continuous self-control efforts. Vigilance, ostracism, and resisting temptations also require continuing self-control. Researchers have concluded that after as little as *one act* of self-control, a person's ability to control other unrelated behaviors is weakened. Apparently, there is an *aftereffect* to efforts to get or to stay in control. Coping with stress leads to decreased ability to delay gratification and resist temptation because resources are degraded. According to studies the type of stressor does not seem to matter (controllable or uncontrollable) and neither does the effort involved, the difficulty of the task, or the person's mood. The executive factor of inhibition is limited and can be consumed (Baumeister, Gailliot et al. 2006; Muraven and Baumeister 2000; Williams 2007).

These studies are particularly interesting in regard to aggression. When individuals engaged in self-regulation were subsequently provoked, they *increased* aggressive responding. It may be that young people have limited ability to stop aggressive or disruptive behavior after having their self-regulatory energy depleted (DeWall, Baumeister, Stillman, and Gailliot 2006). Continuing efforts at self-control caused a decrease in the energy resource.

Recently, researchers have proposed that a reduction in glucose may account for this phenomenon (Gailliot, Baumeister, DeWall, Maner, Plant, Tice, et al. 2007). Brain activity depends on glucose for energy and effortful striving, which in turn depends on well-functioning executive processes, and executive processes may be strongly affected by levels of glucose. Self-regulation or the ability to control thinking, emotions, impulses, and adherence to social rules requires considerable effort. Self-control itself relies on glucose levels, and fluctuations in glucose have been connected to impulsivity; aggressive behavior; and the ability to concentrate, to cope with stress, and to regulate emotion (Gailliot et al. 2007, p. 326). In a series of laboratory studies, Gailliot et al. (2007) demonstrated that participants' glucose levels dropped after efforts at self-control. They associated the lowered glucose levels with poor self-control during the next task because adding a (glucose) snack re-energized the participants and increased their subsequent self-control.

The positive aspect of this work is that we now not only understand that a student's ability to control emotion and behavior may not be entirely tied to motivation. We also have some evidence that indicates that increasing one's energy by adding glucose or introducing exercise can strengthen self-regulation. Subjects in another series of laboratory studies who practiced self-regulation regularly showed the most improvement. Interestingly, strengthening self-regulation generalized to different types of self-regulation. Students who participated in study programs designed to engage their self-regulation ability studied better and reported less distress during testing later on. It appears that self-control is much like a muscle that can grow stronger with regular exercise, as long as exercise is interspersed with relaxation (Baumeister, Gailliot et al. 2006; Muraven and Baumeister 2000).

Programs that Address Emotion Regulation to Varying Degrees

Many different curricula on the market today address students' social emotional development. These programs have different degrees of evidence to support their efficacy, and there are a number of groups and agencies that have evaluated the various programs available, although they have used different criteria to determine effectiveness.

Identifying an evidence-based program is insufficient. Schools must implement the programs as they are written if they expect similar results, and in order for social-emotional programs to be maximally effective, the general school climate must be positive (Elias, Kress, and Hunter 2006). Fortunately, school psychologists do not have to spend a great deal of time on research to determine whether or not a particular program has evidence to support its use, for, as noted above, there are several groups who have already evaluated the programs on the market (see Fig. 6.6).

A few of these programs are described below with various degrees of evidence to support their use in schools. They are aimed at different age groups to provide a sampling of the curricula available. The aspect of each curriculum that has to do with emotions and emotion regulation is emphasized. Of the programs described, the Second Step program has the most support and Making Choices is relatively new with considerably less support.

Second Step

Second Step is a classroom-based social skills program for children four to fourteen years of age that is designed to reduce impulsive and aggressive behavior and increase social competence. Empathy is taught by helping children learn to identify and understand their own emotions and those of others. They learn how to evaluate behavioral consequences in terms of fairness, safety, and impact on others, to accurately identify feelings, and to de-escalate anger by leaving the stressful situation (Fogt and Piripavel 2002). Impulse control, problem solving, and anger management are addressed as

---

Resources for Program Evaluations

Safe and Sound: An Educational Leader's Guide to Evidence-Based Social and Emotional Learning (SEL) Programs, (2004); Blueprints for Violence Prevention, Institute of Education Sciences; OJJDP Model Program Guide (http://www.dsgonline.com/mpg2.5/mpg_index.htm)

PAVNET Programs Database (http://www.nal.usda.gov/pavnet/prog.html)

Promising Practices Network (http://www.promisingpractices.net/programs_topic.asp)

SAMHSA Model Programs: See '*Comparison Matrix of Science-Based Prevention Programs: A Consumer's Guide for Prevention Professionals*' (2002) (http://www.model-programs.samhsa.gov/)

Blueprints for Violence Prevention (http://www.colorado.edu/cspv/blueprints/index.html)

Hamilton Fish Institute: Violence Prevention Programs (updated 2005). (http://ham-fish.org/cms/view/9/)

Social Development Research Group: Research Findings on Evaluations of Positive Youth Development Programs (1998) (http://aspe.hhs.gov/hsp/PositiveYouthDev99/)

Prevention Research Center for the Promotion of Human Development: A Review of the Effectiveness of Prevention Programs (Revised 2000) (http://www.prevention.psu.edu/pubs/docs/CMHS.pdf)

National Center for Mental Health Promotion and Youth Violence Prevention (http://www.promoteprevent.org/resources/resource_pages/program_functions/evidence_based.htm)

Center for Social Emotional Education (http://www.csee.net/pageview.aspx?id = 38)

Safe, Supportive and Successful Schools: Step by Step (2004) Sopris West

---

well. The program includes an optional parent component and has received high ratings from the Substance Abuse and Mental Health Services Administration, the U.S. Department of Health and Human Services and the U. S. Department of Education (http://www.modelprograms.samhsa.gov/pdfs/Details/SecondStep.pdf). Participating students improved their social behaviors to a greater degree than their inappropriate behaviors decreased. Middle school students decreased their tendencies to believe that acting aggressively is a way to solve problems (Merrell 2002).

PATHS

The *PATHS Curriculum* (Promoting Alternative Thinking Strategies), which is designed to prevent or reduce behavioral and emotional problems, includes lessons on developing self-control, feelings and relationships, emotional understanding, interpersonal problem solving, building positive self-esteem, and improving peer communications/relations. It has been shown to improve protective factors and reduce behavioral risk among a wide range of elementary school-aged children and has also been shown to improve students' ability to control impulsivity (Riggs, Greenberg, Kusché, and Pentz 2006). Several studies using control groups have been conducted to evaluate the effectiveness of the PATHS curriculum. Use of PATHS significantly increased the children's ability to: (a) recognize and understand emotions, (b) understand social problems, (c) develop effective alternative solutions, and (d) decrease the percentage of aggressive/violent solutions. Teachers also reported reduced behavior problems and decreased symptoms of sadness and depression.

The *FT/PATHS Curriculum* is a revised version of PATHS designed to be the universal prevention component of the *Fast Track Program*. Goals include the prevention of aggression and promotion of social and academic competence. The FT/PATHS maintains the critical components of the original program. After one year of implementation, children in the first grade were less aggressive as rated by classmates and less disruptive as rated by their teachers; moreover, according to observers, the classroom atmosphere improved (Greenberg, Kusché and Mihalic 1998).

Dinosaur School

Dinosaur School is being implemented and evaluated as a universal intervention in Head Start, kindergarten, and first-grade classrooms. Preliminary analyses suggest that the program is promising, as it has been seen to have positive effects on student compliance and social contact and to decrease aggressive behaviors (Joseph and Strain 2003a,b,c).

SCERTS

The *SCERTS Program*, which is designed specifically for children with autism spectrum disorders, supports development in regard to communicating with others and establishing relationships and regulating arousal to support engagement. It also supports learning for students as they work toward goals. The program has a major component relating to emotion regulation. Prizant, Wetherby, Rubin, Laurent, and Rydell (2005) view emotion regulation as *essential* for the development all children, not only for those with disabilities. They consider self-regulation and respondent mutual regulation in their model, which has to do with providing supports in terms of the response that others (parents and teachers) provide when a child is over- or underaroused. A limited number of studies have been conducted to examine the effectiveness of visual schedules and visually cued choice making and instruction for children with autism spectrum disorders (Mirenda 2001). Beneficial outcomes have been reported, but there have not yet been any broad well-controlled studies. SCERTS uses visual supports as a basic component.

Strong Kids/Strong Teens

Strong Kids is a curriculum with social and emotional learning and resiliency goals designed for children from the fourth through the eighth grade. *Strong Teens* targets students in grades nine through twelve. The lessons are given once a week for twelve consecutive weeks and have been demonstrated to improve a child's knowledge about positive social-emotional behavior and reduce negative emotional symptoms in each age group (Merrell, Carrizales, Feuerborn, Gueldner, and Tran 2006a,b). The lessons involve increasing awareness and appropriate expression of emotions, connections between feelings and events, empathy training, cognitive restructuring, appropriate expression of anger, learned optimism, attribution retraining, empathy training, conflict resolution, goal setting, relaxation, and getting help if you need it.

beyondblue

The curriculum connected with *beyondblue* is a very interesting national research initiative from South Australia designed to prevent depression and promote emotional well-being and social connectedness. This high school program is delivered weekly over three years with the goal of building protective factors within the adolescent. The first-year program has to do with self-knowledge, emotions, and emotion regulation, including coping skills for dealing with stress. The second-year's curriculum involves relationships and the third year's teaches self-talk, problem solving, time management, and planning (http://www.beyondblue.org.au/index.aspx?link_id=4.64).

Making Choices: Social Problem Solving for Children

Making Choices: Social Problem Solving for Children is a kindergarten through grade five cognitive problem-solving curriculum designed to promote social competence and prevent conduct problems among elementary school students. This school-based program is aimed at reducing aggression by increasing children's skills in both processing social situations and interactions and by regulating emotions. Children learn a seven-step cognitive problem-solving sequence, which integrates *social* information processing with emotion regulation. The steps include: (a) understanding and regulating emotions, (b) encoding social and environmental cues, (c) interpreting cues and intentions, (d) setting relational goals, (e) formulating alternative strategies, (f) selecting prosocial strategies, and (g) enacting a selected strategy. An initial three-year study with third-grade students has had positive results (Fraser, Galinsky, Smokowski, Day, Terzian, Rose, et al 2005).

A New Project

The Association for Applied Psychophysiology and Biofeedback (AAPB) is currently working on a new project that is designed to teach children to self-regulate through the use of a workbook to assist educational and health professionals (http://www.aapb.org/i4a/pages/index.cfm?pageid = 3664). The initial focus is on middle school children. Volunteers from the Pediatrics and Education sections of AAPB have written handouts and learning modules for this curriculum, which will cover six topic areas: (1) biological self-regulation, (2) emotional self-regulation, (3) stress management, (4) social self-regulation, (5) spiritual/moral self-regulation, and (6) neural self-regulation.

Promising Resources

It appears that no powerful, evidence-based school curriculum that addresses primarily emotion regulation has been in use long enough to have a strong research base. However, there are several sources to help school psychologists discern what is important in a program designed for prevention or intervention. Several highly promising resources include the learning objectives from the SCERTS model, some of the lessons from *beyondblue*, the outline of the project by the AAPB, and the Strong Kids/Strong Teens curricula. These programs appear to address issues involved in emotion regulation well, and together they provide an interesting and important package of skills and knowledge.

Chapter 7
Emotion Regulation and Social Functioning in the Context of the Peer Group

Social Functioning

Students react emotionally to the challenges of learning and performing in class, as well as to their relationships with their teachers and the emotional climates of their classrooms, but the school environment is more complex than this and extends beyond the walls of the classroom. Classrooms are filled with children who must learn to live and work together in the classroom and in other school environments both within the building and on the playgrounds and athletic fields. From the student's point of view these other relationships and environments are just as important and sometimes more important and more emotionally challenging.

Social functioning is central to a child's adjustment and success in several areas. It determines whether or not a child will *like* school and how successful he or she will be in school; it even has an influence on academic competence. Children who are not successful socially are at risk for anxiety and behavior problems.

Students who are strong in effortful control of their emotions, attention, and behavior can manage anger, are both sympathetic and empathetic, and behave positively in their interactions with others. They are competent socially and are well liked by their peers. Children who are competent in regard to emotion regulation have high levels of play interaction, and when presented with conflicts are better able to take turns and share. They are less likely to grab another's toys or to show temper on the playground. Boys and girls who are emotionally flexible can come back after an altercation or stressful encounter, and the peer group accepts them. The peer group considers their less controlled peers 'immature,' and such children are not well liked. Temperamental reactivity determines popularity early on and popularity may be difficult to change. This is a serious concern and emphasizes the fact that it is very important to improve emotional reactivity with poorly regulated students in the early grades (Fantuzzo, Sekino, and Cohen 2004; Spinrad et al. 2006).

Emotion dysregulation places children at risk for isolation from peers or rejection by peers (Sanson et al. 2002). Gross (1998b) wrote, "...emotion regulation is almost always a social affair" (p. 279). There is a specified set of abilities related to social skills, which includes: (a) emotion regulation, (b) attention regulation, and (c) emotional reactivity. According to Sanson et al. (2002), intense irritability and mood, high-uncontrolled arousal, difficulty carrying a task or activity through to completion, and weak approach or sociability predicts poor social skills. There are strong relationships among these childhood characteristics. Young people who are drawn to social interaction but who are poorly regulated tend to exhibit more externalizing behaviors along with irritability and anger. Children with poor regulation and low sociability tend to exhibit internalizing behaviors, including distress and anxiety. Negative emotionality involves not only anger but also fear and anxiety.

Children who are not able to *tone down* the intensity of their emotional reactions, to keep the *duration* of intense emotion under control, or have emotional displays too frequently are not going to be able to achieve their goals in play or in other social relationships. When they become overaroused, their behavior will interfere with their relationships.

A student's social status or popularity is related to how well he or she understands emotions in others and controls anger. Popular students resist provocation by taking planned, assertive action rather than losing their tempers. They understand their peers' intentions because they recognize others' emotions and interpret them accurately. Popular students can handle their own negative emotions (Hubbard and Coie 1994). The peer group admires children who are 'cool' and do not get upset when others provoke them (Leary and Katz 2005; Levine 2005).

The Influence of the Peer Group

It is not only parents and teachers who influence a child's ability to regulate emotions; the peer group plays an important role as well. Peers act as "trainers" for one another. Children are strongly influenced by the peers they come into contact with as they play and learn. They also acquire emotional regulation as a result of the complex demands they must learn to deal with through peer interactions. As students go through school, they must learn to keep excitement under control and master the skills of negotiating when there is difficulty without losing control. Peers like children who can regulate their emotions easily and well and look for them as playmates and teammates. Older students use more effective strategies for accomplishing this regulation than younger ones (Hubbard and Coie 1994). The peer group is a key source of emotional knowledge and practice, as peer norms influence students' behavior (Bronson 2000).

Among preschoolers, a child's reactivity along with the ability to relate to his or her emotions is connected with both conflict and cooperation with peers. When young children become very distressed owing to frustration in peer interactions and react loudly, they are more likely to experience conflict with their peers. Those who can distract themselves when frustrated are less likely to experience conflict (Calkins et al. 1999). Some young boys can get easily disorganized and out of control during rough-and-tumble play. In both preschool and kindergarten, boys who are weaker in emotion control and seek out and spend a lot of time with others who are like them become less socially competent. High reactivity along with weaker attention and emotion regulation are related to acting-out behaviors. Disorganization in the group can lead to dysregulated emotional behavior (Fabes, Martin Hanish, Anders and Madden-Derdich 2003; Fox 1998; Sanson et al. 2002).

Children who find it very difficult to control the intensity of negative emotions, in particular, become more and more isolated from their peers (Fabes et al. 2002). Girls and boys who become overstimulated and cannot deal constructively with their emotions may withdraw, disrupt others' play, or act out aggressively. Those with social deficits have considerable difficulty de-escalating their emotions and do not focus on calming themselves. Of emotion regulation and emotion intensity, the former is a stronger predictor of social difficulties (Melnick and Hinshaw 2000). Once again, this makes the case for intervention. Students who are weak in emotion regulation need intervention.

Some students learn quite late that feelings do not have to be acted out, a delay that may relate to weaker executive ability. Executive skills are needed in order to refrain from action and to correct social errors. A child must be able to evaluate his or her own behavior in relation to group norms and then change that behavior based on the reactions of the group. For some children, social difficulties may be related to several different problems with executive functions including: (a) social checking for cues, (b) ability to change behavior midstream (to switch set), (c) planning, (d) generating alternatives or options for behavior, and (e) changing goals. All of these require checking one's emotions and emotion intensity long enough to initiate thinking.

Attention regulation is the *link* between emotion regulation and cognitive responses, and students who have difficulty with it are delayed in developing social competence. Attention regulation includes the ability to: (a) pay attention to cues in the environment, (b) sustain attention to the action, (c) refocus by distracting oneself, and (d) think about the situation differently.

Blocked goals, which occur when a student cannot finish what he is doing or cannot obtain what she wants immediately, are common triggers for anger and emotion dysregulation (Parke et al. 2002; Semrud-Clikeman 2003). Children with ADHD-combined type (inattention and impulsivity) have difficulties with emotion regulation; those with the inattentive type of ADHD alone have more difficulty with social knowledge; and the less impulsive ADHD students have less difficulty with regulation (Maedgen and Carlson 2000). However, even children with subclinical attention difficulties have trouble with peer relationships (Rielly et al. 2006).

Children who continue to have difficulties regulating emotion when they begin school and during the early grades are more likely to have problems in social competence. This is because intense and negative reactions along with the ability to control emotions and attention are so strongly related to social competence in this age group (Smart and Sanson 2001). Children who react with negative emotions and do not regulate their emotional responses also have trouble verbalizing their negative feelings, and being without adequate emotion vocabulary they tend to act out. Not only do their peers then reject them, but their teachers describe them as less friendly and more aggressive (Buckley and Saarni 2006). High negative emotionality in stressful situations leads to problems for all students, girls as well as boys (Sanson et al. 2002).

The ability to tone down or recover from an angry outburst or from intense excitement is related to a child's ability to remain engaged in the play action. It is also related to conflict resolution. Socially competent and popular students utilize behaviors that hold off the negative behaviors of their peers, which prevents them from experiencing as much negative emotion themselves. Less competent children either do not have or do not use this skill; however, it is also possible that they have a different threshold for responding to anger (Denham et al. 2002).

Emotion regulation continues to be important into adolescence. Teens who have difficulty coping with negative emotions may seek social support, which for some is a way of 'repairing' mood (Verissimo 2005). Adolescents with different behavior profiles cope differently when they experience peer stress. Unfortunately, unpopular and more aggressive adolescents tend to use negative coping strategies. Girls at this age who are withdrawn use strategies that minimize the emotional impact associated with the problem, employing an avoidant strategy when there is conflict, rather than negotiating to find areas of agreement. Interestingly, very popular aggressive girls use problem solving and cope actively (Bowker, Bukowski, Hymel, and Sippola 2000). Teachers believe that cooperation and self-control, including emotion control, particularly in regard to controlling one's temper with peers as well as with adults are crucial for success during adolescence (Lane, Pierson, and Givner 2004).

Display Rules

Children learn how and when to express emotion through social interactions with their peers. The ways in which emotion is displayed will determine the types of responses that they will get from others. The ways in which emotion is displayed must *fit* the peer culture as well as the more general culture if the child is going to be accepted by the peer group (Shipman, Zeman, Nesin, and Fitzgerald 2003). Students actually create their own group cultures, which have norms that include how emotional events will be interpreted. They create their own rules about how emotions can be expressed or not expressed and about how they are to be controlled (Denham et al. 2002). There is a hidden protocol in schools with norms, shared beliefs, and rules that are seldom expressed openly, yet students are expected to conform to these rituals in order to be accepted (Lavoie 2005).

Display rules must be learned in the peer group. Most adults appreciate the complexity of these rules and do not try to teach them. Students have to learn when it is appropriate to express emotion and when it is not okay to do so. There are rules for which emotions can be displayed, under what circumstances, and in which contexts. For example, fear cannot be shown in the presence of a bully. Boys do not cry when things do not go their way. Girls do not show their friends that they are angry. In order to understand display rules, a student has to be able to perceive these unspoken rules, which are learned through teasing and rejection.

Figuring out the rules and discovering that rules of interaction are often emotionally negotiated can be very complex, more so for some children than others (Hubbard and Coie 1994; Macklem 2003). Games on the playground do have rules, but they change frequently during the game, and they apply more to some children than to others. Students with less emotional control often appear to be subject to more rigid rules. Their tendency to become upset may reinforce the more powerful players, or the socially stronger players may use their power in the group to reject peers who overreact to the unfairness of the situation.

Given that the most socially powerful young participant(s) controls the game, the unfairness of this situation may trigger intense anger in a child with poor emotion control, and anger expressed in this situation can trigger teasing. Understanding the unspoken rules around anger is particularly difficult. The display rules for anger are more complicated than those for other emotions (Hubbard and Coie 1994). Children must have sufficient emotion control to be able to figure out the painful lessons being taught by the group and adapt their behavior sufficiently to prevent repetition of the negative interaction (Macklem 2003).

In compliance with the peer culture, the group interprets events that elicit emotion in the same way and agree on the rules about the expression and regulation of feelings and the accompanying behaviors that emotions generate. This is accomplished over time through play, through games, or through being teased and isolated from the group. The rules are never actually spoken out loud. Children must learn that it is risky to show fear when being provoked or to show anxiety when meeting a new potential friend. During the first few years of schooling children learn how to project an "emotional front." They learn about the "cool rule," which requires emotion regulation in many social contexts. In order to be socially competent, a child must learn to be cool, guarded, and not easily triggered emotionally (Denham et al. 2002). The cool rule is described in Fig. 7.1.

Children learn that an emotional display in reaction to negative experiences in the group is an unfortunate mistake (Denham et al. 2002). Peers model control skills and provide opportunity for the practice in learning to control emotions that children need to be successful. Students who attend and learn display rules are successful, but those with high social anxiety, deficits in social perception, nonverbal learning disabilities, autism spectrum disorders, and even subclinical or unidentified weaknesses have difficulty learning them.

The Cool Rule

According to Dansei (1994), the concept "cool" originated in the jazz clubs of the 1930s. It was later used to describe the musicians and patrons of the jazz clubs and was further popularized by Camel's cigarette ads. Being cool involves a set of bodily movements, postures, facial expressions, use of one's voice, head tilt, language, dress, music, and other age-specific *group* interests and behaviors. Pountain and Robins (2000) point out ancient origins of the word cool from the rebellious, oppositional attitude it represented in the 1950s and 1960s to its more mainstream use by the 1980s and 1990s.

The cool rule for students relates to hiding intense emotion. A student who is *conforming* to the cool rule is well controlled emotionally. Emotional outbursts are quickly repressed and embarrassment is avoided at all costs, no matter how anxious or angry a student may be (Dansei 1994). Looking cool at the mall is very important and as long as the subject matter at school is cool, it is embraced.

Another term for the unspoken rules and norms of the peer culture is "hidden curriculum." Very complex and contextual, it involves body language, communication, behavior, and appearance. It differs by age, gender, group, environment, and culture. The hidden curriculum and rules of the peer culture are never directly taught. Teaching is indirect, intuitive. Peers assume they are "obvious" and that "everyone knows them" (Myles, Trautman, and Schelvan 2004). When the rules are broken, the reaction of peers is strong. Some children have deficits in this type of learning; others are so preoccupied that they miss some of the rules; and still others loudly protest the rules. These students need direct instruction.

Fig. 7.1 The cool rule

Often children who are ignored or rejected by the peer group exhibit behaviors that are highly aversive to peers such as: (a) repeating things over and over, (b) continuing to talk when the play has started, (c) fooling around during the game, (d) pestering for attention, (e) not responding when told to "get lost," (f) trying to get to play when the game has already started, (g) not respecting space/materials, (h) not attending closely to the play action, (i) behaving in a silly way (play interaction is serious business), and (j) arguing negatively during game (Macklem, 2003). Students who are regularly excluded from peer group activities lose the opportunity to learn about the peer culture that is so critical for social interaction, general happiness in school, and social success.

Empathy

Empathy is an emotional reaction to another person. Those who feel empathy for another share that individual's feelings in a particular situation. Empathy is involved in behavior that is considered 'responsible' in the school culture. However, experiencing the same feelings as another does not necessarily result in empathy because a person can experience either *empathy* or *sympathy* (Bear et al. 2003). In order to feel empathy, an individual must be able to:

- Identify or sense the emotion that the other person is experiencing.
- Assume the perspective of the other person.
- Experience the same emotion or emotions without becoming overwhelmed by them.

Studies by Feshbach and Feshbach (2004) indicate that individuals who are more empathetic will be less aggressive.

Students' tendencies to be upset and distressed when they encounter another person experiencing distress or to feel empathetic concern indicate that emotion can be aroused in more than one way and have more than one effect. (Goodvin and Torquati 2006). Students who tend to experience intense emotions and to experience negative emotions frequently, do not react to peers or siblings with sympathy. In order to respond with sympathy, young children must be able to regulate the intensity and negativity of the emotions they experience. Children who are not very emotional may be more likely to pay attention to how others feel and may find it easier to focus their attention on others. Those who are sympathetic are skilled in their interactions with others (Teglasi 1998b).

Children who become very distressed when they see others upset tend to have more difficulty regulating emotion. Upset and distress occur when the child reacts to the another's emotion too intensely in a stressful situation. Personal upset is associated with overarousal. Children who are more capable of regulating emotion and feel less intense emotions tend to be more sympathetic and more empathetic. Importantly, researchers suggest that empathy depends on two variables: emotional intensity and frequency of experiencing negative emotions in particular. Intensity and negative emotionality are stable characteristics of an individual's temperament. Theoretically, a young person who is low in regulation and high in intensity will react with distress, whereas one who is able to control emotions will respond to others with sympathy whether or not he or she has an intense temperament.

Negative emotionality would push a child to feel distress. Young people who tend to react with anger or anxiety are more likely to respond with distress to another's predicament or upset. Those who respond with a moderate level of sadness might be more likely to experience sympathy, even though they may also feel distressed. Children who can: (a) control their emotions, (b) shift attention away from distressing stimuli, (c) focus on something positive, and (d) control emotion-related behavior are more likely to respond with sympathy to another's distress (Eisenberg et al. 1998).

Effects of Rejection on Emotion Regulation

The peer group does not tolerate breaking the rules of the culture that they have created. It not only teaches individual students about emotion regulation but also actively regulates behavior through rejection. Children who try to get into the group at the wrong time or in the wrong way according to the rules of the peer culture are rejected 60 percent of the time and may have little under-standing of why they are not accepted. Close observation of children in ele-mentary school and their interactions with one another can help adults discern some of the rules of the group. These rules are seldom taught directly and boys and girls are expected to learn them through interaction. Some of the "dos" and "don'ts" are listed in Fig. 7.2.

An important rule of the peer culture involves being able to accept a "no, you can't play," or "you can't join the group" (Lavoie 2005). Rejection and verbal harassment from the peer group is very painful and results in negative emotions (Fox 1998). Moreover, children who are rejected or who withdraw from the group have fewer opportunities to practice the skills they need to control their emotions (Fox and Calkins 2003), which places them at a considerable disad-vantage. Moody young people and those who are emotionally negative much of the time are unpleasant to be around and tend to be rejected more often than others. Importantly, being excluded or rejected can result in a decrease in emotion and behavior regulation even if a child had previously been well controlled (Baumeister, Dewall, Ciarocco and Twenge 2005; Denham et al. 2002).

When children are excluded, they exhibit significantly less helping behavior and cooperation, and even when they simply think that they may be excluded from the group prosocial behavior is significantly reduced. After experiencing exclusion, individuals tend to shut their emotions down to protect themselves from further hurt, but this in turn prevents them from acting with empathy. Social exclusion triggers aggressive and impulsive behavior (Twenge, Baumeister, DeWall, Ciarocco, and Bartels 2007). Interestingly, Gailliot et al. (2007) describes individuals who have experienced rejection as "wary." Although rejected indivi-duals would like to make friends, they do not want to be hurt further. An opportunity to be accepted and become a part of the group is balanced for them against the risk for being taken advantage of or being hurt again. If others initiate interaction and are cooperative toward the rejected individual, interaction can proceed. However, if trust is again broken, a rejected individual is not likely to easily give it another chance.

In order to avoid rejection, children must learn to keep anger under control and express it with caution. They must learn to monitor their reactions to another's failure, for bragging and elation when winning is socially risky. They must also learn to keep feelings of envy to themselves, as this too may bring on teasing. Boys learn to be very careful with whom they share their fears. Girls learn to be careful to avoid angry displays of emotions. Having a good friend is extremely important, as children and adolescents need models of emotion regulation, cues in regard to others' reactions, and emotional support when things go wrong in the peer group. A friend may teach a student to "reframe" (change the way one is thinking about something) upset with com-ments, such as "it's not worth getting all upset about" or "don't cry over spilt milk" or "it's not worth crying about." Friends give appropriate warnings when a child is not conforming to the display rules of the peer culture with comments

---

Examples of Peer Group Norms

Elementary Level Peer Norms

Do

1. Take games seriously. Do not 'clown around.'
2. Say something positive to teammates (nice try).
3. Stop talking when others are no longer interested in what you are saying.
4. Pay attention to what is going on in the game.
5. Respect others' space.
6. Ask before you take something another student is using.
7. When the group says "no" or "get lost," move away without making a fuss. Try again when a new game (or inning) starts.
8. If the children appear annoyed, do not continue to try to get into the game.
9. If the rules don't seem fair, don't argue too much during the game; rather suggest a new rule instead of arguing.
10. Only try to get another child's attention once or twice.
11. If you win, don't make a big deal out of it.
12. If you lose, say, "Let's play again," or "Let's play something else."
13. Once rules of the game are agreed upon, don't try to change them.
14. Stand an arm's length away from the person with whom you are talking.

Don't
1. Don't spoil the game by pointing out every rule that is broken.
2. Don't brag if you win.
3. Don't walk away from a game when you are losing.
4. Don't walk away from a game when you get tired of playing.
5. Don't repeat things over and over.
6. Don't act silly when the group isn't interested.
7. Don't try to play with the same kids every recess unless you are best friends.
8. Don't nag. Ask once or twice then do something else.
9. Don't 'hog' the playground equipment (balls etc.)
10. Don't lose control if you make a mistake. Say, "no big deal."
11. Don't tattle about things that are 'no big deal.'
12. Don't make comments that embarrass or upset other kids. If you make a mistake say, "Sorry, I didn't think first."
13. Don't whip balls too hard.
14. Don't interrupt others already talking

Fig. 7.2 Examples of peer group norms

such as "stop it, everyone's looking," or "you're acting like a baby," "the kids don't like it," or "calm down or no one will choose you next time." Friends give advice such as "stop talking about it; you're making it worse," or "don't think about it; it's just upsetting you," or "let's do something else; we didn't want to play anyway" (Denham et al. 2002).

Bullying

Bullying is a serious problem in schools, although awareness of the consequences of bullying is certainly increasing among school staff. One in every three students is involved in one role or another in bullying, with victimization as high as 60 percent at the middle school level. The elementary to middle school transition is a period of particular risk for students involved in bullying. Sixth-grade students who are victimized by bullies are at risk for maladjustment, a risk that is higher for girls during this period (Paul and Cillessen 2003). Not only the victims but also the bullies are at risk for adjustment problems. Students involved in bullying during this transitional period feel that the school climate in general is negative whether they are victims or bullies (Nansel, Haynie, and Simons-Morton 2003). School transitions in general are risky periods for students who are victims of bullying, but they are not the only risky times. Being bullied in the first years of school is especially harmful, and victims during this early period are also at risk for maladjustment (Arseneault, Walsh, Trzesniewski, Newcombe, Caspi, and Moffitt 2006).

Children involved in bullying suffer long-term effects, with outcomes including anxiety, depression, and other negative effects that last for years (Elias et al. 2006; Macklem 2003; Smokowski and Kopasz 2005). Bullying also has short-term effects on children's feelings of self-worth and their sense of being able to control what happens to them (Murphy and Quesal 2002).

Teasing and provocation may be considered milder forms of bullying. Gleeful taunting is seen as early as preschool, and the peer group does not like it (Miller and Olson 2000). Children who behave in unusual ways when provoked or teased, such as saying things that do not make sense, make it clear to the group that they are reacting to what is going on around them, which can be quite reinforcing to the teasers. A common reason given by juveniles who tease others is that the victim is "weird" or "immature," and this leads to even more teasing and provocation. Children who react in age-inappropriate or peer-culture-inappropriate ways and who are most distressed tend to have difficulty in their interactions with others that they consider their friends as well as with those who provoke them. The *disorganization* that occurs in these girls and boys when stressed in social situations results in less fun for them and difficulties in the few somewhat positive relationships they do have. As a consequence, they tend to exhibit less positive social behavior in general (Leary and Katz 2005), which isolates them even further and may intensify the rejection.

When some children are provoked, they exhibit more aggressive reactions, although girls tend to make fewer negative comments than boys and may be more aware of their emotional behaviors. Girls may also be more capable of self-distraction than boys at some ages. Young people with the lowest thresholds for negative emotions exhibit more impulsive aggression than their peers, which further alienates them from the group (Davidson, Putnam, et al. 2000; Masters, Ford, and Arend 2005; Underwood, Hurely, Johanson, and Mosley 1999; Underwood, and Bjornstad 2001). Children who respond by fighting or crying are more likely to continue to be victimized, as bullies seem to be looking for a reaction of emotional distress in their victims. The behaviors associated with weak regulation of emotions include not only aggressive behaviors but also passive victimization and hypervigilance (Buckley and Saarni 2006), and children with poor emotion regulation are easy targets for bullies (Macklem 2003).

Victims of Bullying

Emotion regulation is especially important when considering victims of bullying. A full 10 percent of the *total* school population, kindergarten through twelfth grade, is victimized over time. Girls who exhibit anxious solitude (isolate themselves because they are anxious) tend to be victimized and respond to that victimization with depressive symptoms. Victims of bullying may be more vulnerable than their peers, or they may not have learned to regulate emotions as well as others. Some children have been encouraged to internalize when stressed. As they grow older, fearful children tend to be targeted as easy to upset, and their anxiety makes them vulnerable (Rubin, Burgess, and Coplan 2002).

Emotionally vulnerable children who become disorganized when they are stressed and internalize when they are bullied are considered incompetent by their peers. In fact, dysregulated children do not process social cues well. They may blame themselves for the teasing they are subjected to from the group (Gazelle 2006; Menesini 1999; Rodkin and Hodges 2003; Salmivalli, Ojanen, Haanpaa, and Peets 2005), which makes it difficult for them to problem-solve or to generate a more successful strategy for dealing with being bullied.

Girls who are victimized tend to seek support from peers or adults, whereas boys may not do this as readily unless they experience emotion *very* intensely. Girls often believe that social support is the best strategy for dealing with bullying incidents and for helping themselves feel better. Teachers have to be much more aware of children's need for help in modulating negative emotions, especially after being teased (Hunter, Boyle, and Warden 2004). Kochenderfer-Ladd (2004) found that the specific emotions children experienced are related to how they dealt with bullying. Those who experienced anxiety and/or embarrassment tended to look to others for advice. When embarrassed, some children tried to talk to the bully to get the behavior to stop. Juveniles who become enraged tend to look for revenge, but the bullying does not stop. These are the children who are most at risk for experiencing depressive symptoms. Risks and coping strategies for victims of bullying are listed in Fig. 7.3.

Some students are both victims and bullies and are often referred to as aggressive or provocative victims. The peer group feels that these students provoke the teasing or bullying and then turn around and respond aggressively (Macklem 2003). Although they may have other weaknesses, aggressive

---

Victims of Bullying

Although bullying can be a serious problem in some schools, a good deal of bullying also occurs at a low level and can be subtle. However, even low-level bullying angers and alienates students. Low-level victimization also results in a hostile school environment (Crothers 2007).

Risks for Students Who Are Bullied

- Depression (strongest relationship)
- Low self-esteem
- Anxiety
- Physical and psychosomatic complaints
- Behavior problems
- Self-blame
- Feelings of helplessness

(Smith, Talamelli, Cowie, Naylor, and Chauhan 2004)

Coping Strategies for Victims

A study reported by the British Psychological Society (2004) found that students who had been bullied for a long time used wishful thinking or avoidance strategies to cope with it. Girls, younger students, and new victims tend to seek social support. Some students who felt they had a chance to learn something from the experience tried to manage or alter the situation (Hunter and Boyle 2004).

When students told a teacher or had a friend help them, the bullying decreased. When they fought back or walked away, the victimization increased. For older students nonchalance was a constructive strategy (Smith et al. 2004). Social support is a buffer and seeking social support is a coping strategy. Children who seek support are looking for help in dealing with their own emotions (threat perceptions and emotion regulation) as well as practical advice (Boyle, Hunter, and Turner 2005; Hunter, Boyle, and Warden 2004).

Fig. 7.3 Victims of bullying

victims have particularly significant problems with emotion and behavior regulation (Schwartz 2000). Provocative victims exhibit reactive aggression—a type of negative behavior in which a child responds aggressively when he or she believes that the behavior of the other child is threatening (Kempes, Matthys, de Vries, and van Engeland 2005). Reactive aggression tends to be impulsive behavior.

When multiple studies of students' aggressive behaviors are systematically reviewed and combined (meta-analytic studies), reactive aggression is found to be slightly more strongly related to emotional dysregulation, peer victimization, and sociometric status as well as to other indices of adjustment (Card and Little 2006). Students who exhibit reactive aggression have a negative view of their classmates and playmates, and in turn tend to have low status in the peer group (Brown, Atkins, Osborne, and Milnamow 1996). Their angry aggressive displays escalate the bullying interaction rather than stop it

(Salmivalli et al. 2005; Toblin, Schwartz, Hopmeyer, and Abouezzeddine 2005; Wilton, Craig, and Pepler 2000).

Interventions

There are several different types of interventions to consider when addressing peer group issues. There is agreement in the literature that comprehensive efforts to build competency and teach skills to create positive school climates are more effective than isolated interventions or interventions for small groups of students. This is particularly true in connection with antibullying interventions and intervention to build social-emotional learning (Elias et al. 2006).

It may be important to point out that children with varying abilities in emotion regulation and varying degrees of reactivity may respond differently to different types of interventions. Eisenberg et al. (1998) have made it clear that interventions that improve a child's capacity for emotional and behavioral regulation are needed for children who experience very intense negative emotions. Improving these children's ability to regulate, as well as improving their coping strategies, may increase their sympathy for peers and reduce their tendencies to respond aggressively to provocation. This approach would be most successful for intense children who have adequate understanding of emotions. Children who do not tend to become overaroused but who cannot or do not read someone else's emotions very well first have to learn to attend to and correctly interpret the others' emotions. Teaching the precursor skills first would increase their sympathy and empathy for others.

Universal Programs to Improve Empathy

A handful of programs have been developed that are designed to improve empathy. Teglasi (1998b) identified four of them:

- The Child Development Project
- The Empathy Training Program
- Interpersonal Cognitive Problem Solving
- Promoting Alternative Thinking Strategies (PATHS)

This is only a partial list, however, and several more programs could enumerated.

The Caring School Community™ (CSC) is a research-based grades K–6 classroom and schoolwide program based on building respectful relationships and common purposes. The primary elements include: class meetings, a cross-age "buddies" program, activities to be used at home, and activities to be used by the whole school to develop a strong sense of "community." The main focus is to strengthen connectiveness to school by developing and establishing common norms and goals, solving problems, and learning to empathize with one another. Evaluations have been consistently strong (http://www.devstu.org/csc/results.html).

The *Interpersonal Cognitive Problem-Solving Program* is a universal intervention designed to provide elementary school children with structured training in interpersonal cognitive problem-solving skills. The goal is to teach children how to generate solutions to problems through a strategy of formal dialogue (Shure 2001a, b). Independent evaluators have supported the cognitive and behavioral benefits of the program.

Promoting Alternative Thinking Strategies (PATHS)

Lessons from the *Promoting Alternative Thinking Strategies* (PATHS) program are comprehensive. They include: instruction in identifying and labeling feelings; expressing feelings; assessing the intensity of feelings; managing feelings; understanding the difference between feelings and behaviors; delaying gratification; controlling impulses; reducing stress; self-talk, reading, and interpreting social cues; understanding the perspectives of others; using steps for problem solving and decision making; having a positive attitude toward life; self-awareness; nonverbal and verbal communication skills (http://guide.helpingamericasyouth.gov/programdetail.cfm?id = 409).

Programs that Include Empathy Training Components

Several additional programs include empathy training within broader parameters. Through the *Second Step Program*, students learn to identify their own and others' feelings; recognize that people may react differently to different situations; predict feelings of others; learn the difference between accidents and things done on purpose; share feelings; and learn about individual differences. The *Dinosaur Social Skills and Problem-Solving Curriculum* covers topics such as learning about rules; empathy training; problem solving; anger management; how to be friendly; how to talk to others; and how to be successful in school. Hair, Jager, and Garrett (2001) also suggest two older programs, the *Cognitive/Affective Empathy Training Program* and the *Communication Skills Training Program (CST)*, which trains for self-disclosure and empathy through a structured educational course. One study demonstrated that participants increased self-disclosure and empathetic responsiveness (Avery, Rider, and Haynes-Clements 1981).

An Unusual Program

The *Roots of Empathy Program* has an unusual twist. It is an evidence-based K-8 Canadian classroom program that has shown strong effects in reducing levels of aggression among school children while raising social/emotional competence and increasing empathy at the same time. Goals include the development of empathy, emotional literacy, and reduction of bullying while increasing positive behaviors and preparing students for responsive parenting. The program involves a curriculum and weekly visits by a parent and infant. National evaluations show significant reductions in bullying and increases in social understanding and prosocial behavior (http://www.rootsofempathy.org/Research.html). Specific lessons involve identifying, labeling, and talking about feelings; perspective taking; and respecting others.

Antibullying Programs

Although there are several antibullying interventions that have the effect of decreasing bullying, the interventions that are more complex and involve multiple disciplines are more effective than curricular changes alone (Vreeman and Carroll 2007).

The schoolwide *Olweus Bullying Prevention Program* is designed to prevent or reduce bullying among students 6 to 15 years old. It attempts to restructure the school environment to decrease both opportunities and rewards for bullying behaviors. Olweus conducted the first systematic intervention study against bullying and more recently has directed several new large-scale intervention projects. The program is considered a model because it has been rigorously evaluated (Olweus 1993; Olweus and Limber 1999). An evaluation done in the 1980s showed reductions in bullying of 50 percent or more as well as improvements in school climate (Olweus, Limber, and Mihalic 1999). The Oslo Project Against Bullying resulted in reductions in self-reports of bullying of 43 percent among fourth- to seventh-grade students (Olweus 2004). Parallel studies in the United States have not demonstrated the same degree of success, but Shinn (2003) explains that more variance should be expected in heterogeneous contexts.

Steps to Respect is a schoolwide program designed to reduce bullying. The cognitive behavioral curriculum includes a specific intervention for involved students. Classroom instruction starts in the third grade and focuses on children's beliefs, but also teaches skills for responding to bullying and increasing peer acceptance. The program supports effective action through adult training, school policy, and guidelines for bystanders, with instruction in social skills, emotion regulation, and calming techniques. There are also coaching processes for both bullies and victims. Program evaluation has demonstrated improved bystander behavior and reductions in bullying and general aggression. A study using a random control design, objective observations, and unbiased analytic techniques provided strong evidence of effectiveness (Frey, Edstrom, and Hirschstein 2005).

Curricula for Small Groups

The *Coping with Stress Course* (CWS) targets teenagers at risk for depression who are already experiencing depressive symptoms. Students learn to identify and challenge negative thoughts that contribute to the development of future mood disorders. CWS uses cartoons, role-plays, and group discussions. Two studies utilized randomized assignment of participants and found significant reductions in interviewer-rated and self-reported depression symptoms for treatment teens when compared with those in a control group (http://www.promisingpractices.net/program.asp?programid = 151).

The *Peer Training Program* (Paluck and Green 2006) uses a combination of instructional and peer influences to build empathy for others. The goal is to train adolescents to use the positive power of peer pressure to motivate other students to reflect upon and to take action against prejudice in their schools. Once trained, the *peer trainers* lead workshops, interactive classroom presentations, and group discussions. They work with elementary school children, using classroom activities and books that represent the experiences of diverse peoples, and assist schools in responding to name calling, bullying, and harassment (www.adl.org).

Cognitive/Affective Empathy Training (CAET) is a small-group program designed to improve levels of empathetic response and decrease levels of aggression in aggressive adolescents. CAET addresses the interpretation of others' feelings, role-taking, using an appropriate level of affect, and event analysis. Students continue on to the next topic only after reasonable gains are made in the current one. Research by Pecukonis (1990) involving aggressive adolescent girls found that the training program increased participants' level of affective empathy.

Interventions Involving Teachers

Feshbach and Feshbach (2004) are developing a cognitive-affective teaching approach that influences the way students are taught to understand different ethnic and cultural backgrounds. Initial evaluation suggests that this approach results in diminished aggression as well as increased prosocial behavior and cognitive empathy.

Newman-Carlson and Horne (2004) targeted teachers in efforts to reduce bullying at the middle school level. They provided program manuals and other materials, offered training sessions, and established teacher support groups that encouraged supervision and treatment integrity. Supportive teachers proved to be quite effective in strengthening prevention and intervention work.

Chapter 8
Regulating Positive and Negative Emotions

Adaptive and Nonadaptive Reactions to Stress

Coping with Stress

School is stressful for many students. Sources of stress include academic performance, negative teacher interactions, negative peer interactions, and impaired academic self-concept. The demands that produce stress for children include:

- Grading
- Competition around grades.
- Lack of time.
- Difficulties around task management.
- Pressures to adapt to new environments.
- Worry about class work.
- Changing environments (differences in expectations as compared to home as well as from teacher-to-teacher).
- Increasing difficulty of content as the child goes through school.
- Need to use new specific learning techniques.
- Performance and test anxiety.
- Worry about getting along with peers.
- Fear of being chosen last on any team or being left out entirely.
- Fear of being different from others.
- The necessity of continually self-regulating emotions and behavior.

Anxiety and the ability to cope successfully are related to academic stressors, and the complications of social adjustment and the need to develop positive relationships generate further stress (Kariv and Heiman 2005).

When they have been stressed, students attempt to cope. Coping refers to efforts to manage the specific environmental demands that are stressful or exceed an individual's resources. Coping involves what an individual thinks and does as he or she is being stressed and is influenced by one's interpretation of the situation and its demands (Folkman, Lazarus, Dunkel-Schetter, DeLongis, and Gruen 1986). Coping has two functions—to regulate the emotions that are being experienced and to deal with the stressor to reduce its

G. L. Macklem, *Practitioner's Guide to Emotion Regulation in School-Aged Children.* © Springer 2008

impact—so emotion regulation may be the foundation for coping behavior (Semrud-Clikeman 2003). Wide ranges of both positive and negative coping strategies have been identified, and are listed in Fig. 8.1.

In general, active coping strategies result in improved emotional adjustment when a student is dealing with chronic stress (Taylor and the Psychosocial Working Group 1998). Socioeconomic status (SES) is a factor, and students at different socioeconomic levels may feel the same stressor differently. The coping strategies that children use may also differ by SES (Taylor et al. 1998). Students in lower SES environments may experience more threats in general that are less controllable. Uncontrollable stress is more difficult to deal with than stress that is controllable (Kavushansky, Vouimba, Cohen, and Richter-Levin 2006).

Theorists explain coping dimensions of several classes or types. One is *emotion-focused* coping. Here the individual attempts to cope with the intensity or duration of the emotion that is being experienced in relation to the stressor. For example, emotion-focused coping might involve looking on the 'bright side' of the situation. Another dimension is *problem-focused* coping. In this case an individual tries to deal with the stressful situation by minimizing it or resolving

---

Coping Strategies

- Taking action (active coping).
- Thinking about how to deal with the stressor (planning).
- Seeking emotional support from someone.
- Putting aside other activities to concentrate on the stressor.
- Reinterpreting the situation more positively so that it is less stressful.
- Wishful thinking.
- Seeking information.
- Holding back (passive coping).
- Venting feelings.
- Blaming others.
- Denial.
- Disengaging by distracting oneself.
- Sleeping or daydreaming.
- Giving up.
- Accepting the stress.
- Mental disengagement from one's goals.
- Focusing on emotions.
- Turning to negative behavior (drinking alcohol or taking drugs).
- Engaging in religious activities.
- Making jokes about the stressor.

Fig. 8.1 Coping strategies (Carver, Scheier and Weintraub 1989; Taylor and the Psychosocial Working Group 1998)

the impact and effects of the event. A person might think to oneself, "this certainly isn't the worst thing that could happen but I need to find someone to talk with about it." A third dimension is *avoidance* coping. Individuals may engage in avoidance coping by: (a) avoiding a situation, (b) denying that something is happening, (c) losing hope, (d) distancing themselves, (e) evading the problem, and/or (f) getting involved in unrelated activities to reduce the stress.

Approach coping versus avoidance coping and engagement versus disengagement coping are also discussed in the literature. In stressful situations it is necessary for students to not only cope with the stressor itself, but also to deal with the emotions that the stressor generates.

Coping Styles

Students seem to develop coping styles, some of which are more global and others more situational. Children cope well when they can do something that feels familiar as compared to taking a novel action. When an individual uses one kind of strategy more than others, it may be a function of both style and the type of stressful event to which he or she is attempting to adjust. For example, people who experience emotion intensely and tend to react to emotional events before they occur by anticipating them and worrying about them seem to prefer emotion-oriented strategies. It is important to note that coping strategies are neither all good nor all bad, and different strategies can be adaptive in particular situations (Carver, Scheier, and Weintraub 1989; Kariv and Heiman 2005; Livneh 2000; Taylor et al. 1998; Zeidner, Matthews, and Roberts 2006).

When the academic load is heavy, students tend to use problem solving to reduce stress if and when they consider the situation controllable. They then use emotion-focused strategies to deal with the perceived residual stress (Kariv and Heiman 2005). Emotion coping can be useful in certain situations, for example, dealing with medical issues such as chronic pain (Austenfeld and Stanton 2004). Emotion coping strategies such as relaxation can be adaptive when students must deal with anxiety-producing tests. In real-life complicated situations, individuals may use both problem-focused and emotion-focused strategies (Nezu, Nezu and Lombardo 2001b).

Some coping strategies perpetuate the negative feelings or moods that a person is experiencing and thereby cause an increase in the stress Students who are skilled in regulating their emotions may find it easier to dissipate the negative mood and feelings using a coping strategy such as distraction. Avoidance strategies can cause problems for students, for when they avoid situations that stress them intensely, they may suffer a loss of confidence; they also prevent themselves from engaging in situations that may be of benefit (Zeidner et al. 2006). One complication is that a situation is interpreted as more stressful if an individual does not feel confident in dealing with it. If the student feels that a situation can be managed, he or she is more likely to use adaptive coping strategies. Active strategies generally produce better results, whereas avoidance coping tends to be less effective (Kariv and Heiman 2005). Maladaptive coping results in anxiety, worry, physical symptoms, and negative feelings. Effective coping results in very few negative consequences and solving the problem decreases or eliminates the stress (Nezu, Nezu and Lombardo 2001b).

Active coping is very similar to problem solving, or problem-focused coping, except that the latter often includes planning, suppression of competing activities, and restraint. When a student eliminates competing activities to concentrate on the stressor at hand, other things are put aside so that he or she can deal with the problem, and self-restraint helps one from acting prematurely. It should also be noted that seeking support can imply problem solving, as in the case of soliciting understanding so that one can problem-solve. Seeking someone to listen can also be used just to vent (Carver et al. 1989), which is not as useful or productive.

Temperament can be a complicating factor in coping with stress. Students who tend to be negative are generally pessimistic and may feel that increased responsibility can be a threat. This type of stress may elicit defeatist thinking, "I'll never be able to get this much homework done" or "My teachers will think I'm not very smart and I'll get a bad grade." The result can be overwhelming and cause the student to procrastinate. Avoidance problem solving can clearly result in increased distress, as can impulsive problem solving (Nezu, Nezu and Lombardo 2001b).

Children and preteens learn coping strategies of all sorts, including problem solving, seeking support from adults, and self-instruction. By middle adolescence, students tend to cope using less effective or maladaptive strategies. The coping capacity of young people in early and middle adolescence appears to *decrease* rather than increase. This has been noted among eleven- to fourteen-year olds. This age group shows increases in ruminating and decreased use of distraction. Hampel and Petermann (2005) consider that this places young people in the this age group at risk and emphasizes the need for preventive programming in middle school. Girls in particular try to cope by using peer resources and report experiencing more somatic stress than boys. Passive coping such as resignation and rumination, which is associated with both anxiety and depression, are problematic as they increase risk for internalizing disorders.

Avoidance strategies are also related to depressive symptoms and place students who use them at risk for additional stress. Adolescents who are depressed or have behavior problems use more avoidance coping strategies than their peers and are at risk for poor adjustment. Boys at this age may turn to aggression to cope. Active coping aimed at changing the nature of the event or situation or changing how one thinks about it by reappraising it is important for long-term adjustment (Ebata and Moos 1991; Hampel and Petermann 2005; Taylor et al. 1998). These approaches must be part of any curriculum that teaches coping strategies. It should also be noted that several studies show that emotion-oriented and avoidance coping strategies are

Coping Strategies	
Strategies to Teach or Strengthen	**Strategies to Reteach or Extinguish**
Distraction	Avoidance
Dissipate negative moods	Defeatist thinking
Eliminate competing activities	Ruminating
Seek positive support	Seeking a listening post
Self-instruction	Resignation
Change the nature of the event	Impulsive aggression
Change thinking (reappraisal)	Let it all hang out
Accept the situation	Blame oneself
Refocus	Blame everyone else
Plan pleasant activities	Use drugs to change mood
Put things in perspective	Catastrophizing
Relaxation and meditation	Denial
Exercise	Pounding pillows
Cognitive reframing	Hiding feelings
Problem solving	Suppression

Fig. 8.2 Strengthening or reteaching coping strategies

associated with relapse of depression (Christensen and Kessing 2005). Problematic coping is related to behavior problems, in that children who use physical or emotional avoidance tend to act out. The more emotionally reactive a child is, the more likely that he or she will misbehave (Shipman et al. 2004). Some coping strategies have to be taught or strengthened, whereas others need to be redirected or depressed. Both types of strategies are listed in Fig. 8.2.

Specific Emotion Regulation Strategies

By the time they enter first grade, children have already developed a number of emotion regulation strategies (Richards and Gross 2000). They have also learned to influence emotions in others by showing affection, helping, and giving. However, they must be able to recognize an emotion in themselves and others and know that the emotion needs to be regulated before they can access and use a strategy (Masters 1991). Positive strategies that preschool-aged children use include crying, seeking support, doing something else (Lance 2003). Students in elementary school can redirect their own attention, avoid situations, think about something else, or problem-solve (Denham et al. 2002).

Typically, developing students vary significantly in how often they use various strategies (Gross, Richards, John 2006). Some use only a few, but use them consistently. Others use a large number of strategies and change them as needed in different contexts. Flexibility in the use of strategies is adaptive. Some strategies are healthier than others. Some are costly. "Letting it all hang out" is one of the worst strategies to use when having difficulties with peers, as it leads to rejection by the peer group.

Strategies can be characterized in different ways. There are somatic strategies such as relaxation and meditation that attempt to alter behavior. Yoga induces relaxation and has been used in treatments for anxiety and depression (Scime, Cook-Cottone, Kane, and Watson 2006). A plan of daily exercise over several months has been shown to improve a range of regulatory behaviors (Oaten and Cheng 2006).

There are also cognitive strategies, including: blaming oneself, blaming others, ruminating, catastrophizing, refocusing, rethinking the situation, accepting the situation, planning, and putting things into perspective (Behncke 2002; Garnefski, van den Kommer, Kraaij, Teerds, Legerstee, and Onstein 2002). Mental rehearsal is a strategy used by athletes to enhance performance. It is effective for sports that require specific arousal and attention, such as basketball free throwing, tennis, and soccer (Behncke 2005). There are cognitive emotional regulatory strategies that deal with feelings and mood.

Antecedent- and Response-Focused Emotion Regulation

Antecedent-focused emotion regulation involves strategies that change or modify the situation causing the distress, changing the way triggers are judged or paying attention to something else. These strategies are used at the "front end." One example is to reappraise the situation causing the stress, as in a situation where a child told that he can't play says to himself, "I didn't want to play anyway." This strategy involves *reappraisal* of the situation so that the child no longer considers it such a big a deal. Another example might be when a child strikes out in a softball game and momentarily feels bad. A girl might decide to look at her temporary failure as if it was a challenge and try harder the next time. Changing the way one judges a situation is called *cognitive reframing*. Older children use this strategy more often than younger ones. The older child is actively trying to keep emotions from 'spilling out' in the first place (Gross 1998b; Richards and Gross 2000).

Response-focused strategies are used after one has already reacted emotionally so that the emotion has to be regulated back down to a controllable level. Thoughts, behaviors, and feelings all have to be controlled (Gross 1998a; Richards and Gross 2000). Response-focused regulation occurs at the "back end" and is described as expressive suppression. Strategies are designed to 'mop up' the excessive emotion (Richards and Gross 2000). Examples of response-focused strategies include hiding disappointment when a gift is not what one had hoped for, hiding excitement upon winning the game, or taking deep breaths to calm down before stepping up to hit the baseball. The goal is to change the emotion after it has already been felt. Emotional avoidance can be momentarily useful as it gives an individual time to start the problem-solving process, but it can be negative when it either does not work or lasts too long and feels bad (Westphal and Bonanno 2004).

Exploratory emotion regulation is used in childhood through play, books, or videos. The child using exploratory regulation acts out a role and tries out solutions (Westphal and Bonanno 2004). Young children use exploratory emotion regulation spontaneously, but it can be utilized as an intervention with older children. At a more sophisticated level, it can be used during small-group interventions in the form of role-play or theater.

Less Healthy Down Regulation Strategies

Children may have learned strategies to decrease or down regulate negative emotions that may not be as healthy as other strategies. Parents may have modeled the less healthy strategies, or the child may have developed an unhealthy strategy in response to a combination of parenting styles, his or her own temperament, and the intensity of the stressor. Suppression and rumination are strategies that can make a situation worse; they can take too much of a child's energy; and they do not address the cause of the stress. Moreover, there are 'costs' to overuse of these strategies. Moreover, the habit of self-criticism has negative consequences.

Suppression

Different forms of emotion down regulating have different consequences. When a children decide to try to hide their feelings, a demand is placed on both language and thinking. We consider well-controlled children as cool and those who have poor regulation as hot headed (Richards and Gross 2000). When individuals try not to think about something that upsets them, the effort to suppress unwanted thoughts and feelings actually increases the intensity and frequency of experiencing them (Rassin 2003; Sloan 2004; Wegner 1994). When suppression is used to stop thinking an upsetting thought, the thought is linked to the *mood* that the individual would like to avoid. The risk is that the distracting thought becomes connected to the thought that the person is trying to suppress forming a bridge back to the negative thought, which leads to suppression becoming the problem (Wegner 1992).

Young people who use suppression to deal with intense emotion experience fewer positive and more negative emotional experiences. (Kashdan, Barrios, Forsyth, and Steger 2006). There is also another cost to using suppression as a strategy to regulate emotion, as it affects memory for verbally encoded information. Individuals who use this strategy have difficulty recalling the verbal memory aspects of situations in which they find themselves. They 'forget' bits of information from arguments. When adults confront children who use suppression, they find that these boys and girls become frustrated, misinterpret the events they experienced, and are unable to recall events as clearly as others describe them. The effort to hide emotions appears to require a high degree of self-monitoring to keep them repressed, which, in turn, makes it difficult to encode verbal information in memory. Monitoring one's body so that emotion does not reveal one's feelings to the world interferes with memory for details of the emotional experience. The use of suppression, in addition to affecting auditory memory, is also associated with: (a) decreased social support, (b) decreased optimism, (c) increased agitation, and (d) increased symptoms of depression (Gross, Richards and John 2006; Richards and Gross 2000; Westphal and Bonanno 2004).

Rumination

Rumination is another emotion regulation strategy that is not very healthy. Individuals who ruminate mull over problems repeatedly and, at times, quite frequently (Law 2005). Rumination is a passive focus on how one feels and what might have caused it, as well as on what will happen next (Nolen-Hoeksema and Jackson 2001). Young people who ruminate are likely to be avoided or pushed away by their peers. Rumination interferes with attention, concentration, and problem solving. It also prolongs symptoms of depression (Broderick 2005), leads to temporary increases in negative emotions, and is negatively associated with forgiveness. Short-term increases in rumination are related to short-term increases in anger, and when ruminating about issues of trust, individuals become angry. Ruminating and feeling angry can lead to thoughts of revenge or serve to motivate revenge (McCullough, Bono, and Root 2007), which may help explain why some children who are bullied become aggressive.

Rumination is associated with dysphoria, anxiety, and behavior problems (Matheson and Anisman 2003; Silk et al. 2003). Students who ruminate excessively have difficulty concentrating and experience unwanted thoughts when trying to complete their schoolwork, which slows them down when they are engaged in academic tasks such as reading and answering questions. Reading comprehension is reduced and detailed work such as proofreading becomes difficult. Mood, thinking, and problem solving become negative and difficult (Lyubomirsky, Kasri, and Zehm 2003).

Ruminating is not effective for depressing negative emotions or mood (Silk et al. 2003). Moreover, when it is used to depress anger, it is quite ineffective, for instead of decreasing anger, it increases both anger and aggression. Doing nothing at all works better than venting anger (Bushman 2002). Peled and Moretti (2007) found that not only do angry feelings predict aggression, but also recurrent angry thoughts predict aggressive behavior even when the child does not act on them initially. Rumination appears to increase in adolescence. There are connections between anger, rumination about anger, and aggressive behavior, just as there are connections between sadness, ruminating about sadness, and depression. Anger rumination and sadness rumination are different in that they are associated with different emotional problems.

Some children engage in both anger rumination and sadness rumination. Those who experience sadness rumination are less likely to act out if they can control anger rumination. Girls experience more sadness rumination and more anger rumination during adolescence. Ruminating about a provocation increases the likelihood of displaced aggression following a minor annoyance or trigger, and ruminating about a prior provocation increases the likelihood that a new *minor* annoyance will increase displaced aggression. This explains why a child may appear to be overreacting to an incident after having a really difficult day. Rumination exacerbates aggression because it maintains the aggressive mood. If a mildly annoying incident occurs later, it is experienced in an exaggerated way. A child who becomes angry and continues to think about the anger over time by focusing on the bad mood can subsequently react aggressively to a minor incident that ordinarily would not provoke any aggressive reaction at all (Bushman, Bonacci, Pedersen, Vasquez, and Miller 2005).

Avoidance

Avoidance coping leads to rumination and increased stress. Avoidance is often driven by fear and is connected to interpreting situations as threatening. When anxiety is the predominant negative emotion being experienced, anxiety can also be driven by shame and embarrassment because the child is aware of the fact that others are not reacting in the same way or because he or she feels that reacting to anxiety is immature. Avoidance can lead to trying to hide symptoms of anxiety and exacerbate the feelings that avoidance is being used to dampen. Avoidance also blocks the child's ability to learn to deal with anxiety because exposure is blocked and the child loses the opportunity to either try out strategies or to challenge negative thinking associated with anxiety (Wells 2003). Avoidance coping strategies place a child at psychological risk and lead to socially inadequate behavior (Boo and Wicherts 2007; Holahan and Moos 1987).

Some young people are more sensitive to anxiety input than others. Anxiety sensitivity is the extent to which one believes that body symptoms (racing heartbeat, sweaty hands, etc.) can have negative consequences. Children with high anxiety sensitivity are more aware of their own internal physiological signals than other children and are also more emotionally reactive when they experience these symptoms.

Anxiety sensitivity is a risk factor for anxiety disorder and symptoms of depression in children (Eley, Stirling, Ehlers, Gregory, and Clark 2004; Joiner, Schmidt, Schmidt, Laurent, Catanzaro, Perez, et al. 2002). Students with high anxiety sensitivity can often be found in the office of the school nurse, reporting somatic symptoms. Importantly, anxiety sensitivity is associated with avoidance coping strategies (Andersson and Hägnebo 2003).

There is a relationship between avoidance and the perception of parental criticism. Use of avoidance is more common in girls who felt criticized by parents. The higher the levels of perceived criticism, the more likelihood that the girls will use avoidance in late adolescence to deal with stress, and the greater the distress they experience in adulthood (Rosenthal, Polusny and Follette 2006).

Avoidance may not always be a negative coping strategy. Faith, Leone, Ayers, Heo, and Pietrobelli (2002) found that when obese students experienced criticism about their weight when engaged in physical activities, avoidance coping strategies diminished the negative relationship between weight criticism and enjoyment of the activity. Thus in such a case avoidance can be an effective strategy.

Negative Self-Thinking

Negative self-thinking, or self-critical thinking, can cause problems as well. Negative self-thinking is associated with depressive and anxiety disorders. When a child thinks critically about him or herself frequently and spontaneously, and finds this type of thinking difficult to control, it becomes a habit. This unhealthy habit can result in poor self-worth apart from whatever the child is thinking about. Whether or not a child's self-critical thoughts have become habitual can be ascertained by asking how frequently he or she engages in this kind of thinking, whether or not the thoughts seem to be under control, and whether or not they are difficult to control (Verplanken, Friborg, Wang, Trafimow, and Woolf 2007). Researchers have developed a short-term tool for this purpose (Verplanken et al. 2007, p. 541).

Healthier Down-Regulating Strategies

Engaging in Pleasant Activities

Healthier down-regulating strategies include getting involved in a positive activity (behavioral distraction), enhancing positive emotions and optimism, and active problem solving. Broderick (2005) suggests that getting involved in pleasant activities or interesting projects works better than rumination because these activities use working memory. If working memory is engaged in this way, there is less of it available for negative thinking or worrying about emotions or moods. In the same way distraction works better than avoidance. Reijntjes, Stegge, and Terwogt (2006) demonstrated that ten- to thirteen-year-old children who were socially competent and less depressed used more active, problem-solving coping strategies when stressed.

Positive Reappraisal

Another positive and healthy strategy is changing one's thinking, as in positive reappraisal. Individuals who use positive reappraisal choose to think of the stressful situation differently, changing its meaning for themselves. This can transform the situation or event from negative to neutral. Positive reappraisal is effective in minimizing the negative impact of frightening or hurtful experiences. It is also less emotionally costly to the person who uses this strategy as compared to suppression and avoidance (Powers, Smits, Leyro, and Otto 2006). Reappraisal is used just as one first begins to react to a stressful event, stopping the outward expression of emotion and decreasing the likelihood of a behavioral reaction. Moreover, it has no impact on memory for the stressful event (Gross 2002).

Mindfulness

Detached mindfulness (Wells 2004) refers to taking a detached view of what is happening to oneself without thinking about it. The individual using this strategy does not interpret, analyze, or try to control his or her emotional responses. Thinking or worrying must be monitored and stopped; attention is redirected to something nonthreatening and this interferes with negative emotions. Practice for using this strategy might include allowing one's mind to wander using free-association exercises and imagery tasks where visualizing a calm scene depresses feelings of anxiety.

In general, cognitive strategies deal with the cause of the stress, which is positive and helpful (Behncke 2002; Richards and Gross 2000). Strategies one brings into play early in the process as negative emotions are being generated are more effective than those that are generated in response to an emotional experience that is in full swing and difficult to fight (Gross 2002).

Approaches to Improve Self-Regulation

Cognitive behavioral therapy (CBT) has good support as an intervention for use with children and adolescents to improve self-regulation. Examples of cognitive behavioral interventions include (Delaney 2006):

- Questioning whether or not one's thoughts are totally true.
- Looking for the facts in a given situation.
- Brainstorming alternative explanations for what one finds troubling.
- Thinking of the worst possible outcome and comparing that with the current situation.
- Making a chart with advantages and disadvantages of choices.
- Practicing new behaviors and new thoughts in front of a mirror.

- Making a record of one's automatic thoughts.
- Inserting 'thinking' between feelings and actions.

Cognitive behavioral interventions also teach self-talk to change thinking. These interventions involve a "how-to-think" protocol for young people to use to change behavior. Reframing, changing one's thinking, and reappraisal are the central strategies for dealing with negative emotions. Although interventions have been more successful with adolescents (Cartwright-Hatton, Roberts, Chitsabesan, Fothergill, and Harrington 2004; Quakely, Coker, Palmer, and Reynolds 2003), there have been some successful adaptations of CBT for use with children (Bailey 2001; Kendall 1994; Kendall and Southam-Gerow 1996), as well as adaptations for cognitively delayed individuals (Suveg, Comer, Furr, and Kendall 2006).

Cognitive behavioral interventions, or cognitive behavioral therapy (CBT), have been demonstrated to be effective in ameliorating a variety of problems experienced by children and adolescents with subthreshold symptoms as well as those with serious disorders. Figure 8.3 offers a sampling of the effects of using

Effects of CBT	Type of Problem or Disorder	Research
Decrease anxiety	Mild-moderate anxiety disorders Subthreshold anxiety symptoms	Dadds, Spence, Holland, et al. 1997
Decrease anxiety and depression	Children with anxiety disorders	Mendlowitz, Manassis, Bradley, Scapillato, Miezitis, and Shaw 1999
Improve social functioning and school performance	Anxious children	Smith 2002; Wood 2006
Improve rate of recovery and decrease self-reported depression	Symptomatic adolescents	Clarke, Rohde, Lewinsohn, Hops, and Seeley 1999
Reduce school Phobia, SAD* and GAD*	Symptomatic children and adolescents	Silverman 2003
Improve on-task behavior and reduce disruptive behavior	Children with ADHD	Bloomquist, August, and Ostrander 1991; Smith 2002
Ameliorate anti-social behavior	Older elementary students and adolescents	Bennett and Gibbons 2000
Help boys deal with provocations	Aggressive boys	De Castro, Bosch, Veerman, and Koops 2003
Improve emotion understanding and regulation	All children	Suveg, Kendall, Comer, and Robin 2006

* Separation Anxiety Disorder and Generalized Anxiety Disorder

Fig. 8.3 Effects of cognitive behavior therapy

Cognitive Behavioral Therapy with children and adolescents of va. Problems that have been addressed using these approaches range from understanding to significant reductions in symptoms associated wit disorders.

School psychologists and other mental health workers have to explore the evidence to support an intervention before implementing it. "Efficacy studies" are conducted under ideal conditions, where all of the factors or variables are controlled (Chambless and Hollon 1998), whereas "effectiveness studies" are carried out in the real world. Programs can be designed and tried out in a very scientific manner in order to determine whether or not they will affect student behaviors. Then, the programs must be tried out in schools, where teachers implement them as well as they can. If the programs are successful in the real-world school conditions they are considered to be effective.

When we look at cognitive behavioral interventions, we find that they have good support. They are efficacious for treating posttraumatic stress disorder in children, although the research needs to be expanded. CBT for obsessive compulsive disorder is considered to be possibly efficacious at this time. Several treatments for social phobia are thought to be possibly efficacious, including the Social Effectiveness Therapy for Children program for students aged eight through twelve years, which focuses on social-skills training with generalization sessions. CBT for childhood phobia is efficacious when it includes an exposure component to gradually introduce the fearful child to the object or situation. Contingency management, modeling, and self-instruction training are efficacious interventions, whereas, there is less support for imagined and in vivo desensitization (Oswald and Mazefsky 2006).

Dialectical Behavior Therapy

Dialectical behavior therapy (DBT) is a specific cognitive behavioral intervention that was designed for the treatment of individuals with borderline disorder. It is based on the idea that borderline disorder is characterized by emotion dysregulation, so emotion regulation is a core therapeutic feature (Harned, Banawan, and Lynch 2006). DBT is not used in schools, but some of its concepts and aspects might be helpful if they were redesigned for use in schools.

Children and adolescents with borderline disorder are extremely vulnerable emotionally and do not have or do not use emotion regulation skills. They are highly sensitive and easily triggered. Moreover, once triggered, their arousal is both high and intense, and it takes them far more time than their peers to calm down. They experience negative emotions frequently including anxiety, shame, depressive symptoms, and anger that can be intense. When they are functioning better and are more stable, they may continue to experience mild depressive symptoms (Sanderson n.d.). Emotion regulation training for these young people is designed to reduce their vulnerability. Some of the specific skills that are taught include: (a) how to interpret and describe emotions, (b) experiencing emotions and letting them go again, (c) changing emotions by acting the opposite of how you feel, and (d) increasing positive emotions (http://www.dbtselfhelp.com/html/emotion_regulation_handouts.html).

Recent Approaches to Help Children and Adolescents

Mindfulness approaches are beginning to be used in schools. Mindfulness has to do with paying attention to the present moment without judging it. It involves being aware of emotional experiences in a way that allows the student to feel and accept emotions. As mindfulness correlates with emotion regulation, it makes sense that mindfulness skills might be important in learning to regulate emotion (Erismana, Salters-Pedneaultb, and Roemera 2005). Focusing attention on the *here and now* involves awareness of both one's body and one's thoughts. The skills involve learning to distance oneself from negative thoughts enough to be able to determine if they make sense. Mindfulness is often compared with experiencing thoughts and emotions on 'automatic pilot.' Broderick (2005) believes that mindfulness is the key to therapeutic change in CBT.

Mindfulness interventions have been studied for effectiveness in a wide range of disorders in adults and show clinical promise, although the research is still in its infancy (Broderick 2005; Dimidjian and Linehan 2003; Leventhal 2003). The use of mindfulness interventions with school-aged children is also in the research stage, although a number of programs are being developed and some schools are piloting them. Early reports indicate that children can learn the skills and can use them to reduce stress (Ott 2002). The current school-based interventions are adaptations of Kabat-Zinn's Mindfulness-Based Stress Reduction program. Several programs are being rigorously evaluated, including the MAPs project (Mindful Awareness Practices) at the University of California-Los Angeles, which is currently exploring mindfulness in relation to ADHD, mood disorder, and obsessive compulsive disorder in children, and Bright Light Foundation's ME program (Schoeberlein and Koffler 2005).

There are two approaches to using mindfulness techniques: narrow programs and broader programs. The former emphasize mindfulness to focus on controlling attention and improving academic success; the latter focus on the development of social and emotional skills. The broader programs also aim at improving school climate, increasing prosocial behaviors, developing empathy, and improving academic learning (Garrison Institute Report 2005). Schoeberlin and Koffler (2005) describe programs such as: the Education Initiative at the Mind Body Medical Institute at Harvard University, eveloped a K–12 curriculum to deal with stress, teach relaxation, ngthen coping skills; the HeartMath system; and other social emotional learning programs that use contemplative techniques. Social-emotional learning programs that meet this criterion include the PATHS curriculum, Resolving Conflict Creatively, and the Open Circle social competency program. These broad programs teach students to recognize and regulate emotions and develop empathy; they also teach decision making (Schoeberlein and Koffler 2005).

Research on the use of mindfulness programs with school-aged children is ongoing, and the programs developed for use in the early grades have been shown to improve attention (Napoli, Krech, and Holley 2005) and reduce anxiety in fearful children (Semple, Reid, and Miller 2005). Semple (2005) demonstrated improvements in attention, reductions in anxiety, and improved reading comprehension in children of middle school age, although this group treatment was conducted in a clinic and not in a school. When attention problems were reduced, behavioral problems were reduced concomitantly. Another clinical project combined tai chi with mindfulness-based stress reduction with middle school children. This effort, along with others, provides evidence that mindfulness skills can be taught to children effectively (Wall 2005).

One aspect of the mindfulness movement is acceptance and commitment therapy (ACT), which is beginning to receive some research support (Hayes, Luoma, Bond, Masuda, and Lillis 2006). ACT emphasizes acceptance of feelings. The approach for young people includes mindfulness, cognitive diffusion, and metaphor. It is recommended for use with small groups of middle and high school students who need more intensive intervention. Students must decide what is important to them and to behave with those goals in mind. They are taught to accept thoughts, feelings, and moods without avoiding them or experiencing a need to act on them as if they were absolute truth.

Treatments for Internalizing Problems

The tendency to internalize problems is increasing significantly in school-aged children. Schools contribute to depressive symptoms in students through academic stress and failure and by not adequately addressing peer victimization and rejection. Depressed children are at a particular interpersonal disadvantage because studies indicate that teachers, peers, and families reject depressed children. Sadly, schools do not see internalizing problems as a high priority, whereas they readily attend to disruptive and externalizing behaviors (Herman, Merrell, Reinke, and Tucker 2004).

One type of intervention to help students with internalizing disorders is emotion-focused therapy, which distinguishes among different types of emotion and is designed to help children become aware of and accept their emotions. Emotion awareness, emotion regulation, changing emotions, and thinking about them are the goals of this intervention. The therapist is considered an "emotion coach" (Greenberg 2006). Hromek (2004) described a school-based emotion-coaching approach. The content of the once weekly intervention would include:

- Identifying coping strategies.
- Exploring alternatives to aggression.
- Developing an anger management plan.
- Identifying physiological responses to emotion.
- Identifying early warning signs.
- Emotion control strategies that work for the particular student.

Work would involve goal setting, progress review, and encouraging optimism. Calming scripts are taught for use in crisis situations.

Interventions for Depression

No efficacious treatments for depression are available as yet (Oswald and Mazefsky 2006). Interpersonal therapy is considered to be possibly efficacious and research is ongoing. Interpersonal therapy includes strategies to educate students about depression, to clarify feelings and expectations, and to teach communication skills. Self-control therapy is also considered possibly efficacious for students and teaches self-control, self-monitoring, self-evaluation, and self-consequence or reinforcement.

There are additional treatments for depression in childhood and adolescence that are considered possibly efficacious, including the *Penn Resiliency Program for Children and Adolescents* (Gillham, Reivich, Jaycox, and Seligman 1995). The is a school-based program that has been successful with both Caucasian suburban and inner-city Latino students, but less effective with inner-city African American students. It has been shown to decrease anxiety symptoms in children and early adolescents, which is valuable given that anxiety often precedes and predicts depression later on (Gillham et al. 2006).

The *Coping with Depression for Adolescents Course* (Clarke, Hawkins, Murphy, Sheeber, Lewinsohn, and Seeley 1995; Clarke, Hornbrook, Lynch, Polen, Gale, Beardslee, et al. 2001) is possibly efficacious as well. The focus of the course for use in schools includes training in relaxation, increasing pleasant events, controlling negative thinking, and improving social skills. Problem solving and communication skills are also taught (Oswald and Mazefsky 2006). In modified form this course has been used to prevent the onset of depressive symptoms in students with subclinical symptoms of depression with strong results (Gillham et al. 2006).

Crisp, Gudmundsen, and Shirk (2006) describe the *Adolescent Mood Project*, a cognitive behavioral intervention for adolescents that has been delivered with success in a community setting and has been modified for use in schools. The intervention has three modules: cognitions, activities, and relational issues. Students are given a personal mood manager, which is a handbook and a workbook. In pilot studies, students' scores on the Beck Depression Inventory decreased and 15 out of 20 students who participated in the intervention no longer met the criteria for any of the depressive disorders after treatment. School staff reported positive changes in students.

Contextual emotion regulation therapy (CERT) is a new intervention for depressed children that focuses on teaching elementary-aged students to regulate mild depressive symptoms, and it has produced some positive results (Kovacs, Sherrill, George, Pollock, Tumuluru, and Ho 2006). Additionally, schools can help by teaching and modeling verbal and nonverbal communication that is not depressive, stop children who are excessively seeking reassurance, and can teach both problem-solving and self-management (think aloud) strategies. Moreover, it is important for teachers and counselors to provide labels for emotional experiences to assist students in identifying emotional aspects of their lives and to increase their emotion-based vocabulary.

Interventions for Anxiety

The interventions for anxiety disorders have good empirical support. The *Coping Cat Program* and the *C.A.T. Project* are cognitive behavioral therapies for school-aged children. There are data to support the use of these programs for students with generalized anxiety disorder, separation anxiety disorder, and social phobia. The components of these programs involve recognizing feelings and physical reactions to anxiety, recognizing negative self-talk, and learning to use positive self-talk. Modeling, evaluating progress, and self-reinforcement are emphasized as well. The lessons include a good deal of practice in using the skills. Efficacy research has determined that this program is promising or even efficacious (Oswald and Mazefsky 2006).

The Coping Cat program works well with parents as consultants to their children, as well as in small groups. *Coping Koala* and *Coping Bear* are the adaptations in the program that have been made to fit populations in different countries. The Coping Cat program has been recently refined in Australia into programs called *FRIENDS for Children* (7–11 years) and *FRIENDS for Youth* (12–16 years). Research results have been very positive (Dadds, Holland, Barrett, Laurens, and Spence 1999); Dadds, Spence, Holland, and Barrett 1997; Shortt, Barrett, and Fox 2001).

McLoone, Hudson, and Rapee (2006) reviewed three school-based interventions for students with anxiety disorders, *Skills for Social and Academic Success*(SSAS), Cool Kids, and FRIENDS. This group considers Cool Kids and FRIENDS to be appropriate for broad treatment of the various anxiety disorders, and SSAS to be a more specific intervention for children with social phobia. Cool Kids is designed to be implemented by school-based mental health workers and can be delivered in eight small group sessions and two parent meetings. A manual and student workbooks are available. An evaluation of the

Cool Kids program showed that symptoms decreased in economically disadvantaged students as reported by self and teacher reports, as compared to students waiting for service (Mifsud and Rapee 2005), but independent evaluation is necessary. Masia-Warner, Fisher, Shrout, Rathor, and Klein (2007) evaluated the twelve-week SSAS intervention. Adolescent participants reported significant reductions in symptoms of social anxiety, still evident six months after completing Cool Teens. Researchers at Macquarie University's Anxiety Research Unit have developed a computer-facilitated intervention for adolescents with anxiety disorders. Initial work suggests that some adolescents may respond to the use of a CD-ROM. Work with this approach has only just begun (Semple et al. 2005).

Generalized anxiety disorder (GAD) is the most challenging anxiety disorder to address. Students with GAD report: (a) intense emotions, (b) poor understanding of emotions, (c) heightened negativity, (d) difficulty engaging in goal-directed behavior when stressed, (e) poor impulse control, (f) excessive worrying (as a primary strategy for controlling emotion), and (g) poor regulation skills (Mennin et al. 2005; Salters-Pedneault, Roemer, Tull, Rucker and Mennin 2006).

Students with GAD focus on the *process* of worry versus the *content* of worry. They use worry to structure, control, or suppress their emotional states and do not believe that they can change their moods. Emotion regulation therapy (ERT) is a new intervention for GAD that utilizes cognitive behavioral treatments such as relaxation, self-monitoring, reframing, and decision making with emotion-focused interventions (Mennin 2004). This treatment has not yet been adapted for use in schools as research is in the early stages.

Treatments for Angry Externalizing Behaviors

Anger, which is commonly considered a negative emotion, can be expressed appropriately or inappropriately. Appropriate and justified anger can be adaptive when it is expressed appropriately. When underregulated and inappropriate for the situation, anger can be problematic. Anxiety and guilt are often experienced at the same time as anger, and together this combination of emotions can be very distressing. There are fewer strategies for controlling anger than there are for other strong feelings (Phillips, Henry, Hosie, and Milne 2006). Anger is not limited to children with externalizing disorders. Individuals with social anxiety experience more anger and express it less well than their peers. School psychologists should also be aware of the fact that cognitive behavioral interventions may be less successful with children who suppress anger (Erwin, Heimberg, Schneier, and Liebowitz 2003).

In certain situations mild anger can be positive. When younger schoolchildren face challenging tasks, anger is more likely to result in persistence to complete the task than sadness, which is more likely to result in pulling away

---

Students' Anger Intensity and Use of Display Rules

Research protocols can often be excellent sources of ideas for the development of tools to use in practice. Dearing et al. (2002) developed a questioning protocol for his study that may be useful in practice.

If students are going to learn about anger, they have to learn about it very close to the time they experience it. School psychologists can set up small group experience to generate mild anger as in a competitive game (some students find it difficult to lose games), or when they cannot reach their goals (a game of chance or when required skills are a little beyond a child's ability). This is the time to assist students in becoming aware of *how they are feeling* and *how that feeling is expressed* to the group. After an experience in which a student reacts with or experiences anger, ask:

> "How angry did you feel?"
> "How did you know that you were angry?"
> "How did your body (face, shoulders, hands) feel?"
> "Did you feel a little angry, or some angry, or a lot angry?"

Assign values to the last question (+1 a little angry, +2 some angry, +3 a lot angry). Next, show students a series of facial expressions (purchased, drawn, or collected from magazines).

> "Sometimes kids' faces look the *same* as how they feel, and sometimes their faces look *different* than how they feel. I'm going to show you some faces, and I want to point to how you looked."
>
> "The last question I asked you was about how you felt; now I am going to ask you about how you looked. Did you look (1) happy, (2) not at all angry, (3) a little or some angry, or (4) a lot angry?"

You can get a measure of the *use of display rules* used by the student by *subtracting* the level of anger expressed from the level of anger felt.

> ### KEY
> (a) Positive numbers mean that children reported expressing less anger than they reported feeling; (b) negative numbers mean that children reported expressing more anger than they reported feeling; and (c) zeros mean that children reported expressing the same amount of anger that they reported feeling.

Fig. 8.4 Students' anger intensity and use of display rules

from the task (Cole, Dennis, et al. 2004). However, intense, frequent anger is different. Anger is the most challenging emotion to control, and intense uncontrolled anger is a serious problem resulting in acting out and behavior disorders. An approach to determining students' anger intensity and use of display rules can be found in Fig. 8.4.

Once anger is present, anger builds on anger. "Trigger arousal"—the initial energy surge when anger is experienced that gives students the feeling that they cannot control it—decreases slowly. Anger can distort an individual's perception of others. For some children who react with anger frequently, anger can provide a kind of success. They begin to believe that it is an effective tool to get what one wants in the peer group. They also believe that anger is not disapproved of by their peers (Lochman, Dunn, and Wagner 1997). This is because strong arousal can be energizing, making the child feel good and feel powerful. Anger mobilizes action and relieves stress, which makes it very hard to change. Anger is hard to give up. Therefore, helping children understand that they have a choice in whether or not they get angry in the first place may be quite helpful. With practice, they can choose not to get angry.

Anger can also be destructive. It can affect information processing and impair the processing of complex information. Once angry, the child looks for cues that others are going to act unfairly toward him or her and reacts strongly to any perceived threat, even when it is mild and would not bother a typical juvenile with better anger control (Lochman et al. 1997; Novaco 1996).

Most anger reduction programs use a combination of techniques to manage anger with good short-term but less consistent long-term benefits (Skiba and McKelvey 2000). Anger management is often delivered to students in groups because anger is an interpersonal emotion (Phillips et al. 2006). The steps of training for anger management are common to many curricula. The three strategies that have the most research support for treating anger include (Holloway 2003):

- Relaxation
- Cognitive therapy
- Developing skills and practice using specific tools and strategies

The steps that are common to the various curricula include the key component of increasing the students' motivation to participate by convincing them that they have to change their management style. Without this step, anger management is not likely to be effective. Helping students become aware of the environmental triggers and their own personal body signals that indicate that they have become aroused is an important component of training. Self-talk strategies, problem solving, and relaxation are additional components of many programs (Rutherford, Quinn, and Mathur 1996). Small-group interventions for anger management that include only angry or angry and aggressive students are risky in that students can negatively reinforce others' feelings (Holloway 2003). Groups consisting only of angry and aggressive students are likely to fail in reducing anger issues.

Cognitive behavior therapy has been shown to be effective for training students in anger management (Williams, Waymouth, Lipman, Mills, and Evans 2004). Cognitive behavioral interventions have been used to help aggressive boys deal with provocations. The most effective aspect of the intervention in one study related to strategies involving self-monitoring and regulating of emotions. These strategies reduced aggressiveness, whereas asking the boys to consider the other child's emotions and intentions actually increased aggressiveness, as did asking them to wait 10 seconds before responding or answering a question. In typically developing children, considering the other child's emotions and intensions decreased aggressiveness (De Castro, Bosch, Veerman, and Koops 2003). School psychologists must conduct careful investigatory work before forming groups in schools.

Feindler and Ecton's (1986) anger management program includes education about the cognitive and behavioral components of anger, teaching techniques to manage anger, and practice in applying skills. A *Hassle Log*—a self-monitoring tool to record anger triggers of members of the group and records of how they handle their anger—is central to the program. Specific skills that are taught include:

- Relaxation
- Self-assertion
- Self-instruction
- Thinking ahead
- Self-evaluation
- Problem solving

Kellner and Tutin (1995) modified this approach for use in one school by including badges for group identity and a simplified *Mad Log*, in which each student could make an entry both at lunchtime and just before dismissal. Students were encouraged to record incidents of anger whenever they occurred. They could use decals, write the words "happy" or "angry," or draw a face to show how they were feeling during the incident, and classroom teachers helped them fill out the logs each day. Students learned about the physiology of anger, how to identify body signals telling them that they were indeed angry, and how to control their reactions. A master list of physiological symptoms was kept.

The group kept a "trigger list" as a running record so that they could refer to it often. A list labeled "How My Anger Was Managed" was devised to develop coping strategies. Strategies that were taught included relaxation, deep breathing, and counting exercises. Students participated in role-play, and a mirror was used for self-observation so that they could monitor their body movements and facial expressions. They were guided to analyze what they saw through questions such as: "Who is angry?" "Why do you think he/she is angry?" "What do you think he/she is feeling in his/her body?" "What can he/she do about being angry?" "What will happen if he/she does that?" Alternative strategies were generated for expressing anger appropriately.

Dearing and colleagues (2002) examined three aspects of anger management: (1) generating strategies for down regulating angry expressions, (2) strategies for managing internal feelings of anger, and (3) exhibition of appropriate display rules in elementary school students. They based their work in part on the distinction between the internal experience of anger as opposed to the external expression of anger (Eisenberg and Fabes 1999). Display rules guide children's judgments about whether or not to show the anger they are feeling. It appears that a child's accommodation to display rules for anger is not directly related to either social preference or aggression, rather all three aspects of anger regulation are related to social competency and/or aggressive behaviors (Dearing, Hubbard, Ramsden, Parker, Relyea, and Smithmyer 2002). Children's ability to generate strategies for regulating emotion is an important skill to be taught in the overall process of emotion regulation (Garber et al. 1991).

Anger Management

A number of programs are currently available to address anger. The degree to which anger management is part of the curriculum varies from program to program.

The *Second Step Program*, which was developed by the Committee for Children in Seattle, Washington, has an anger management component. It has consistently been positively evaluated when delivered from preschool through fifth grade in regard to effects on anger reduction and antisocial behaviors (Lochman et al. 1997). *Anger Coping*, a school-based program designed to teach perspective taking, social problem solving, and conflict management skills, has research support for use with boys (Lochman 1992). Etscheidt adapted this program to help aggressive juveniles improve their self-control and found that teaching a sequential problem-solving strategy resulted in decreased aggression (Etscheidt 1991; Smith 2002).

Aggression Replacement Training (ART), developed by Goldstein and Glick (1987) for adolescents, has a behavioral component (structured learning), an affective component (anger control training), and a cognitive component (moral reasoning). It is designed to teach adolescents to understand what causes them to feel angry and provides them with techniques they can use to reduce their anger and aggression. The *Anger Control Training Curriculum* (ACT) teaches what not to do and how not to do it by controlling anger. It includes what a child can do in place of acting aggressively (Goldstein and Glick 1987; Hogan 2003). The *ThinkFirst Curriculum* developed by Larson and McBride (Larson 1992) is a secondary prevention program (for a small group of students identified as having difficulties or a disorder) that teaches anger management using cognitive behavioral problem solving. It includes dealing with direct and indirect provocations and teaches assertive behaviors. It can be used at both middle and high school levels in a small-group format (Hogan 2003; Jahnke 1998; Possell and Abrams 1993).

The *Tools for Getting Along Curriculum* is an anger management program for fourth and fifth graders that teaches a problem-solving model. Students learn to recognize anger in themselves and each other and to de-escalate it. Role playing and skill rehearsal are used along with a Hassle Log. Early evaluation of this curriculum showed that participants increased their knowledge of problem-solving strategies, and teachers rated targeted students as less aggressive. This is not a pull-out program, but rather has been successfully implemented in the classroom (Lochman et al. 1997).

In general, many of the anger management curricula utilize short-term interventions, whereas longer-term interventions or booster sessions are generally recommended in the prevention literature. Moreover, prevention literature suggests treatment that is supplemented with other interventions may have greater effects than a curriculum that teaches anger management alone (Skiba and McKelvey 2000.). School psychologists must be sure to use the best practices whenever they implement interventions and must include:

- A preintervention assessment
- Progress monitoring
- Measurements to determine whether or not interventions are effective
- Booster sessions

When this process is followed, they will find their work far more effective than if they implement a curriculum without these additional safeguards and supports.

Chapter 9
Strategies for Parents and Teachers

Strengthening Skills for Parents and Teachers to Help Students Regulate Emotions

Engaging Adults to Help Children

Parents shape early emotion regulation in their children (Gross et al. 2006), so a key way to provide interventions for students may be to influence their parents. School psychologists can implement this in several different ways:

- Offer a single workshop.
- Provide a series of parent training sessions.
- Offer a training course to parents together with their children so that hands-on supervised practice or coaching and feedback can occur.
- Offer counseling (versus training) to parents.
- Offer counseling to parents and their children together.
- Collaborate with a parent or parents to help a given student.
- Collaborate with parent(s) and teachers to help children.

Parents may need assistance in regulating their own anxiety levels or anger management so they can help their children. They may also need help in learning to coach their children in managing emotions rather than ignoring, punishing, or intensifying those expressions of emotion.

Teachers may also be in need of services and can be assisted in several different ways. They can be provided with information and assistance through in-service presentations, a training course, or individual consultation.

It is important, on the one hand, to help parents understand the elements of positive parenting and, on the other, to have teachers understand didactic styles that promote and encourage healthy emotional development. Along with positive models, parents and teachers have to be made aware of the several adult behaviors that are *not conducive* to developing good emotional control, such as overreacting themselves.

A particularly important variable in helping children develop good emotion regulation has to do with how adults react to children's negative emotions. Punishing, minimizing, or not supporting children's expressions of negative emotions will cause them to experience these emotions at a *higher intensity* than they would have otherwise reached. In fact, when young people are subject to frequent stress, they express negative emotions more often. Moreover, the children who experience negative adult reactions to expressing sadness or anger tend to demonstrate less social competence later on (Fabes, Leonard, Kupanoff, and Martin 2001; Jones et al. 2002). When mothers and teachers *disapprove* of children who display negative emotions, the effects are not at all positive.

The use of shame or humiliation to stop the negative display, such as teasing or nagging the child who is showing temper, has the effect of further enraging him or her and prolonging the episode (Furlong and Smith 1998; Shore 1994). Sometimes, adults who are trying to suppress emotional behaviors in children are using inappropriate behavior to reduce their emotional intensity. Unfortunately, the situation becomes even more critical when the adults are stressed themselves (Melnick and Hinshaw 2000). Reactive adult efforts to suppress a child's outburst are easy to understand. Children who are expressing emotions loudly and inappropriately threaten adults' sense of competency, especially when the incident is occurring publicly.

Reacting to Negative Emotions in Children

When children who are easily aroused have angry exchanges with their parents, they become even more upset. When this continues to occur, the children learn a confrontational interpersonal style that they will use with other adults and their peers in school and elsewhere. This parental behavior often occurs when the parent is depressed, and such parents elicit high levels of guilt and anger in their children, who respond by being even more defiant (Denham et al. 2002). Children who have intense temperaments are at higher risk in these less regulated families. In some families high levels of emotionality can be found in both parents and their children (Sloan 2004). In these families, parents think it is best to change the display of emotion as quickly as possible, so they tend to dismiss the child's feelings, making it clear to the child that his or her feelings are not important (Katz and Windecker-Nelson 2004).

Easygoing parents on the other hand may be tempted to let their children show temper, thinking it may be beneficial. These parents may actually encourage the expression of anger, telling their children to hit a pillow or "get the anger out" in other ways. They forget that once aroused, it might take a child as long as 20 minutes to become stable again (Harrington 2005); thus they may be inadvertently 'training' intense expressions of anger and both prolong and intensify its expression. Many parents have significant difficulty understanding how to react to their child's expressions of negative emotions. It is very important that parenting responses to children's expressions of anger be discussed when school psychologists consult with parents. Suggestions for helping parents understand their child's temper tantrums can be found in Fig. 9.1.

The feelings and thoughts that parents have about their own and their child's emotions make up what has been termed their "meta-emotion philosophy." Parents may have a healthy and positive philosophy or an unhealthy one (Gross et al. 2006). The way in which they react to an expression of negative emotions is important; in fact, the ways they allow expression of emotion in general is important. In some families, parents have strict sanctions on emotional expression, and their children learn to hide their feelings rather than regulate them (Denham et al. 2002). Repression of emotions is not healthy for children. Most of the time, parents who punish highly reactive boys get reactive angry rebellious children in return (Jones et al. 2002). Moreover, when parents are highly controlling, their children may lose the opportunity to learn to be independent. Other parents may not react to their children's emotional life in any manner at all, a behavior that can be seen in parents who have children with conduct problems. Ignoring parents are not very aware of their own or their child's emotions, in spite of the fact that he or she may be exhibiting a high level of emotionality (Katz and Windecker-Nelson 2004).

Researchers have paid particular attention to the parenting styles of people who have highly anxious children. Anxious children engender complementary adult behaviors. These reticent children influence their parents, who then

---

The Intense Anger of Temper Tantrums

Temper tantrums are common among preschool-aged children, and are also seen in older children with handicapping conditions and behavior disorders. Temper tantrums in young children are signs of acute distress. Older children may be persisting in this delayed manner of expressing distress (Koch 2003).

Temper tantrums are common in children from 18 months through five years of age, increasing to 91 percent around age three and decreasing to 59 percent by age four. The longer the tantrum, the more different behaviors exhibited and the greater likelihood that crying will be involved. Anger rises quickly and peaks near the onset of the tantrum. High degrees of anger are often directed against individuals within reach and involve kicking, hitting, and pulling or pushing behaviors (Potegal and Davidson 2003). Seventy-five percent of tantrums in this age group lasted 5 minutes or less.

If adults intervene early, they have a good chance of stopping the escalation of behaviors. The presence of familiar adults may prolong tantrums. Once the behaviors reach intensity, intervening will intensify the tantrum. If the child stamps his or her feet or falls to the floor in the first 30 seconds, the tantrum will be shorter. Stamping is the lower level of anger, shouting and throwing things are the intermediate level, and screaming and kicking are the highest level of anger. The length of the tantrum appears to be related to the degree of distress that the child experiences; such distress involves crying, help seeking, and sadness. Tantrums involve anger and distress, but not anxiety according to Potegal, Kosorok, Richard, and Davidson (2003).

Fig. 9.1 The intense anger of temper tantrums

become overprotective, a parenting style that is associated with internalization of emotion (Fox and Calkins 2003). Parents and teachers of anxious children tend to encourage less adaptive social responses. The parents, in particular, model anxious behaviors themselves and are overcontrolling (Suveg, Zeman, Flannery-Schroeder, and Cassano et al. 2005).

Kagan and Snidman (2004) describe a small group of parents who punish their talkative high-energy anxious boys, which exacerbates their excitability. In turn, the boys become more stressed and irritable or they withdraw. Parents who protect high-reactive children have children who are increasingly fearful. Although comforting young children is appropriate, when parents and teachers overuse comforting or continue to comfort as a primary reaction to upset as children get older it prevents them from learning the critical skills involved in self-regulation of negative emotions. Parents and teachers are not with children all of the time. Children have to master regulatory skills to use on their own when they are in the peer world by themselves.

Matching Children's Temperaments

It is clearly important for adults to correctly 'read' a child's temperament and emotional style and to respond appropriately. There are *bidirectional* influences between a child's temperament and adult responses. For example, inconsistent management on the part of the parent or the teacher may actually increase negative emotions in children (Lengua and Kovacs 2005). Adults have to be aware that a child's behavior will 'pull' him or her to respond in certain ways that may not be the most helpful. Particular responses to a child can exacerbate or modify the behavior. A range of adult behaviors is needed that are sensitive to the child's responses that will also teach skills. This may not be intuitive for all adults. Dennis (2006) points out, for example, that parents are tempted to encourage avoidance at times when problem solving is needed. Examples of three different parenting strategies and the various effects of using those strategies can be found in Fig. 9.2.

Some parents and teachers may need assistance in learning to use the interactive style that would be most helpful to their children. Parenting practices that support increasing emotion regulation include:

- Encouraging children to be independent.
- Reminding children that they are capable so that they will believe that they can control themselves.
- Coaching.
- Encouraging.
- Supporting.
- Modeling emotion regulation.

Both persistently nudging and directly instructing children in how to manage emotions and to use specific strategies are positive for helping them learn to

---

Parenting Anxious Children

Pushing Strategy

This parenting approach involves demanding that children deal with their fears and anxieties themselves with the goal of making them 'stronger,' for example, saying "Stop acting that way." "Get yourself under control." "Boys don't cry." This approach is very controlling and teaches children to hide their feelings or to suppress them. It can exacerbate anxiety and does not teach the child how to deal with anxieties and fears.

Protecting Strategy

This parenting approach involves warmly protecting the child from anything stressful. The goal is to prevent upsets and to keep the child comfortable and feeling safe. This protective strategy certainly makes both the child and the parent feel good in the short run; however, it does not teach the child how to deal with anxiety and fears when the parent is not there. It does not prepare the children for the real world and may undermine their sense of confidence, making them feel powerless.

Pulling Strategy

This parenting strategy involves scaffolding the child's skills over time so that he or she can deal with anxiety and stress. It is firm but encouraging, is low key, and may include humor. It involves giving support, but the support is given by talking from an arm's length away. The child is supported, but is also given strategies to deal with the anxiety and is reminded to use them, and is reminded of past successes: "Remember when you shrugged your shoulders, took a deep breath, and tried to do it last week...it worked didn't it?"

Fig. 9.2 Parenting anxious children

regulate themselves (Apter 2003; Bronson 2000; Melnick and Hinshaw 2000). Parents are encouraged to be emotional coaches, to listen to their child, to recognize and label the emotions being expressed, to set limits, and to teach strategies (Smith and Furlong 1998).

Discussions about Emotion

Talking about emotions and about strategies for regulating emotion are particularly important. Parents and teachers have to use emotion language, teaching the words or labels for various emotions. Positive emotion words as well as negative emotion words are important. Emotions have to be talked about in a variety of ways, including talk about the child's emotions, the adults' emotions, and the emotions of people with whom the child interacts (Cicchetti, Ganiban, and Barnett 1991; Suveg et al. 2005). Children need to learn about the various causes of emotions and the consequences of responding to them in different ways (Shipman et al. 2004). These "emotion discussions" facilitate the child's awareness and understanding of emotions. Talking about negative emotions is critical because learning to cope with negative emotion when aroused is far more difficult for young people than learning to cope with positive feelings

___

Facilitating Regulation

egulating Commentary versus Avoidance-Inducing Commentary

hild is upset and reacting strongly to a negative event, an *avoidance-inducing*
cc... t might be, "This is really hard isn't it," or "I have a special treat in the car for you."

A *problem-solving* or *regulating comment* is more helpful in that it offers an emotion regulation strategy, or it provides a rationale for using a strategy that the child is already familiar with.

A regulating comment would be, "Time to calm down now, think about something else."

A problem-solving comment would be, "If you don't share that with the others, the kids aren't going to want to come to play again. Tell the other child that he can have it as soon as you are finished with it, or tell him he can use it for a little while." If the child chooses to share later, be sure to remind him that he needs to share at the appropriate time.

___

Fig. 9.3 Facilitating regulation through commentary

___

Talking with Children about Negative Emotions

White and Howe (1998) wrote: "...educators who encourage children's emotional expression, who model the expression of positive emotions, and who talk about emotions with children would be expected to foster the ability of the children in their care to engage in emotional regulation and socially competent behaviors with educators and peers" (White and Howe 1998, p. 85).

It is important to help children understand that negative thoughts multiply and the more you think about them the worse you feel (Wenzlaff and Eisenberg 1998).

Books

There are many avenues for talking about negative emotions in school settings. Books can be used as the base for talking about emotions. After reading a story ask open-ended questions, ask how the main character dealt with feelings, and what strategies the characters used to handle their emotions.

Discussion Points

Some concepts to discuss with children include:

- You are more powerful than the emotion.
- There are no rights or wrongs when it comes to emotions, although there may be negative behavior
- Positive and negative emotions can occur at the same time.
- We can limit the length of time we experience negative emotions.

Writing

There is increasing interest in using writing therapeutically (Robinson 2000). This may be a positive strategy for some students who find it easy to write but difficult to talk.

Critical Times

School transitions, local and national traumatic events and individual family crises are times when children need to talk about negative emotions.

___

Fig. 9.4 Talking with children about negative emotions

(Ramsden and Hubbard 2002). Examples of regulating commentary versus avoidance-inducing commentary can be found in Fig. 9.3.

A good example is the case of anger. A child's ability to regulate anger is predicted by overall language ability, and language becomes a major tool for emotion regulation (Bronson 2000; Marion 1997). Some adults simply have to be made to understand the importance of discussions about emotion or may need encouragement or modeling to be better at engaging in discussions with young people. Suggestions for talking with children about negative emotions can be found in Fig. 9.4.

School psychologists can provide this information and insight in a one-shot parenting evening meeting. If discussions are particularly difficult for a parent or group of parents, they can provide them with opportunities to engage in discussions with their children at school privately and give them constructive feedback (Suveg et al. 2005). They can model emotion discussion for teacher's on-the-fly, by visiting classrooms and modeling emotion discussion with the whole class, or they can provide helpful information more formally through consultation. Fig. 9.5 describes dialoguing.

Dialoguing with Children: A dialogue is a conversation between two or more people. When talking with children, a dialogue is more powerful than stating rules or simply telling them what to do. When talking *with* students rather than *at* students, use words with which they are already familiar. Encourage them to think and share their own ideas about how to manage interpersonal situations. At the same time, teach them to evaluate their solutions to conflict or difficulties in terms of the consequences that might result if the solution were tried out (Spivack and Shure 1976, pp 22–34).

When children encounter problematic interpersonal situations, a dialogue or conversation might consist of somewhat open-ended questioning, which teaches children to problem-solve. Questions such as (Spivack and Shure 1976, 60–65,78–81):

"Do you know why this is happening?"
"How can you find out?"
"How did it make you feel when. . .?"
"How do you think __feels when. . .?"
"What might happen if. . .?"
"Can you think of a way to. . .?"
"That's one way or one idea, can you think of another. . .?"
" Is that a good idea?"

Spivack and Shure used this type of questioning technique in their early research. Shure formalized a technique called *ICPS Dialoguing* (Shure 1999). She has demonstrated that it is possible to modify children's behavior by changing their thinking about situations,. Her research has had positive effects on the thinking of children as young as four years of age (Shure 2001).

School psychologists can find ICPS Dialoguing and other important processes and lessons in Shure's curricula: *I Can Problem Solve (ICPS): An Interpersonal Cognitive Problem Solving Program 1992.* The curriculum comes in three levels: preschool, kindergarten/primary, and intermediate elementary with training manuals for teachers and school personnel.

Fig. 9.5 Dialoguing with children (Spival and Shure 1976; Shure 2001a, b)

Emotion Coaching

"Emotion coaching" has become a popular term in the parenting literature. The specifics for emotion coaching include:

- Attending to and respecting the emotions that the child exhibits.
- Direct teaching of self-soothing and calming down.
- Showing interest in how the child feels.
- Modeling and talking about remaining engaged with others when the situation is stressful.
- Pointing out what caused the emotion.
- Answering children's questions quickly.
- Specifically helping children manage anxiety, sadness, and anger.

This parenting style is just as important for parenting adolescents as it is for parenting young children (Katz and Windecker-Nelson 2004). Parents have to encourage expression of negative emotion to a *moderate* but not to a fully permissive degree. This encouragement should be *accompanied with teaching strategies* so that children do not feel overwhelmed or powerless to control themselves (Jones et al. 2002).

Specific emotion regulation strategies need to be taught and reinforced at critical periods of development. Those strategies include:

- Comforting oneself (Calkins 2004),
- Seeking help (Calkins, 2004; Joseph and Strain 2000**b**; Masters 1991),
- Distracting oneself (Calkins 2004),
- Refocusing or shifting attention (Bridges, Denham and Ganibon 2004),
- Problem-solving (Joseph and Strain 2003**b**),
- Changing goals (Joseph and Strain 2003**b**),
- Taking a walk to calm down (Masters 1991),
- Looking for the 'silver lining.' (Masters 1991),
- Getting involved with something else (Masters 1991),
- Deep breathing (Joseph and Strain 2003**b**) (Joseph and Strain 2003**c**),
- Trying a different way (Joseph and Strain 2003**b**),
- Talking 'strategy' to oneself, and (Joseph and Strain 2003**c**),
- Distracting oneself by refocusing attention (Silk, Shaw, Skuban, Olan and Kovacs 2006).

These strategies have to be taught to juveniles directly and explicitly. They have to be practiced, modeled, and their use reinforced. Children who have a large repertoire of strategies that they can recall and use when they are upset are in a good position to be able to control intense emotions (Bridges et al. 2004). A tool to determine which strategies a student typically uses, and to what degree, is shown in Fig. 9.6.

Use of Coping and Regulating Strategies

Please rate this student in regard to whether or not and to what degree he or she uses the following strategies to cope with upsetting events and /or situations.

	Usually	Often	Occasionally	Never
1. Works hard to resolve the situation.				
2. Looks to the adult to solve the problem.				
3. Walks away from the situation.				
4. Blames everyone else.				
5. Thinks positively about the situation.				
6. Looks for emotional support from others.				
7. Holds back.				
8. Makes angry negative comments.				
9. Tries to put things in perspective.				
10. Asks for help in solving the problem.				
11. Daydreams and avoids dealing with stress.				
12. Vents feelings loudly, fusses, or cries.				
13. Formulates a plan to change the situation.				
14. Seeks positive support from adults/peers.				
15. Gives up easily.				
16. Gets angry and strikes out.				
17. Takes deep breaths or counts to ten.				
18. Asks what should be done.				
19. Denies that the upset is a problem.				
20. Stamps feet, clenches fists.				
21. Exercises, goes for a walk or bike ride.				
22. Moves near adults.				
23. Hides feelings.				
24. Yells at others.				
25. Formulates a plan to change the situation.				
26. Finds someone to listen.				
27. Gives up goals, disengages.				
28. Seeks revenge.				
29. Reinterprets the situation.				
30. Asks for comforting.				
31. Avoids thinking about it.				
32. Acts with impulsive anger.				

Key

Problem-Solving /Active Strategies #s 1, 5, 9, 13, 17, 21, 25 and 29.
Seeks Support #s 2, 6, 10, 14, 18, 22, 26 and 30.
Avoidance/Passive Strategies #s 3, 7, 11, 15, 19, 23, 27 and 31.
Aggressive Strategies #s 4, 8, 12, 16, 20, 24, 28 and 32.

Fig. 9.6 Use of coping and regulating strategies worksheet

Working on young people's gut reactions to others or to ambiguous situations (attributional biases) is important so that they do not assume that others are "out to get them." This involves having them learn to interpret social cues correctly, having an optimistic attitude, and controlling how much anger they allow themselves to experience in a stressful situation (Furlong and Smith 1998). Children need practice asking questions when upset instead of acting out impulsively or saying something that they may regret later on. Engaging in people watching is a fine way to learn about others, to learn how to behave in social situations, and to learn to control emotional intensity (Lavoie 2005). The benefits of 'people watching' are found in Fig. 9.7a and the technique is described for school psychologists and parents in Fig. 9.7b.

Fitea, Colder, Lochman, and Wells (2006) found that sixth grade is a critical stage at which adults have to monitor children. Students may need specific skills at this point in their development to regulate emotional reactions to change, peer isolation and rejection, increasing academic challenge, adults that they do not match well, and being teased.

Both parents and school staff can be involved in meeting children's needs during transition periods, and the way parents and other adults interact with

---

People Watching

Rothenberg (1998) has made a series of important suggestions for helping students with nonverbal learning disabilities.

- Watch a television sitcom and ask the student what is happening
- Turn off the sound on the television set and talk about what is going on given nonverbal cues
- Talking with students after an incident has occurred, asking questions such as "What do you think the other person was feeling? What about her makes you think that she was feeling that way?"

Olivera and Straus (2004) conducted a study in which students demonstrated that participating in or observing a group caused transfer of learning as compared to a situation in which working without interacting or without observing others interact did not. The transfer of learning occurred based on cognitive rather than social factors.

This suggests that social learning from observation and social imitation are more complex than thought in the past. Not only are there perceptual factors, but social beliefs, social goals, and social decision making is involved (Conte and Paolucci 2001).

Observation is not enough; discussion of the behaviors that are being observed is necessary. Asking questions about the behaviors an the goals and consequences of the behaviors that other children exhibit is critically important as is reflecting on whether the child's social goals match the goals of the child being observed.

When the child can understand the behavioral sequences, appreciate the consequences of the specific behaviors, and decide whether or not the behavior might be tried out, the school psychologist can serve as a coach, cuing the child as he or she tries out the new behaviors.

Fig. 9.7a People watching

People-Watching Technique

Spend part of several recess periods watching the games and social interactions on the playground with the targeted student. Point out incidents and children who are managing their emotions well and those who are not.

Comments

"See the student over there who is being told he is out of the game?"
"How is he reacting?"
"Why is he behaving that way?"
"Do you think his behavior will help him with the group or hurt him with the group?"
"What else could he do?"
"What other things could he do?"
"How can he help himself feel better?"
"Can you see someone else who is managing his disappointment well?"

Continue to work on this type of problem solving until the student is able to generate alternative ways to deal with upset and has several good ideas to help himself feel better. Agree on a signal to use to help the student remember to use the strategies. Send the student into the game reminding him to use the strategies and watch for your signal if he forgets to use them.

Teach parents to use this teaching tool so that they can use it after school and on weekends with their child at local playgrounds.

Fig. 9.7b People-watching technique

them during emotionally stressful encounters is particularly important. This is a key opportunity to model the regulation of intense emotion, teach children how to remain engaged when stressed, and model how to tolerate the intense emotions of others (Calkins 2004; Shore 1994).

School Stress

School stress can occur daily and, over time, can exacerbate psychological symptoms (Hampel and Petermann 2005). Teachers have to be more aware of the differences among their students so that their reactions will be appropriate and helpful rather than adding to the students' stress. Of course, teachers themselves are under considerable stress in today's schools and negative displays of emotions by their students can be highly disruptive and distressing for them (Jones et al. 2002).

The differences in schoolchildren that are associated with their individual temperaments have to be understood. It is important to help teachers appreciate how these differences affect classroom behavior so that they use appropriate strategies for interacting with their students (NASP 1998). They have to understand that they have the power to affect social achievement by offering emotional support in the same way that they affect academic achievement by providing a strong instructional environment in their classroom (Hamre and Pianta 2005). Teachers may also need some assistance in identifying children for whom emotion regulation is challenging. They find it hard to identify students who are quietly intense, whereas it is much easier to distinguish emotionally reactive students. They find it challenging to deal with children who are hostile (Fainsilber and Windecker-Nelson 2004: Furlong and Smith 1998).

Teachers have to respond empathetically to children who have meltdowns and become flooded with emotion. They should be taught techniques to support these children, rather than be left feeling overwhelmed or frustrated. Two strategies that have been helpful in this regard, which can be shared with teachers, are reflective listening and the use of calming scripts Both of these approaches have been found to be effective in helping children regain control (Hromek 2004).

Classroom Climate

Classroom climate has to do with the general atmosphere in the room and the degree to which the class runs smoothly and the interactions are positive. The teacher's response to students and interactions between the teacher and students and among students can support the positive climate. Classroom climate varies from classroom to classroom in a school. Students in classes where the climate is negative are at risk for internalizing symptoms and peer rejection, with some children at greater risk than others: anxious boys, for example, are at particular risk for peer rejection and girls are at risk for victimization by classmates.

In classrooms where the climate is positive, these students are both supported and protected (Gazelle 2006). Teachers who are keenly aware of emotions are able to discriminate students' emotions, can take a student's point of view when listening, and can stay in control themselves are more empathetic with their students (Feshbach and Feshbach 2004). A tool for teachers to assist students in identifying their own anger triggers can be found in Fig. 9.8.

Strategies for Teaching Emotion Regulation

Teacher interventions that are helpful for students as they develop emotion regulation include stress reduction (Napoli 2004), emotion coaching (Hromek 2004), and modeling and directly teaching coping skills (Pincus and Friedman 2004). Teaching anxious students, for example, requires attention to their specific needs. Fifteen recommendations for teaching anxious students are listed in Fig. 9.9.

Reading books about dealing with emotions and engaging in role-play in which students have a chance to get into a role, feel the specific emotions, and learn about solutions are very helpful (Westphal and Bonanno 2004). These opportunities are provided by social-emotional learning curricula that

Would this make me angry?

Place a check mark beside your triggers.

1. I lose the game.   ____
2. My friend is mean to me.   ____
3. My friend says something that isn't true about me.   ____
4. Somebody takes something that belongs to me.   ____
5. My brother (sister) won't leave me alone.   ____
6. A classmate tells the teacher on me.   ____
7. A kid gets in line in front of me.   ____
8. I get picked last for the team.   ____
9. Somebody gets me out on purpose.   ____
10. I don't get invited to a birthday party.   ____
11. Someone says, "No girls (boys) allowed."   ____
12. I don't get invited over to play.   ____
13. The teacher says, "That's wrong."   ____
14. The teacher says, "Do it over again."   ____
15. Someone says, "You can't play."   ____

Fig. 9.8 Identifying anger triggers worksheet

Fifteen Recommendations for Teaching Anxious Students

1. **Schedules** are very important. Keeping the anxious student on a schedule is critical. Schedules allow students to know what to expect.
2. **Physical activity** makes the anxious student feel better and is extremely important. Even a walk around the room or doing an errand can reduce stress.
3. **Down time** is very important. Don't fill all of this student's time. Allow the student some time for quiet reading or drawing. Reading to the class is relaxing for most students. A relaxation exercise can be used for the entire class. A quiet time, however short, can be provided by playing music in class.
4. Make sure that whatever the student is experiencing emotionally is accepted by all staff. The goal is not to get rid of anxiety, but rather to reduce it or prevent it from getting out of control. At the same time, **don't reward** anxiety by offering protection without also teaching a self-management strategy.
5. Help this student **set goals.** Setting goals to control anxiety and to use strategies that you are teaching is important. Help this student understand that effort can result in success. Give rewards for efforts to control anxiety that interferes with having fun and/or learning. "You can't learn math by talking about it; you must do it!" Rehearse and practice ahead of time when the child will have to deal with a stressful event. Keep the rehearsal low key, and practice not only the actions, but how you would like this student to think about the event ("It will be new and different, but I can handle it. "I may feel a little tense, but if I feel stressed, I will take deep breaths and try to relax.").
6. Anxiety interferes with **organization.** Help this student learn organization strategies and remind the student to use them.

Fig. 9.9 Fifteen recommendations for teaching anxious students (handout)

7. When the student is extremely stressed, give the student an **activity with a goal** such as drawing a picture, cleaning his desk, straightening or collecting papers, or writing a list. Offer praise for efforts to control anxiety.

8. Listen to the student's thinking for if-then statements such as 'if I do x, y will happen.' The 'x' part of the statement is often correct, but the 'y' part is not. Correct this thinking and other negative self-talk. Thoughts can cause anxiety; students need to be taught to challenge thoughts. A student who thinks, "If I make a mistake, I will fail first grade," needs to think, "This may take awhile to learn but I am getting better at it." Correct **'should'** statements and jumping to conclusions.

9. Teach the student to ask for a **'break.'** Phrases such as "I need a break," "I need more time," "Can I have another minute please?" may protect the child from being overwhelmed or feeling as if he or she is being confronted.

10. Keep the **emotions** in the classroom **at a low level**. It is important not to raise your voice (yell) when interacting with this student. Use a calm, quiet voice so this anxious student can hear what you are saying. Confrontation is overwhelming; give warnings when transitions are coming; make comments such as "Others are going to 'x.' If you continue to waste time, is that going to be okay?" Give choices where possible.

11. When the student is relaxed, **comment** that the student looks relaxed: "You are so relaxed when you are drawing!" Describe how that looks and what the child is doing. This gives the student a verbal picture of calm feelings. It will help the child have more cognitive control over the feelings.

12. **Model** positive thinking and problem solving. Negative thinking contributes to the perception of stress. As you model positive thinking and problem solving, you are directly instructing students on how to think about stressful events and on how to feel about making mistakes and how to 'fix' them. High anxiety immobilizes a student, who then does not engage in problem solving or use coping strategies. Talk about your own feelings in emotionally difficult situations so the student will have the language to do so as well. Teach and model **"one thing at a time"**. thinking. Model coping behavior and stress management techniques. Great acting while you are talking out loud is great teaching. Don't just lecture. Insist on practicing and role-play.

13. **Stories** are very helpful. Stories are not confrontational. The goal of reading stories is help students learn about managing stress. A good story not only explains about stress, but tells the student how to deal with it– what actions to take. The best stories tell the student what the stress is, what to **think about it,** and then **what to do** about it. If you can't find a story to fit the student's difficulty, write one!

14. **Written communication.** Once a student can read, you can use written communication instead of 'talking at' the student, which increases anxiety and shuts down thinking. When an older student is upset or out of control, ask him or her to write down the argument or question. Then you can write your reply. With a younger child, ask the child to draw a picture of what is upsetting her/him. Draw a solution in response. You can also use stress cards. Write the strategy that the child is practicing on a card (or draw pictures), and then tape it on the desk as a visual reminder. At the end of the day, don't bombard the student with how did the day go or with additional criticism if the student had a difficult day.

15. Positive comments are very important in teaching anxious students. Use lots of positive comments, about six to ten positive statements to every criticism. A positive comment does not have to be a compliment (although if you use a lot of compliments, students will use a lot in return to you and toward their peers). A description of what the student is doing at the moment is very pleasant and reinforcing because it offers positive adult attention (I see you are. . . .). These descriptive comments help a student feel valued.

Fig. 9.9 (continued)

incorporate "scripts" to assist teachers and school psychologists to deliver the curricula with integrity. The goal is to help students learn to be flexible in their ability to mobilize emotions (Diamond and Aspinwall 2003).

Specific strategies that teachers need to be aware of include emotional literacy so that children develop an emotion lexicon. "Feelings words" should be taught and defined regularly. Students have to be shown how listening to another person's voice in literature can tell them how that person feels. Teachers can use emotion vocabulary in their day-to-day teaching. They can use stories to discuss emotions by asking students, "How do you think this character feels?" A question such as "What happened in the story to make him feel this way?" will direct attention to causes for feelings and emotions.

Asking questions such as "What can she do?" directs students' attention to the need for problem solving. Stories can be used to teach perspective taking. Teachers and school psychologists can use real events to help children attend to others' emotions: "How do you think Jake feels with his dad away?" Additionally, teachers can stress the differences between purposeful aggression and accidents. Another critical lesson is teaching the difference between feelings and acting upon those feelings:

- It's okay to be angry but not to hit.
- It's okay to be jealous but not to sabotage a friendship.
- It's okay to be upset but not to knock over the board game.
- It's okay to feel sad but not to say mean and hurtful things to classmates.

Teachers, like all adults who work with children, need to problem-solve *out loud*, sharing the steps they take to cope or calm down. Modeling taking a deep breath, taking a break, talking to a friend, and staying in control when excited are helpful, although describing what you are doing while you are using the strategy is even better (Joseph and Strain 2003b). Children have to be taught *reparative* behaviors when they have expressed inappropriate emotions (Fainsilber and Windecker-Nelson 2004). They need to master a few scripts to use in such situations: "Sorry, I lost my cool; I'll try this again;" "Give me a minute; I'm a bit stressed;" "I really didn't mean that"; "I was upset; I didn't mean to upset you too." These scripts can be included as part of universal social-emotional learning curricula.

Young people need help in distracting themselves from paying too much attention to negative experiences and in reappraising the meaning of events that make them sad, angry, or frustrated (Westphal and Bonanno 2004). They have to be helped to set emotion regulation goals and to self-monitor their progress toward those goals. Suggestions for children who tend to see the "glass half empty" (who are pessimistic or who exhibit mild negative moods) can be found in Fig. 9.10.

Shifting a negative mood to a more positive one takes considerable practice. Children need both strategies and reminders, once they have mastered several strategies, in order to be successful in ameliorating mild negative moods. It is not so much a matter of rewarding them for making progress in controlling their emotions, but rather helping them learn strategies over time and repeatedly practicing using those skills that makes the difference (Kazdin 2006).

Shifting Negative Moods

When students experience frequent but mild negative moods and tend to see the 'down side' of events, they may be helped with a variety of simple interventions. These tools can also be used as a booster for other interventions.

Daily report cards have been used successfully with students with behavior difficulties. They are helpful in generating positive motivation and attitudes when they generate discussion and positive feedback. They additionally improve parent-school communication (Chafouleas, Riley-Tillman and McDougal 2002).

Mild negative moods can be elevated using daily report cards with reinforcements. The main purposes include: helping students understand the 'face' that they are presenting to others, to help students understand that moods can be worked on in the same way as other behaviors, and to help students understand they have some control over their moods.

Teaching children to 'smile' whether or not they feel low will result in others treating them positively. Smiling may also momentarily elevate mood (Kleinke, Peterson and Rutledge 1998; Schnall and Laird 2003).

Teaching students to report positive school experiences, as well as negative school experiences when they return home each day, may be important in making sure that parents are not inadvertently rewarding negativity (Freeman, Pretzer, Fleming and Simon 2004, p. 374). Students can take a few minutes at the end of the day to reflect briefly on the day's events. Two positive events are generated for every negative event. This can be done individually (and written down so the student has reporting cues) or the entire class might benefit from this type of reflection.

Fig. 9.10 Shifting negative moods

School psychologists can provide additional training outside of the general education classroom for students who are having particular difficulty in regulating their emotions. In order for skills to transfer back into the classroom, the student must feel safe in the classroom and must be supported in using new skills. The school psychologist may have to go into the classroom or out onto the playground and coach the student to use the skills taught elsewhere. Going into the classroom to work with a student also models the coaching technique for the general education teacher (Besley 1999). Coaching techniques for teachers are listed in Fig. 9.11.

It is important to keep in mind that teaching needs to continue over time. More intensive interventions work best when the intervention or curriculum is delivered over time, when the student feels that the training is relevant, when the goal setting relates to both the individual and the group, and when progress is carefully monitored (Skiba and McKelvey 2000).

When teachers are faced with a very challenging group of students and the entire climate of the classroom is affected, they have to take steps to de-escalate the prevailing emotional level. They can do this by changing activities to something less stressful, such as reading, telling stories, or drawing, or bring students together in a circle to talk. Teachers can bring in other staff such as the school psychologist to work with students, while at the same time giving themselves some breathing space so that they can regroup (Bradley, Ama, Gettman, Brennan, and Kibera 2004).

Coaching Techniques for Teachers

1. When a student makes a negative comment, consider it an opportunity to talk about emotions and to teach about emotions.

2. Label negative emotions that a student exhibits (if the student is very young) or help the older student label the emotion being expressed for himself or herself.

3. Listen empathetically to the student's description of his or her feelings giving the student time to experience and accept his or her feelings.

4. Give the student permission to 'feel' the emotion, indicating that emotions are not 'bad' but rather are normal and experienced by everyone.

5. If the student is in a public place (corridor, cafeteria, playground, classroom), it may be important to move an upset student to a place where the student will not be on display in front of his or her peers. Set limits if the intensity of the emotion being expressed is extreme. If a student is out-of-control (or close to that stage), use distraction rather than trying to reason with the student.

6. When the student seems to be under some control, ask the student if the emotion is uncomfortable.

7. Suggest that the student limit the intensity of the emotion that is being experienced or the length of time that the negative emotion is being exhibited.

8. Offer to teach strategies for dealing with the intensity of the emotion or offer to set up an appointment with the school psychologist.

9. Teach two or three strategies for calming down.

10. If problem-solving would be helpful, engage the student in exploring solutions or in determining how to prevent the situation from happening again.

11. Give the student concrete reminders or cues to remind him or her to use the strategy or strategies after they have been taught.

12. Help the student practice using the strategies until the student is more confident and comfortable.

13. Ask the student if he or she would like others to remind him when he might use the strategies. A trusted peer could be the person to remind the student to use strategies if that would be comfortable for the student you are trying to help.

14. Give homework that involves practicing the strategies or solving the problem(s).

15. Remind the student that you will be checking in to make sure that things are going well and the student remembers to practice the strategies.

Fig. 9.11 Coaching techniques for teachers (handout)

Diverse Populations

School psychologists have to keep in mind that there is significant diversity in many American schools today, more so in urban areas. These professionals have to be acutely aware of the relationship between emotion regulation and culture so that they can appropriately service children and their families. They must appreciate the fact that individuals' understanding of healthy adjustment and even of mental health is cultural. Some parents and children do not consider mainstream American regulatory norms for emotional display or emotion regulation familiar, important, or appropriate for their families.

Many families in America may not hold the same values that child development professionals consider critical. Behaviors that concern school staffs may not be of concern to families whose cultural expectations differ, and what may worry us may not be of concern to families whose cultural background is different from ours (Cole and Dennis 1998; Rubin 1998). These differences must be respected. Owing to the complexity of American society, we may be quite limited in our ability to know how another individual feels. Our critical judgments about a given child's competence and adjustment may be incorrect at the least to detrimental in the extreme.

At the most basic level, cultures differ in the number and kinds of emotions that they identify or recognize. Some cultures do not even have words for particular emotions (Satcher 2005). People express emotion in a variety of physical ways, but these tendencies are not very strong and are easily overridden by cultural rules and norms. This can make it very difficult for us to identify the emotion being expressed by a child or parent whose cultural background is different from ours. Emotion concepts can be very broad or finely distinguished, depending on an individual's culture. The display rules for emotions are cultural, and these in turn determine the ease with which emotions are expressed. The ways in which individuals resolve emotions also depend on culture (Ratner 2000).

The culture that is dominant in American schools is "individualistic," and anger is appropriate and functional. 'Reasonable' anger (a cultural value in itself) reflects independence, protection of rights, and self-expression (Holodynski and Friedlmeier 2006). Contemporary Americans believe that personality, which in American culture is considered a constant trait, motivates behavior. If they are slighted or their goals are blocked, Americans become angry and do not let it go quickly. They find it difficult to regulate this type of anger (Ratner 2000).

Americans tend to exaggerate their expressions because they do not value emotional moderation to the same extent as *some* other cultures. When Americans judge another's expression of emotions they may believe that the other person is experiencing less intense emotion than they are expressing. This would not make much sense from the perspective of some other cultures (Matsumoto 2002; Tsai and Levenson 1997). On the other hand, individuals in some other cultures are even more expressive than those who fit the current American model. As another example, socially anxious behaviors or inhibited behaviors are considered problematic in American schools, but this is a culturally dependent value judgment. The same behaviors might be interpreted as 'reserved' by individuals of another culture and quite appropriate (Holodynski and Friedlmeier 2006).

Culture determines how people feel, how they express emotion, and which emotions they value. Reactivity, control, and perception are cultural. Parents begin the training of their children according to the rules of their respective cultures about experiencing, expressing, and regulating emotions (Denham et al. 2002). These display rules reflect how easy or difficult it may be to express emotions and lead to differences in intensity and regulation. Parents teach context-dependent feelings rules to their children (Ratner 2000), but children may not master cultural display rules until they are of school age (Fox and Calkins 2003), so schools also influence a child.

When a student's culture does not match the school culture, the influence of the school culture on their child may not be appreciated or understood by the family. It can be very stressful for children who must behave emotionally one way in school and another way at home. Some children who are trying to adjust to two different strong sets of cultural expectations may feel a bit 'schizophrenic' or confused at times. If we in turn make judgments about how we think a child 'really feels,' we may just be adding to this distress.

Emotion regulation predicts adjustment in a wide variety of cultures (Matsumoto 2002), and cultural beliefs influence whether or not a child's behavior is considered difficult or problematic (Smart and Sanson 2001). There appear to be cultural differences in the manifestation of disabilities. For example, the degree of comorbidity in cases of depression is culturally dependent, as is the way in which disorders progress, the way they are treated, and the outcomes (Tsai and Chentsova-Dutton 2002).

Although there are critical differences, it appears that the importance of emotion regulation is universal. It should be noted that although we may never become proficient in understanding other cultures, improving emotional regulation in our general school populations may be helpful in teaching children to appreciate and tolerate the cultural differences that do not match each of our own (Matsumoto 2002). This can only happen if we teach respect and model acceptance of differences.

Gender Variables

There are gender differences in self-regulation that can be observed in children as early as three years of age (Zhang, Jin, and Shen 2006). Gender, as well as culture, complicates our ability to judge whether or not an emotional expression or response is contextually appropriate (Rottenberg and Gross 2003).

Parents socialize girls and boys differently in regard to emotion expression and regulation. Girls are socialized to express more emotion than boys. Parents talk more to girls about emotions, are more emotionally responsive to girls, and display a wider range of emotions to them. They help girls more, smile more to them, and use a wider variety of emotion words in general and positive emotion words in particular when they talk with them. Parents may allow boys more autonomy, but they minimize boys' expressions of sadness and pay more attention to boys' negative behaviors once they reach puberty, even though girls may behave just as badly. Parents attend to boys' expressions of anger and minimize a girl's anger expression (Ratner 2000).

During the preschool period, girls talk more than boys about their emotional experiences and use more "emotion words" than boys when they talk about things that happened to them that were frightening (Fivush, Brotman, Buckner, and Goodman 2000). Girls have greater understanding of conflicting relationships and are more influenced by the quality of relationships they have with their siblings than boys (Brown and Dunn 1996).

Mothers tend to be the ones who socialize (trains according to culture) negative emotions, particularly anger. Fathers reward their daughters for expressing fear and sadness but punish boys for expressing those same emotions, and both mothers and fathers use more emotion language when discussing sad events with girls. Parents personalize the discussion when talking with girls (Fivush et al. 2000; Garside and Klimes-Dougan 2002).

Gender differences continue to be socialized throughout life, so they can be identified during adolescence and beyond. During adolescence, for example, girls show higher levels of anxiety and other negative emotions just before taking standardized tests, whereas boys show higher positive emotions and higher self-esteem in the week before testing (Locker and Cropley 2004). Gender differences are seen from adolescence into adulthood in regard to the strategies that females use (versus males) to deal with stress. Females use more rumination and catastrophizing, as well as more positive refocusing, or seeing the positive side of things, than males (Garnefski, Teerds, Kraaij, Legerstee, and van den Kommer 2004).

Identified Children

Children with autism spectrum disorders (ASD) have particular difficulties with emotion regulation. Even if they are functioning well enough to be able to identify the other person's emotions, they still have difficulty determining the implications of emotional states for behavior. Some children with ASD may notice that another child is in distress, but not know what to do about it so they cannot respond empathetically (Loveland 2005). These children have difficulty determining the social reasons behind their peers' facial expressions (Dennis, Lockyer, and Lazenby 2000). Children with ASD have a low threshold for reactivity and emotional upset. When emotion is intense and elevated, they may exhibit behavior that could be misinterpreted as deliberate misbehavior (Prizant, Wetherby, Rubin, and Laurent 2005).

Children with ASD have to be taught to remain on an even keel across various settings and activities. As they function differently at different levels of arousal and excitability, their various behaviors have to be identified. They need support in order to use strategies at each level of arousal. The SCERTS model provides structure for these interventions and goals (Prizant et al. 2003).

Chapter 10
Adapting Interventions for Use with School-Aged Children

Need for Adaptations

Many of the intervention techniques for improving regulation of emotion and mood were developed for adults. School psychologists today work with students from age three through twenty-two, and the same tools, strategies, and techniques are not appropriate for all age and ability levels. A number of programs and curricula have already been described that have some evidence or research base, but adaptations of the more specific tools and techniques are needed so that they can be used effectively with younger children.

Adapting Intervention Tools for Practice

Tools used in assisting students to regulate emotion and behavior may have to be adapted to increase the likelihood that they will be employed. It is particularly important to adapt tools for young children. For example, Venham and Gaulin-Kremer (1979) used stylized cartoon faces or characters to stand for different emotional states, and the children used these to demonstrate how anxious they were in a stressful situation. The pencil and paper tool illustrated in Fig. 10.1 can be used to help a student identify and convey this or her emotional intensity. There is more research on the typical interventions for anxiety, depression, and anger management when used with adults and adolescents than with younger children, but solid inroads have been made adapting them for children.

Cognitive Behavioral Therapy

Cognitive behavioral therapy (CBT) is an organized set of interventions that are designed for each student who needs them (Gosch Flannery-Schroeder, Mauro, and Compton 2006). CBT has the potential to affect the brain, and recent research demonstrates that it may be able to modify the neural circuitry

Fig. 10.1 Intensity

underlying anxiety (Paquette Lévesque, Mensour, Leroux, Beaudoin, Bourgouin 2003). CBT interventions for children and adolescents must be adapted to the young person's ability and developmental level.

Affective education is the first body of information to be taught. Children must learn to identify and label emotions and feelings and to see how these thoughts and feelings are connected to sensations in their bodies. If they deny or are unaware of somatic symptoms or feelings of anxiety, it must be addressed immediately. Some girls and boys may need concrete experiences to pay attention to their bodies. Asking a child to balance on a board a few inches off the ground (taking proper safety precautions) can initiate a discussion about which parts of one's body may be tense. Using language that is at the child's level of understanding and visuals such as pictures or drawings of faces depicting various emotions can be helpful. Sharing feelings through modeling may facilitate talking about emotions.

The goal of cognitive therapy is to help the child experience emotion in ways that fit the situation appropriately and to be able to adapt emotion as needed.

Recognizing and understanding one's emotions leads to efforts to tone down overreactions. When using cognitive therapy approaches with children, it is important to also work with their parents, and the younger the child the more vital it is to actively involve parents. Family interactions and parents' thoughts and beliefs affect children's functioning. Parents may need assistance with positive ways to manage behavior, relaxation techniques to teach to their child, and techniques to help their child learn to regulate emotion (Freeman, Pretzer, Fleming, and Simon 2004). In addition, Freeman et al. (2004) recommends 30-minute sessions with younger children, with simple therapeutic games, stuffed animals, and puppets, which the child can use to communicate concerns. With older children, assignments to be completed between sessions, self-instruction training, and role-playing problematic situations are recommended.

Additional cognitive techniques include scheduling worrying during a specific time of the day and learning to refocus one's attention on things that are not anxiety provoking. Students can help design a schedule so that worrying is restricted to a specific short span of time during a day rather than during academic periods. They practice refocusing as they fill their minds with happy thoughts or calm images whenever they start to think negatively. Getting involved in activities that require concentration is helpful in reducing worrying (Freeman et al. 2004).

Adaptations of Cognitive Tools

Another tool used in cognitive interventions is a number scale, which can be used to help students in several ways. A numerical scale is designed to change internal and external reactions to the emotion that an individual is experiencing. First, it is used to stop thoughts that are centered on how upset the person is feeling, how 'awful' the situation may be, and what 'devastating' things may occur. Second, it engages the student's thoughts on making a judgment in regard to how serious the situation may be and whether or not his or her 'feelings' are valid or are exaggerated for the given context. A worksheet for this purpose is provided in Fig. 10.3. Make a vertical number scale listing the numbers 5, 4, 3, 2, 1 with number 5 at the top as in Fig. 10.4, with or without the pictures. Construct the scale with the student as explained in Fig. 10.5.

The numerical scale must be designed for the age level and general cognitive ability of the child. For very young, preschool, or handicapped children, the numerical scale can be associated with pictures indicating the different levels of emotion, and the descriptors of the levels must be simple and memorable. For children of elementary school age, the pictures and the descriptors can be more complex. A sample scale for anxiety reduction is pictured in Fig. 10.4.

Putting Your Feelings in Perspective Script

This number scale helps students decide how worried or upset they ought to be when something stressful happens.

Do you remember the story of Henny Penny? Look at number 5, "The sky is falling." Let's think of the most upsetting things that could possibly happen. (Make certain that these items are personally and extremely stressful for the student and are highly unlikely to occur; for example, a parent dying which would raise fears of abandonment). Select three events or circumstances.

Now let's look at number 4, "a terrible storm is coming." Items that belong in this category are very serious and would make the student very upset but would not be as horrible as the items listed for number 5 (e.g., parents divorce, a parent or the student herself becoming extremely ill, failure, a pet dog being hit by a car).

Look at number 3. Think of situations or events that would make you feel *very* uncomfortable (e.g., being teased, forgetting your homework, failing a quiz, being left out, the teacher is angry, not getting invited to a party).

Look at number 2. The things that belong here are the things that make us feel somewhat stressed (striking out, getting chosen nearly last, someone cuts you in line).

Finally, look at number 1. The things that belong here are the things that you can handle and little things that make you feel okay or good (getting a sticker, the kids say "good hit," someone tells a joke that isn't funny, you ask for something and the teacher says "Oh, all right" but she isn't really happy about it).

Keep in mind that the descriptors for each level will be highly individual. What is stressful for one student will not be stressful for another. Work this through carefully.

Fig. 10.2 Putting feelings in perspective script

For high school students, the number of degrees of emotion can be larger, although even older children may respond better if there are fewer degrees when faced with intense emotion. The descriptors can be more sophisticated, and pictures would only be necessary at this level for some students with special needs, such as adolescents on the spectrum or those with developmental delay.

Students need a detailed explanation of the scale and how to use it. The better the description, the more practice given and setting up cues in the environments the student needs to use the scale, the more successful the strategy. A possible script to use with a student is found in Fig. 10.2.

Students will need considerable assistance in determining which number represents their current feeling, which is why that the various descriptions of each number are generated. A think-aloud strategy is modeled for the student.

"Could this be a 5? No, this couldn't possibly be a 5; no one has died or been terribly injured. Could it be a 4? Well, it isn't as bad as ___, so it couldn't be a 4. Maybe it's a 3? Well, this situation is worse than a 3. I think I could call it a $3^1/_2$, and I can handle things at this level."

This thinking process is modeled repeatedly until the student starts to use it. Engaging this thinking process works very quickly in reducing anxiety. It

Fig. 10.3 Constructing the number scale

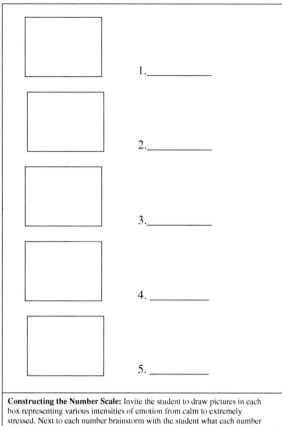

Constructing the Number Scale: Invite the student to draw pictures in each box representing various intensities of emotion from calm to extremely stressed. Next to each number brainstorm with the student what each number will represent.

engages the brain, refocuses attention away from the anxious feelings, and can be used to start the problem-solving process.

Teaching the strategy to parents and teachers and reminding them to cue students to use it increases success. For younger students, a small-sized scale can be taped on to their desks. Older students can keep a card with the numbers and pictures in their pockets. Sample messages or cues for a response card with instructions are pictured in Fig. 10.6.

The initial meeting with a student or group of students generates the meanings of the numbers. The next several meetings involve practice with the scale. Parents and teachers are given the scale with directions for its use, and the student is asked to use the strategy and report back regarding its success. The keys are teaching the strategy as closely as possible in line with the student's personal experience of intense emotion and giving assurances that it has worked for many other students dealing with intense emotions. Importantly,

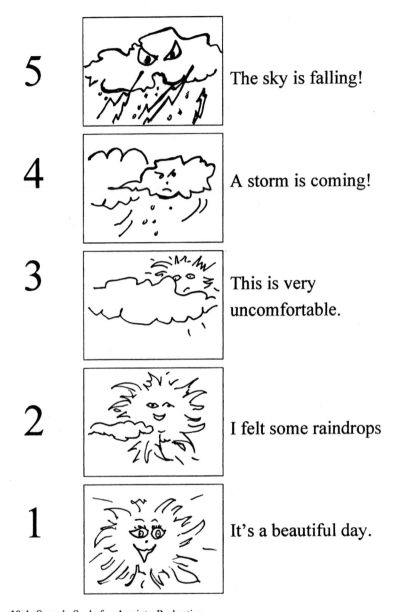

5   The sky is falling!

4   A storm is coming!

3   This is very uncomfortable.

2   I felt some raindrops

1   It's a beautiful day.

Fig. 10.4 Sample Scale for Anxiety Reduction

the strategy can be used to reduce both anxiety and anger. When a number scale is used to teach young people to reduce angry feelings to a tolerable and controllable level, it is important to add strategies to the scale for the different levels or intensities of anger that are experienced. For elementary school students, the numbers, pictures, descriptors of intensity, and the strategies

---

Design and Use of a Number Scale

A numerical scale can be used to help children in several ways. The scale is designed to change internal and external reactions to the emotion that are being experienced. First, it stops thoughts that are centered on how upset the child is feeling, how 'awful' the situation may be, and what 'catastrophic' things might occur. Second, it engages the child's thoughts on making a judgment in regard to how serious the situation may be and whether or not his or her 'feelings' are valid or are exaggerated for the given context.

The numerical scale must be designed for the age level and general cognitive ability of the child. For young children, the numerical scale may be associated with pictures indicating the different levels of emotion, and the descriptors of the levels must be simple and memorable. For elementary-aged children, the pictures and the descriptors can be more complex. For secondary-level students the number of degrees of emotion can be larger, although even older students may respond better if there are fewer degrees when faced with intense emotion. The descriptors can be more sophisticated, and pictures would only be necessary at this level for some students with special needs, such as students on the spectrum or those with developmental delay.

Students need a detailed explanation of the scale and how to use it. The better the description, the more practice given and setting up cues in the environments the student needs to use the scale, the more successful the strategy. Teaching the strategy to parents and teachers and reminding them to cue students to use it increases success. For younger students, a small-sized scale can be *taped on* to their desks. For older students, a card with the numbers and pictures can be kept in their pockets.

The initial meeting with a student or students generates the meanings of the numbers. The next several meetings involve practice with the scale. Parents and teachers are given the scale with directions for its use, and the student is asked to use the strategy and report back regarding its success.

The strategy can be used to reduce both anxiety and anger. The keys are teaching the strategy as closely in line as possible with the student's experience of intense emotion and assurances that it has worked for many other students dealing with intense emotions.

Note: *this strategy has been successful clinically with many individual children over many years and was also successful with an entire classroom of second-graderswho were extremely upset after the Columbine tragedy and after talk of war.*

Fig. 10.5 Design and use of number scale

can all appear on the scale that the school psychologist designs together with the child, as in Fig. 10.7.

Designing the tool is an intervention strategy and opportunity to assist older students in identifying feelings, triggers, and strategies that may work for them. This is accomplished over time, using a journal. As incidents occur, the student identifies the incident or experience that ignites anger and how he or she feels about the experience; later a variety of actions are tried out with the school psychologist until it is clear what may work for that particular child. The tool is generated and placed in a daily notebook for personal reference in school and on the refrigerator at home. When the child feels stressed, the expectation is that one of the strategies will be used; rewards for using the scale may be necessary. Figure 10.8 shows a scale for older elementary and middle school students.

Response Card

5 Get help/get away right away!

4 See counselor today.

3 How stressed should I be (?)

2 Use a strategy.

1 I can handle this. Thumbs up!

Students can be given a 'Response Card' to use once they have mastered the number scale. The Response Card reminds them what they need to do when the stress is more than they can manage, and cues them when they cannot make the strategy work without help.

If stress remains at an intolerable level, the student needs to tell the nearest adult that he or she must find the school psychologist.

If the stress can be somewhat tolerated but is not coming under control, the student needs to obtain an appointment that day. If the stress is bearable, the student needs to ask herself questions about how stressed to feel, using the number scale. Once the student manages to reduce the stress to a number 2 level, relaxation strategies should be utilized. If the stress is reduced to a number level of 1, the student needs to congratulate himself/herself.

Fig. 10.6 Response Card

Emotion regulation can occur before the emotion is triggered, during the expression of a particular emotion, and after the emotion has occurred. Strategies needed before the emotion occurs are aimed at weakening or

5		Too mad to think.	Find an adult. Say, "Help me." Get help right away. Move away or sit in a chair. Hug myself.
4		Feeling really angry.	Walk away. Say, "Stop, I am very angry." Say, "I need to change this." Say, "I need a break."
3		Feeling upset. (agitated, annoyed)	Say, "See you later." Think about something good. Say, "Let's do something else." Take a deep breath. Ask, "How can I make this better?"
2		Just starting to get upset.	Think of something funny. Look for something else to do. Say what is the problem. Ask the person to stop.
1		It's okay.	I can do this. I know how to feel good. I have a plan. Things are getting better.

Fig. 10.7 Anger Reduction Tool Sample for Elementary Level Students

	Feelings	Experiences that trigger my anger	Choices for action!
5	I feel like I am going to explode.	Somebody hurts my family I get kicked out of school and it wasn't my fault. My brother is loved more than me.	Find the nearest adult to help. Walk to the side of the playground. Ask to see the school psychologist. Ask to see the school nurse.
4	I am working as hard as I can not to do something that will get me in trouble.	My brother hits me after I tell him to stop. The teacher blames me over and over all day The kids make fun of me at recess. The kids try to get me out over and over.	Go ride my bike alone. Ask, "What number is this really?" Go for a walk near the building. Say why I am so angry. Start thinking and problem solving.
3	I am getting very irritated	My brother is bragging about how great he is. Teachers say "stop" before I am done. The girls get the ball field and there's nothing to do. It's a rotten day	Leave and listen to music. Think about something else. Walk away from the situation. Take a deep breath and exhale slowly.
2	I am feeling a little sad and a little mad at the same time.	My sister gets the last cookie. I didn't get to try the new activity. My friend is playing with someone else. The teacher wants to talk with me during recess.	Ask, "Is this really a big deal?" Say to myself, "Next time." Find someone else to play with. Say," Could we talk another time?"
1	I know I can handle this.	I broke my pencil, but the teacher has extra ones. I think the work is hard, but I can still do it. I missed the basket when I threw the ball this time. It's starting to rain, but there's lots to do indoors.	Say, "No big deal." Start thinking about *the problem*. Say, "I'll do it next time." Think of something that will be fun.

Fig. 10.8 Anger reduction tool sample for older children

strengthening it, replacing it with alternative emotions, or avoiding the emotion-evoking situation. During the emotion, the strategy needed is to modulate it (Holodynski and Friedlmeier 2006). If a child can dampen the intensity of the emotion that is experienced, control is easier. The variety of strategies that can be taught is broad. By school age, children can be taught to use verbal social strategies, as well as strategies that directly address the cause of another's emotional state (McCoy and Masters 1985). In selecting strategies, it is important to determine a student's strengths and which strategies will work best for him or her (Hromek 2004). Beyond this, since even a single well-learned strategy will not work all the time, children should master several (three or more) strategies to deal with specific problematic emotions.

Mantras

Relaxation strategies can be taught using scripts, a personalized tape, stories, and/or direct instruction. Diaphragmatic breathing and progressive muscle relaxation are key therapeutic tools. A mantra or "cue word" is taught and then used repeatedly, providing practice so the children can relax quickly when they start to feel anxious, to feel angry, or have negative thoughts. Suggestions for using mantras in school are shown in Fig. 10.9.

Use of Mantras

Children need quick strategies that they can use when stressed. Clearly, quick strategies will not work unless they are practiced. Any strategy that a child is taught must be rehearsed frequently if it is going to be accessible when it is needed.

Mantras have been used by adults historically for various purposes. A panel of the National Institutes of Health has concluded that meditation and similar practices such as mantras have important benefits (Powell, Shahabi, and Thoresen 2003; Seeman, Dubin, and Seeman 2003). Frequent repetition of a word or phrase while blocking out intrusive thoughts has been shown to have physiological benefits and to decrease anxiety and anger (Bormann, Oman, Kemppainen, Becker, Gershwin, and Kelly 2006).

Repeating the word "stop" is a technique that has been used by clinicians to disrupt compulsive thoughts and redirect attention (Fazio 2001). Use of mantras to reduce blood pressure and for managing a variety of everyday challenging situations as well longer-term stress has been demonstrated for both typical adults and for adults with both medical and psychological stresses (Bormann et al. 2006).

The advantages of mantras, as a strategy for stress management is that they are easy to remember, easy to use, can be used only once or used repeatedly over time. They do not require a quiet place or special materials, and are invisible. When taught in schools, it may be helpful to call the technique *your calm word, your power word*, or *your special tool*. Students should be reminded to use the technique repeatedly, giving them concrete markers around when to use the strategy, such as at the beginning of each new school period or task. They should also be provided with a card on which to make checks or print a '+' each time the strategy is used, adding a reinforcement for using the strategy as appropriate (such as ten times a day).

Fig. 10.9 Use of mantras

Thought Bubbles: a situation with which a student is having difficulty is depicted in a series of steps using cartoon or stick figures. Together with the student, fill in the thought bubbles. The goal may be to help the student identify his or her emotions or the goal may be to generate an emotion control strategy. Leave only the thought bubble of the main character empty.

Fig. 10.10 Thought Bubbles

Self-Talk

Self-talk is important. By age seven or eight, children can learn to identify their own self-talk. One technique to help younger schoolchildren with self-talk consists of "thought bubbles," cartoons in which figures are drawn with empty bubbles over their heads that the children fill in with their own thoughts (Kendall 2000). Thought bubbles can be used throughout elementary school to help identify feelings, as well as for problem solving. After a child has filled in his or her thoughts, the school psychologist helps make the connections among thoughts, feelings, and behaviors. Self-talk is a particularly important tool for adolescents. A thought bubble worksheet can be examined in Fig. 10.10.

Acceptance

Acceptance refers to taking a new attitude toward situations that a person finds stressful. Using acceptance as a strategy involves trying to stop efforts to avoid or control the anxiety so that it peaks and then decreases. Anxiety can become the problem rather than whatever had triggered the anxiety in the first place, and acceptance disrupts the anxiety cycle. Fighting anxiety makes it worse (Freeman et al. 2004), and this is difficult for young children to understand. Acceptance can be described in analogy with an ocean wave. The child has to let the anxiety wave wash over him or her, and then it will flatten out. The anxiety will decrease naturally.

Another image that may be helpful is to ask the child to imagine that anxiety is a great monster (or fearful animal or some other image that is not too frightening). The child allows it to come closer in his or her mind until it is quite close, and then shrinks the image (letting the air out of a balloon might make this concept more concrete). Ask the child if the shrunken image is still frightening to give him or her a feeling of control over the anxiety. The goal of these interventions is to help the child reduce the intensity or the frequency of distress by more successful coping.

Social Problem Solving

Thoughts and emotions have been described as a "regulatory team" (Schutz et al. 2006, p. 351). Self-questioning can be introduced along with a problem-solving sequence (Gosch et al. 2006). Problem solving is typically taught in a series of steps, with the number of steps varying from one curriculum to another. For example, the *Social Decision Making and Social Problem Solving* (SDM-SPS) program (Elias 1983; Elias, Gara, Ubriaco, Rothbaum, Clabby, and Schuyler 1986) uses an eight-step social decision-making model for students in elementary and middle school and has been rated as a promising program by the Promising Practices Network operated by the RAND Corporation, a nonprofit research organization. This curriculum focuses on building skills necessary to promote social competence, decision making, group participation, and social awareness. It was originally piloted with students when it was implemented for the two years prior to transition from elementary to middle school.

Although it has been demonstrated that children can learn a lengthy problem-solving series of steps, it is very difficult for them to use a multistep sequence of thinking when they are highly stressed, which is when it is most needed. Learning the sequence and practicing it is helpful, but a short set of cues has to be taught for real-life situations. It may be that a fewer number of steps would be more practical in situations such as facing a bully when no one is around to help. The steps of problem solving are listed in Fig. 10.11.

Exposure and Fear Hierarchies

Systematic desensitization is a behavioral intervention with the goal of decreasing anxiety through counterconditioning. For dealing with situational as well as generalized anxieties, additional components should be added to interventions, such as the use of exposure tasks and a fear hierarchy. The latter is a concrete tool individualized for a particular child that lists fearful situations (or objects) from least to most fearful. Fear hierarchies can be used to gradually expose children to feared situations beginning with the least stressful and building up to more challenging situations over time. A

Problem-Solving Steps

Social problem solving can be taught by working problem solving steps into a universal curriculum, through cooperative learning, or as a key component of group counseling sessions. Various programs teach either the behaviors needed, or the cognitive strategies or both (Bear 1998). Most programs combine behavioral and cognitive strategies so students are taught a set of skills, a cognitive strategy to evaluate the situation at hand and how to use the specific skills (Elias and Tobias 1990; Goldstein 1999; Shure 2001a, b).

One of the several curricula on the market is interesting because of the attention that this model gives to emotion regulation. *Making Choices* is a social-information processing skills training curriculum that attempts to integrate emotional-regulation into the model (Fraser 2006; Fraser, Nash, Galinsky, and Darwin 2000). This six-step problem-solving model addresses how a student is feeling, how others feel, and calming down at each step of the problem-solving process. Understanding and regulating emotions becomes an additional step in the process.

Studies using this curriculum at the third grade level showed students improved their ability to regulate emotions and to process social problems. In addition, there was a reduction in students' inappropriate behaviors. Program effects were enhanced when parents were involved and when the curriculum was integrated into the general education program (Fraser 2006; Smokowski, Fraser, Day, Galinsky, and Bacallao 2004).

The various models use variations of six steps of problem solving.

- Understanding the problem
- Generating and evaluating solutions
- Picking a solution likely to work
- Trying out one solution
- Determining whether or not the solution worked
- Planning ahead

They vary in regard to the number of steps and the degree to which the steps are broken down. Although it is clear that students can memorize a complex series of steps, in real life and under stress, fewer steps may be easier to generate and use. The process will be more effective when the emotion that accompanies interpersonal situations is recognized and addressed as part of the process.

Fig. 10.11 Problem-solving steps

sample fear hierarchy for a first-grade student is shown in Fig. 10.12 along with suggestions for the use of fear hierarchies.

Breaking the fears down into small steps makes the exposure easier. Exposure is not introduced until a child has had some success with contingency management (or reinforcement) systems, has been taught strategies to manage anxiety through modeling, and has learned some cognitive control strategies. A self-control strategy that has had some demonstrated success uses an acronym such as STOP (Ollendick, King, and Yule 1994, pp. 99–100):

- "S" stands for scared.
- "T" stands for thoughts.

Fear Hierarchies

The idea of a fear hierarchy is to come up with a list of social situations that the student fears or avoids. The list consists of different items or situations of increasing intensity of fear. The child and the school psychologist can use the list to plan interventions and develop coping strategies appropriate for each level of fear. The fear hierarchy also serves as concrete evidence of progress as the child learns to deal with each item in turn. Role-play and imaginative practice can be used to learn to deal with items on the hierarchy as well as practice coping with the actual feared situation.

The fear hierarchy should have items at both ends of the continuum. At the low end will be the things that the child can handle, moving to items that make him or her quite nervous, to items that are fearful and are avoided but that the child thinks he or she might be able to cope with, to more intense fears (Martell, Safren, and Prince 2004, p. 96).

For students in fourth grade or above, each item on the fear hierarchy can also be rated in regard to degree of distress that it causes and whether or not the child avoids the situation. When the fear hierarchy has been constructed, a sequence of steps is devised to begin to deal with the situations. The fear situations are imagined; they are paired with relaxation and coping statements such as, "Everyone feels anxious sometimes; it will go away," or "I need to use my strategies." (Leahy and Holland 2000).

First-Grade Student's Fear Hierarchy

10   Going to the cafeteria alone
9   Answering questions in front of the group
8   Answering open-ended questions
7   Going onto the playground without mother or teacher
6   Starting to write
5   Reading out loud
4   Choosing what I will have for lunch
3   Coming into the room in the morning
2   Talking to boys
1   Filling in worksheets

Fig. 10.12 Fear hierarchies: sample for a first-grade student

- "O" stands for other (things I can do or think about).
- "P" stands for praise (a self-reward such as thumbs up or a statement such as "Good for me").

Exposure tasks often are supported with rewards to increase "brave behavior." Typically self-praise is taught as children are encouraged to share successes and to give themselves a "high-five" or a "pat-on-the-back."

When using the fear hierarchy for exposure, the school psychologist first builds the hierarchy with the child. Next, the child is taught relaxation techniques. Finally, the child is helped to work through the hierarchy, relaxing as the stimulus is imagined so that he or she can respond calmly to each step in the hierarchy (Weiten and Lloyd 2006. pp. 533–534). The process has been demonstrated to be very effective.

There are some variations of the approach in the literature. For example, Ventis et al. (2001) used humor to reduce a specific fear of spiders. Children were given a rubber spider and asked to think of as many uses for the rubber spider as possible. They were asked to finish incomplete statements about spiders in a funny way. A humorous spider hierarchy was created. The children provided captions for spider cartoons and nicknamed the spider. They thus learned to connect humor with spiders, which reduced their fears.

Often, a thermometer is used when working with children to demonstrate the hierarchy (Burg 2004; Chapman and Kirby-Turner 2002). Kendall used a "feelings barometer" in his Coping Cat intervention for anxiety (Flannery-Schroeder and Kendall 1996). Chapman and Kirby-Turner (2002) describe several visual/verbal analogue scales. One is simply a horizontal line with numbers and subdivisions. A child can point to the degree of stress that he or she is feeling along the line from 0 to 10. A second scale was a series of "happy face" drawings from sad to happy, and children pointed to a drawing to show how they felt. A fear thermometer was used successfully, and, for older children, a number list can be used vertically on a page from (0) calm to (10) highly anxious.

The youngest students can demonstrate their level of fear simply by holding their open hands apart at differing widths to indicate how stressed they are or how stressful a given situation may be for them. This may be appropriate for very shy, cognitively limited, or emotionally delayed children as well. However, only one method should be used for any given child. Several different scales are pictured in Fig. 10.13.

Emotive imagery is a systematic desensitization tool to reduce anxiety (King, Cranstoun, and Josephs 1989). An adaptation for younger students involves asking them to share what frightens them to build the hierarchy. The images are put into an engrossing *story* beginning with the least frightening to the most frightening story over time. The child identifies a hero who helps conquer the fear and is added to each story. This approach can be used with children as young as six, and has been used with four-year-olds when the adult creates the hero (King, Heyne, Gullone, and Molloy 2001).

Other clinicians have incorporated concrete objects into their treatments for young children. Camp and Bash (1985) used a cartoon bear in their curriculum to teach social problem solving. The bear was used to demonstrate the steps of problem solving by asking a set of questions:

- What is the problem?
- What can I do about it?
- Is it working?
- How did I do?

Images can be used to help students learn to use problem-solving strategies. Chowdhuy, Caulfield, and Heyman (2003) asked students to draw a real or

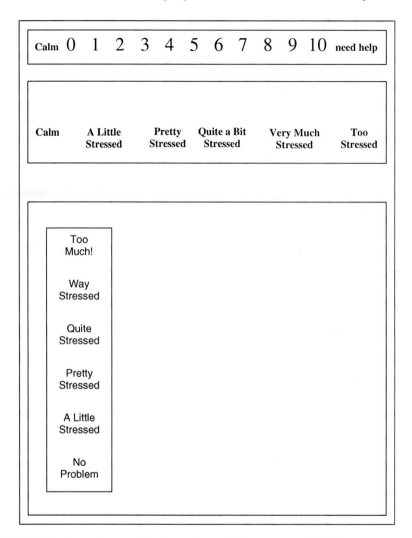

Fig. 10.13 Various analogue scales for students of different ages and abilities

made-up animal and to create a story about it. Students with obsessive-compulsive disorder wrote about how they thought the animal would be affected by worries and what kind of help the animal should look for, and then wrote an end to the story. The students benefited by reflecting on their own experiences and sharing their stories. Heffner, Greco, and Eifert (2003) explored whether or not children preferred metaphorical to literal relaxation instructions and found that they clearly preferred metaphorical instructions to relax such as "pretend you are a turtle going into its shell."

Fig. 10.14 Hero Card

Take a deep breath. Let it out slowly.
Say to myself, "I don't have to get upset."
Think, "I have a choice."
Look away from the action for a few seconds.
Think, "I am okay. I can be in control."

Hero card drawn by Hunter Ward, age 7 years.

Power Card Strategy

A "power card" strategy was designed by Gagnon (2001) to make use of the high level of interests that ASD children have, along with difficulties they have in problem solving. The power hero is used to teach a problem-solving strategy. The child carries around a card with a picture of the hero and instructions for handling a stressful situation as a cue to help manage various situations. There is little research to support this intervention, but it has been very successful in practice with some children with ASD and also with younger typically developing students. Figure 10.14 shows a sample hero card.

Meditation

Meditation and the use of mantras to reduce stress have been used with some success. Travis, Grosswald, and Stixrud (2006) taught children with ADHD to meditate for 10 minutes twice a day and found that symptoms were reduced.

They demonstrated that young people that we might think would have considerable difficulty learning to relax could learn meditation techniques.

"As If" Technique

Kelley (1955) invented the "As If" technique, also called the fixed-role strategy. The child is asked to behave as if he or she were a person who does not care what others think so that it is easier to face social situations that cause intense anxiety. This technique was used with adults who imagined themselves brave movie heroes, and it may work well for some juveniles who have movie heroes (Spiderman, etc.). The technique can be combined with the use of a hero card. Children can be asked to behave as if they were Spiderman (or some other superhero or person they admire) in anxiety-producing situations.

Accommodations for English Language Learners

It may also be necessary to make accommodations for students who are handicapped or who are learning English. Moser (2006) recommends using metaphors, which reduce the complexity of emotion concepts and the intensity of the emotions that are being discussed. She suggests that children create their own personal metaphors, such as an anger metaphor in which anger becomes a dangerous animal or other image. They can then easily use the metaphor to understand that controlling anger is similar to constraining a dangerous animal. After drawing an angry beast or other angry image, they are encouraged to think of strategies for controlling it. They then practice the strategies and with guidance connect the angry feelings to themselves and again practice the strategies to control their own feelings of anger. Children's drawings of angry beasts can be quite frightening as in Fig. 10.15.

Tools for Teaching Strategies

Social Stories is a technique that was created by Gray (1993). The social story is written according to a specified pattern. A situation is described in a matter-of-fact manner to match the student's perception. A story is written to give the student clear cues about the context and provides problem-solving strategies that will be acceptable in the student's various environments (Gray 1996a,b). There is initial evidence that social stories can be used to decrease unwanted behaviors and to increase social behavior in ASD children (Mogensen 2005). Mirenda (2001) located four studies involving a small number of students to determine the efficacy of social stories. These findings were positive and since

Fig. 10.15 Controlling the
Angry Beast

Beast drawn by Hunter Ward, age 7 years.

Beast drawn by Summer Ward, age 5 years

then a number of studies have been conducted, many of which can be located on the website of The Gray Center for Social Learning and Understanding (http://www.the graycenter.org/store/index.cfm?fuseaction = page.display&page_id = 47). Larger studies are needed including studies involving preschoolers. In practice, social stories have been helpful for children with behavior disorders as well as for anxious elementary school children. Figure 10.16 contains a sample social story.

Comic Strip Conversations (Gray 1995b), a strategy for children who need a visual representation of a social story, use cartoon figures and thought bubbles. Evidence for social stories, comic strip conversations, and thought bubbles is limited (Hutchins and Prelock 2006). However, studies with small numbers of students have demonstrated that some children with autism can understand thought bubbles as representations of what one might be thinking (Parsons and Mitchell 1999). There are more recent data, also with small numbers of students, to indicate that children with autism can use cartoon thought bubbles as "pictures-in-their-heads" to learn about the thoughts of others and to attend to their own thoughts (Wellman, Baron-Cohen, Caswell, Gomez, Swettenham,

---

Getting Upset during Games at Recess

I love to play with my friends and classmates during recess.

Sometimes it makes me very happy. Sometimes I get upset.

I feel really mad when another kid wins the game.

I get mad when another kid gets ahead of me or gets a hit and I don't.

When I get mad, I may yell and everyone else gets upset too.

Then kids don't want me on their team. They don't want me to play.

When I feel angry, I can take a deep breath and walk away for a minute.

I can think of something else, like the last time I won.

When I feel upset I can say, "Let's play another game (or a different game)."

When I get mad, I can say, "I need a break."

If I only get a little upset and I don't spoil the fun, the other kids will want to play with me. They will want me on their side.

If I do this, the teacher won't get upset either.

I think I can get only a little upset.

Hint: When the other person wins, you can grit your teeth, smile, and say "Next time" with a 'warning voice'. This will get the mad feeling out in a socially acceptable way.

Fig. 10.16 A sample social story

and Toye, et al. 2002). In fact, children as young as three can understand that the bubbles represent thoughts and can even grasp the concept that the ideas may not be true (Kerr and Durkin 2004). Pierson and Glaeser (2005) have extended the use of comic strip conversations to students with learning difficulties and behavior problems. Although it is not yet clear why comic strip conversations work, they appear to be quite useful in practice (Attwood 2000).

The *Social Autopsy*, a strategy described by Lavoie (2005), was designed for young children and adolescents with learning disabilities. Using this strategy, the adult works with the student to analyze a social situation that has already occurred, to detect the errors that were made, and to plan ahead so that the errors do not reoccur. Together the adult and student deduce alternative strategies. Lavoie strongly recommends that the strategy be taught to all adults with whom the student comes into contact, so that he or she has experience dealing with a number of autopsies in a day in a variety of settings. There is little research on this strategy, but it is clear that it is important to include discussion of regulating emotions and the appropriate expression of emotions when working with a student using a social autopsy (Miles and Simpson 2001).

All of these techniques have been successful with particular young people in practice. Although they were designed to work with disabled students, they work well with typically developing younger students, as well as with older students whose emotions interfere with their thinking.

Quick Tools

Distracting oneself can be useful for individuals experiencing temporary uncomfortable moods or immediate emotional reactions. Doing something one likes or something that requires concentration, such as watching television, reading a book, exercising, listening to upbeat music, or writing, are the best ways to distract oneself. Such distraction might work because these kinds of activities are rewarding. Reinforcing and pleasurable activities diminish negative affect (Abela, Brozina, and Haigh 2002). A complicating factor is that elementary-age students may distract themselves, but they do not use the 'break' that distraction provides to problem-solve so that the underlying emotion returns, as does the depressed mood.

Distraction for children who are clinically depressed may prevent symptoms from increasing, but again it does not eliminate symptoms entirely. Moreover, children are not as likely to use fully engaging distractions or distractions that are reinforcing and highly pleasurable, so they might believe that the strategy does not work for them.

Choices for engrossing distractions may not be available in the school environment, owing to the fact that students do not control their own time or activities. However, for temporarily stressed typically developing children, distraction can help shift thinking and mood and can interfere with ruminating around some event or situation. Distraction remains a temporary fix. There is not enough evidence to support distraction as an effective technique to ameliorate depression in a clinically depressed child or adolescent, except for the fact that it may be somewhat helpful in minimizing symptoms (Jorm, Allen, O'Donnell, Parslow, Purcell, and Morgan 2006).

Quick relaxation strategies may be helpful for many students, but only if they are practiced as well as taught. Students tend to prefer some strategies over others, which is the reason for trying out a number of different ones. Teachers can select and use several daily. For individual students, school psychologists can help select strategies and engage parents in teaching and practicing the strategies. Ten quick relaxation strategies are described in .

Students need more than one quick strategy to use in class. Either teachers or parents can work with them to try out a range of quick strategies, after which they need to choose several and practice those regularly. If the first strategy tried does not work in a given stressful situation, several others that have been practiced and mastered should be tried. A worksheet such as that found

Quick Relaxation Exercises

Quick relaxation exercises do not work like magic. They only work if they are practiced on a regular basis. You can approach teaching these quick relaxation strategies by setting up a series of sessions. First, practice all of them until the student can use them well. Next, ask the student to rate them. Finally, ask the student to choose three strategies that will become his or her 'special' strategies. Use the rating sheet to make these decisions.

It is necessary to continue to practice using the strategies frequently. Some students will need a visual cue from an adult to use one of the strategies at first. Others will need a contingency plan to use them.

Inhale very slowly.
As you inhale slowly, lift your arms up over your head.
Then, gently drop your arms back to your side.
Think ONLY about relaxing.

Count to ten or count backward *slowly* from ten.
If this is not long enough, count by two's or threes or fours (forward or backward).
The task needs to be a little bit challenging but not too hard.

Practice blowing up a very large balloon.
Breath in deeply.
Blow out very slowly until the balloon is huge.
Start with an actual balloon and then pretend to do the same thing without the balloon.

Block your left nostril with one hand.
Inhale deeply through your right nostril counting to 5.
Block both nostrils and hold your breath for 5 seconds.
Block your right nostril and inhale deeply through the left nostril counting to five.

Pick a spot in the room to focus on.
Stare at this spot.
Think about getting heavier and heavier in the chair.
Count five breaths backward.
Think about feeling very, very heavy.

Place your left hand (palm down) in front of you.
Relax the hand.
Press your right thumb on the back of your relaxed left hand between the thumb and the pointer or index finger.
Massage this spot in a circular motion as you slowly count to 15.
Switch hands and do it the other way.

Say 're' while you breath in.
Say 'lax' while you breath out.
Say 're' while you breath in.
Say 'lax' while you breath out.
Say 're' while you breath in.
Say 'lax' while you breath out.

Count the fingers on your right hand slowly.
Do it again.
Do it again.
(Repeat using left hand if you need more time.)

Fig. 10.17 Quick relaxation exercises

| Scrunch up your shoulders.
Drop your shoulders.
Scrunch up your shoulders.
Drop your shoulders.
Scrunch up your shoulders.
Drop your shoulders. | Shut your eyes.
Drop your head forward.
Feel your shoulders lifting as you breath in slowly.
Think, "I'm feeling as light as a cloud.
Think, "I'm floating like a cloud.
Think, "I' can see my favorite place. I feel much better." |

Fig. 10.17 (continued)

| **Choosing the Top Three Quick Strategies** |
| *After practicing all of the strategies for a few sessions, choose the top three strategies to use on a regular basis.* |

Breath in while lifting arms	_____
Counting by threes	_____
Pretending to blow up a balloon	_____
Alternate nostril breathing	_____
Staring at a spot	_____
Massaging your hand	_____
Breath in and out saying re-lax	_____
Counting your fingers	_____
Scrunching your shoulders	_____
Become a cloud	_____

Fig. 10.18 Choosing the top three quick strategies

in Fig. 10.18 is helpful for making a final selection of the top three quick strategies.

Quick relaxation strategies are best for typically developing students and for students with mild to moderate anxiety. Some are more obvious to peers than others, which can be problematic for some students.

Wegner, Schneider, Carter, and White (1987) conducted a series of studies in which they instructed students not to think of *white bears*. The harder the students tried not to think of white bears, the more they thought about them. However, when some of them were given a distracter to think about, they had more success in controlling their thinking.

These studies suggest that something as simple as a picture card might be useful for some students. Giving children a picture card and relaying the story of Wegner et al.'s white bears at the same time is particularly effective in reducing anxious rumination. The children can use pictures of white bears, of their own pets, or of superheroes. These cards can be placed on the children's desks, as it is important to keep them visible. The classic white bears' studies are described in Fig. 10.19 with suggestions for using white bears as a tool for distraction or a cue to refocus attention.

White Bears

Distracting oneself is not difficult, it is a way to keep ourselves preoccupied so that we don't think of our worries. Procrastination is a form of distraction. Self-distraction is more challenging for children, and young children need parents to help distract them when they are upset. However, children need to learn to do this for themselves. Just as a computer does not destroy information by deleting it or even trashing it, our brains do not eliminate thoughts completely when we try to suppress them. Wegner, Schneider, Carter and White (1987) in their studies, which are now considered a modern classic, asked college students to spend five minutes thinking about white bears. They were then told to suppress the thoughts of white bears. They found they were preoccupied with thoughts of the white bears, which they were trying to suppress.

The act of suppressing thoughts doesn't work very well. In fact, if the thought of the white bear resurfaces after efforts to suppress it, there is a rebound effect such that the thoughts of white bears become even more persistent to the point of preoccupation. The surroundings of the place where we try to suppress a thought can become cues to think of the thing we are trying to suppress. Suppression needs to take place in a different environment than the one in which the thoughts were occurring. The original environment needs to be supportive of new thoughts. The mood state during suppression needs to be positive. Students need cues to direct them to the new or replacement thoughts (Wegner 1987, pp. 59-60, and 96-98).

Better and more effective methods are needed to help students get rid of unwanted thoughts. Distraction involves trying to think of something else. This effort requires a mental transformation or metacognitive strategy using stronger distracters, accepting the unwanted thoughts, or concentrating on goals (Wegner 1987; Wenzlaff and Wegner 2000).

Theory suggests that working with a student away from the classroom, talking about and accepting the unwanted thoughts for a specified period, making an effort to induce a positive mood and convincing the student that he or she can control thoughts would be helpful. Deciding with the student what positive image might serve as a distracter and giving the student a cue card to place in his pocket or on his desk would remind the student to think of the distracter(s). If a word were also associated with the cue, the teacher could remind the child to concentrate by stating the cue word.

Fig. 10.19 White Bears

Worry Stones

Below is a script for introducing worry stones and their use.

Script:

"Worrying is hard work. When we worry, we don't have any fun at all. When we worry, we get very tired."

"Sometimes we need a 'friend' to worry for us. A worry stone can be a good friend. Look at these beautiful worry stones."

"It is very important to choose a worry stone that fits your fingers perfectly. Some people like worry stones that are very smooth. Other people like worry stones that are rough. Some people like worry stones that are pretty. Many people like worry stones that are thick and strong, or some people like thin and slippery worry stones."

"Let's find a worry stone that is perfect for you. (Encourage the student to try out several and select one.) The best safe place for your worry stone is in your pocket."

First, ask the child to rub the worry stone in his or her pocket. Second, ask the child to close his or her eyes for a minute, and think about how it feels. Third, ask the child to put all of his or her worries into the rubbing and let the stone worry for him or her. Fourth, remind the child to take deep breaths in and let them out slowly so that the worries can go into the stone. Finally, ask the child to smile.

Fig. 10.20 Worry stones script

There are a number of other temporary and quick tools that can be considered for children who have temporary 'worries' in the normal range. These are not evidence-based interventions. They are more like 'lucky charms' or fall into the category of magic and myth, but when a child is having a tough day, they can be useful. Tools include *Guatemalan worry dolls and worry stones*. A worry doll is given to a child, who tells the doll a 'trouble,' and then places it in a safe place such as a locker, desk, or pocket. There are several children's books written about worry dolls explaining their use as part of the story. A worry stone works the same way. The child can carry it around all day long. The worry stone is carefully chosen from a box of smooth stones and shells. It must be kept in one's pocket, but the child can rub it in his or her pocket, whenever it is needed during the day to reduce stress. Figure 10.20 contains a script for introducing worry stones and their use.

Chapter 11
The Intervention Process

Strengthening Interventions in the School Setting

Planning Interventions to Improve Students' Emotion Regulation

School psychologists can address the emotional development of students in several major ways. Universal programs designed for all students is an especially efficient way of delivering services because not only will the needs of students who are typically developing be addressed, but at least some of the needs of children who may be different, delayed, or emotionally disabled will be met as well. A number of programs and curricula have already been described.

When considering the needs of students who may be at risk or delayed in emotion regulation or who simply exhibit extremely poor emotion regulation, it is important to think in terms of servicing not only the students but their parents as well for the intervention to be maximally effective. School psychologists can become involved in parent training that can meet students' needs by either influencing parenting practices or engaging parents to provide education and training for their children. Most children will have their needs met through one or more of these interventions.

Unfortunately, there remain substantial numbers schoolchildren who require more intensive services to answer their emotional needs. According to the U.S. Department of Health and Human Services (SAMHSA 2003), the number of students who may have a mental health disorder may be as high as one in five. These young people have identifiable issues and need treatment. Moreover, estimates of children younger than school age in need of services run to more than 10 percent, but this may actually be an underestimate, especially in urban areas (Gimpel and Holland 2003). Some of these children can be serviced in small groups, but some may require individual treatment. In any case, for all children: "The acquisition of strategies for modifying the quality, intensity, duration, and frequency of emotions is a major developmental task" (Holodynski and Friedlmeier 2006, p. 87).

There are less data for evidence-based universal curricula than for more intensive interventions in general, but some specific interventions for reducing

G. L. Macklem, *Practitioner's Guide to Emotion Regulation in School-Aged Children.* © Springer 2008

anxiety and for managing anger, such as cognitive behavioral therapy, have support. Although mental health workers in schools know that there are ideal ways to establish small groups for intervention, it is seldom that all of the students who fit the ideal group are available at the same time. More often, and in some smaller schools *most often*, a group will have some children with mild issues and others with significant ones. This is not necessarily inappropriate because students with more significant issues need more positive peer models to set a behavioral and attitudinal standard that they have a chance of reaching. In other words, models should not be too far removed in skill from those who need to learn from them.

Identifying Students Who Have to Improve Their Emotion Regulation

In the school setting, although students who have more extreme difficulty with emotional regulation stand out, tools are needed for identifying the child who has more moderate needs, as well as for choosing the very specific subskills that a child may have to master, as in Fig. 11.1. Monitoring tools are needed, as are identification and outcome measures during and after interventions are implemented.

Equally important, school psychologists have to understand how to adapt strategies for use with students of different ages. Certainly bright adolescents may be able to utilize strategies originally designed for adults, but younger children, children with handicaps, and children who are very stressed need more concrete strategies. Moreover, at least some aspects of curricula and tools that have been designed for specific populations—such as those for students with borderline disorder or autism spectrum disorder—may be useful for a broader spectrum of young people. School psychologists are aware of the fact that generalization of training (use of strategies outside of the training session) has been a major problem in the school setting, given the manner in which interventions have been traditionally provided. Generalization and transfer (carrying over skills taught to other environments) must be directly addressed. Finally, the major steps in providing treatment for problems in emotion regulation have to be specified.

Tools for School Psychologists

Interviews and rating scales can be useful in establishing baseline behaviors and in pre- and postintervention assessment. One must keep in mind, however, that some children find the language of questionnaires and interviews difficult to understand and still others hide their symptoms because they want to be thought

---

Identifying Specific Social-Emotional Skills Weaknesses

In trying to select strategies to teach to children to regulate their emotions, school psychologists need to obtain assessment data from a variety of sources, in multiple settings, using a variety of methods just as they typically do when trying to answer other child-centered questions. Behavior-rating scales used for early screening can identify needs and behavioral observations later in the process of identification will identify more specific needs. School psychologists then design interventions to match specific problems carefully attending to context (Merrell 1999).

Direct observation is particularly important. Elliott and Gresham (1987) proposed that "analyzing children's behavior in natural settings...is the most ecologically valid method of assessing children's social skills" (Elliott and Gresham 1987, p. 96). Observation helps identify those children who have social deficits and those who do not. For example, maltreated children have specific weaknesses in initiation and self-control; whereas, socially anxious children typically only think they have deficits in social skills and observers will not observe weaknesses (Cartwright-Hatton, Tschernitz and Gomersall 2005; Darwish, Esquivel, Houtz and Alfonso 2001).

Children with weaknesses in skills that are critical for school success need to be identified. Skills including sharing, accepting criticism, giving and receiving compliments, understanding others' feelings, listening, following directions, controlling anger, and taking conversational turns should be targeted for observation (Elksnin and Elksnin 2000). Add to this skill list complying with group rules, conversation skills, asking others to join activities, managing conflict and anger, giving others personal space and ability to correct social errors are key skills to note. Observations during unstructured school period (recess, cafeteria, corridors) and observations during small group activities (cooperative learning, work groups, teamwork) are rich contexts for determining social skills weaknesses.

Emotional regulation weaknesses must be identified. Children who are isolated, rejected, withdrawn, emotionally volatile, frequently angry, quick to anger, cry easily, frequently complain, see things negatively or who are exhibiting sad moods must be identified and interventions must be provided for them.

Fig. 11.1 Identifying specific social-emotional skills weaknesses

competent (Gosch et al. 2006). There are several commonly used rating scales that may be useful as long as they are not used alone to diagnose disorders.

The *Behavior Assessment System for Children, Second Edition (BASC-2)* is a set of rating scales along with an observation system for use with students, with parents and teachers is respondents (Reynolds and Kamphaus 2004). School psychologists use these tools frequently, as they have been designed for the entire age range for which they may be responsible (ages two through twenty-one). Two scales that are part of the BASC-2 are of particular interest: the externalization scale and the internalization scale. The former may be helpful in identifying students who are having difficulties with emotion regulation. Several clinical scales indicating the presence of internalizing symptoms, including the anxiety and depression scales, are also helpful. There are content scales available on the BASC-2 computer software associated with both the parent and the teacher scales that are also interesting: anger control, emotional self-control, executive functioning, and negative emotionality. Finally, a measure of anger control and test anxiety can be obtained using the student self-report rating scale.

The ways in which a disorder shows itself in children can vary widely, which makes such identification challenging. Anxiety disorder is a good example: students with anxiety disorders may underreport symptoms when asked because of embarrassment or worries about sharing personal information or because they have become experts at avoiding the specific situations and triggers that provoke their anxiety.

The Behavior Rating Inventory of Executive Function (BRIEF) is a tool designed to measure problems with executive functioning (Gioia et al. 2000). This scale, which covers the age range of two to eighteen years, has measures of ability to inhibit, shift, and monitor behaviors, as well as a measure of emotional control. A factor study of this scale provided some evidence for an emotion regulation factor consisting of the emotional control and shift scales (Gioia, Isquith, Retzlaff, and Espy 2002). This makes the BRIEF an interesting tool to assist in identifying students with weak emotion regulation.

A general symptom questionnaire for use with parents, called the *Pediatric Symptom Checklist* (Applegate, Kelley, Applegate, Jayasinghe, and Venters 2003), addresses specific behavioral and emotional issues. There is a parent report and an adolescent self-report version. The scale is useful in cases of depression and anxiety when the student herself may be a better reporter than parents or teachers. Young people from low-income homes, boys, and children who live in single-parent families show elevated symptoms on this scale (Jellinek, Murphy, Little, Pagano, Comer, and Kelleher 1999). The tool is very short and is considered a screening device.

In addition to these established tools, there are others under development and some that have been used in research that may be useful for school psychologists who are looking for additional help and for treatment planning. Some of these can be located online. Figure 11.2 lists a number of interesting tools that may help explore the emotion regulation abilities of students.

Beyond paper and pencil tools, it is important to evaluate a student's social interaction, the antecedents and consequences for his or her behavior as in a functional behavioral assessment, and a child's sense of control over his or her environment in general. It is also important to look at parenting style and parents' responses to the child's issues as well as to take a good family history (Gosch et al. 2006).

Planning Interventions

Interventions chosen for schools have to be evidence based, and there are a variety of programs on the market from which to choose. Matching the intervention to the school is important. When a planning team is given the

---

Tools Used in Research or Under Development

Emotion Regulation Questionnaire (ERQ)

Gross and John (2003) developed the Emotion Regulation Questionnaire (ERQ). It asks participants to rate the extent to which they typically try to think about situations differently in order to change how they feel. The Emotion Regulation Questionnaire assesses expressive suppression and cognitive reappraisal. Whereas suppression is unhealthy, reappraisal has positive consequences socially and emotionally; it decreases the intensity of emotion and the likelihood of acting on one's emotions, and does not impair memory for the triggers or events (Gross 2002; John and Gross 2004).

**The Global Negative Emotionality Scale
(from the Differential Emotions Scale-IV, DES-IV)**

There are several tools that have been used in research studies to consider. The Global Negative Emotionality Scale from the Differential Emotions Scale-IV (DES-IV) is a tool that purports to measure the frequency with which a person experiences negative affect (Blumberg and Izard 1986).

The Children's Emotion Management Scale-Coping Factor (CEMS)

The Children's Emotion Management Scale-Coping Factor (CEMS) can be used to assess the child's ability to manage negative emotions such as sadness and anger (Zeman, Shipman, and Penza-Clyve 2001).

Achievement Emotions Questionnaire and Test Emotions Questionnaire

The Achievement Emotions Questionnaire (Pekrun, Goetz and Perry 2005) and the Test Emotions Questionnaire (TEQ) (Pekrun, Goetz, Perry, Kramer and Hochstadt 2004) may be helpful for students exhibiting test anxiety.

Cognitive Emotion Regulation Questionnaire (CERQ)

Cognitive Emotion Regulation Questionnaire (CERQ) is a multidimensional questionnaire constructed in order to identify the cognitive coping strategies a person might use after having experienced negative events or situations. More particularly, it refers to an individual's *thoughts* after having experienced a negative event. This tool is still in the research stage (Garnefski, Kraaij, and Spinhoven 2001). The tool measures the cognitive emotional regulation strategies of self-blame, other-blame, rumination, catastrophizing, putting into perspective, positive refocusing, positive reappraisal, acceptance, and planning. The tool may be appropriate for adolescents.

The Child Trait Arousability Scale

The Child Trait Arousability Scale was developed by Mehrabian and Falender (1978). It is an interesting experimental tool, which might be used to help specify the situations to which a child may react which would be helpful in planning treatment.

SUDS: Subjective Units of Distress

The SUDS scale is a simple numerical rating to indicate level of distress and anxiety in a social situation. Ratings are from 0–100 and each is described with an example. It might be useful clinically as a worksheet or monitoring tool for adolescents. Find this tool at http://www.cci.health.wa.gov.au/docs/SHY-10-Exposureplan.pdf

Fig. 11.2 Tools used in research or under development

task of selecting a particular universal program to implement, they should consider:

- Attitudes of school staff
- Time available
- Competing interests
- Funding for training
- Availability of staff for monitoring the program and determining outcomes
- Administrative support
- Community and parental support
- School values

All of these variables are important as programs are reviewed for possible implementation. As school psychologists and other school staff examine these programs, they will want to refer to the several organizations that have already evaluated them according to several criteria such as are described in *Safe, Supportive and Successful Schools: Step-by-Step* (Osher, Dwyer, and Jackson 2004). One should keep in mind, however, that there are actually only a few programs that teach cognitive restructuring or other emotional regulatory strategies to deal with stress (Pincus and Friedman 2004).

When designing interventions, timing is important. Curricula that deal with executive functioning and include verbal self-instruction, emotional awareness, and emotion regulation are particularly important during times of peak development and transitions (Riggs, Greenberg, Kusche, and Pentz 2006). Initial school entry and the transitions from elementary to middle school and from middle school to high school are particular periods of stress. Content of programs must match the school and the developmental needs of its students. For example, prevention and intervention programs targeting conduct problems might be even more effective if they focused on the promotion of inhibitory skills along with emotional goals thus meeting the developmental needs of these students (Dennis and Brotman 2003a).

Important additional considerations involve including ongoing practice and handouts for students so that they and their parents can refer to strategies later on and parents can assist in cuing their use and reinforcing effort at home (Nezu, Nezu and Brotman 2001b). Children's beliefs must also be addressed. Older students' belief in regard to how good they are at solving problems has a stronger effect than their actual skills in problem solving (Printz, Shermis, and Webb 1999). It may be important to change some of their beliefs: for example, teaching students who have difficulty controlling anger that learning anger control skills increases one's sense of *power* (Novaco 1996). This is critically important given how difficult it is to give up angry feelings. In fact, young people can be enlisted to help generate strategies to reduce anger themselves. Figure 11.3 offers suggestions for helping students generate anger reduction strategies.

Since emotion regulation is only a component of several programs rather than the key focus, school psychologists might have to design interventions to

---

Helping Students Generate Internal and External Anger Regulation

Adapted from Dearing et al. (2002) in their innovative study involving a prompting technique for the generation of internal and external anger regulation.

After students have reacted to a situation with anger, ask the following series of questions to help them generate strategies for learning display rules for anger and also for generating antecedent strategies so that they do not experience so much anger in the first place.

> "What is something that you did so that the other student playing did not find out that you were angry?"
> "Did you do anything else?" (Change your facial expression, say something or do something?)
> "What is something else you *could have* done?" (or said?)
> "Tell me another thing you *could have* done?"

Continue to question the student until the student has generated three to five strategies. Assist the student in generating alternatives only if necessary. Next ask the student the following:

> "What is something that you did to make yourself *feel* less angry?"
> "Did you do or think anything else to make yourself *feel* less angry?"
> "What is something else you *could have* done?" (or thought)
> "Tell me another thing you *could have* done?" (or thought)

Continue to repeat the last question until the student has generated three to five strategies. Assist the student in generating strategies only if necessary. *Role-play* the new strategies with the group as soon as students are calm. Lead the group in *relaxation exercises* if the group is not yet calm (explaining their purpose as you go through the short exercises).

Fig. 11.3 Helping students generate internal and external anger regulation

meet very specific needs. This is particularly important when interventions are planned for targeted students who are not making progress in the general social-emotional curriculum and for those who need intensive intervention. For these young people, it is important to identify the key skills and strategies that are absent or weak, along with the best match in regard to: (a) the child's disability, (b) the method of intervention, (c) primary or critical contexts, (d) triggers, (e) goals, and (f) specific strategies that may be most useful to the particular individual.

Matching Interventions to Students' Needs and Abilities

Students have to be matched to intervention approaches. Interventions designed to promote effortful regulation may be less efficacious for internalizing than externalizing children so a different approach would be needed for the former. Direct attempts to reduce negative affect often do not work, and indirect methods are needed (Ciarochi 2006). Self-talk and reinterpreting or reframing are very high-level strategies that require at least average cognitive ability, and they will be more successful with older children (Holodynski and Friedlmeier 2006). For some young people, the problem is motivation. For example, school psychologists have to determine whether or not a student does not *have* good anger control, *is not motivated* to use what he knows, or *does not realize* that the strategies for anger control might help (Ciarochi 2006).

Interventionists must keep in mind that the more novel or complex the strategy they are trying to teach, the greater the demand for executive functions (Gioia and Isquith 2004). Some young people have major executive functioning weaknesses and need interventions designed for younger children or modified versions of interventions designed for children of the same age.

The approach that is taken for an intervention can range from using a carefully scripted manual, which allows one to deliver the intervention almost exactly as it was designed (maintaining treatment integrity), to loose interventions, where the activities are more open ended. With the latter the school psychologist is actually working constantly with minicrises that have been planned, but nevertheless cannot be totally controlled or guaranteed ahead of time. Teaching anger control while engaged in a game would be an example of a planned but not totally controlled intervention.

Planned but less tightly controlled interventions such as theater and theater games for children nine to fourteen years of age, team sports, adventure counseling, yoga, as well as tae kwon do and other martial arts all have some support in the literature (Cole et al. 2005; Lakes and Hoyt 2004; Semrud-Clikeman 2003).

Team sports have been shown to partially mediate depressive symptoms and risk for such symptoms, not only for boys but also for girls (Boone and Ledbeater 2006). Adventure counseling programs work best with single-gender groups as long as students are at least in second grade, although greater gains can be made from the fourth grade on (Lakes and Hoyt 2004). Tae kwon do training for children in kindergarten through grade five has been shown to have positive effects on both emotion regulation and classroom behavior. Moreover, studies utilizing tae kwon do have shown positive effects on students' ability to handle mental math and in increasing positive behaviors with peers (Lakes and Hoyt 2004).

Different strategies are needed at different times and in different contexts. Emotional reactions that parents might accept might not be tolerated in school, and adults may be more forgiving than peers when a student loses control of his or her emotions. Individuals' experience degrees of anger (Kellner 1999). Given different degrees of anger, different strategies are needed for feeling slightly angry versus feeling enraged. Appropriate expression of emotion varies considerably, and this must be taught explicitly to some students. The appropriate intensity of anger to be expressed outwardly in specific situations must be practiced over time. The strategies that work for a particular student must be identified along with goals for the particular individual.

Triggers

Identifying triggers for each student is important. Triggers are situations that frighten us and make us feel anxious or set us off and make us feel angry (Kellner 1999). The physical symptoms that are experienced can be used as cues, or children can be taught to use feelings as cues so that they know when a problem exists and they are in trouble (Nezu, Nezu and Brotman 2001b). Triggers can be used as cues to 'chill out' (Lochman, et al. 1997). Different triggers can be used as signals to use specific strategies that fit the emotion that is being experienced. Children should be taught that negative emotion is a signal alerting us to pay close attention to external information (Forgas and Wyland 2006).

There are some common triggers for elementary-aged students, including having an ongoing activity interrupted, blocked goals, and blocked access to a reward (Fox 1998; Martin and Bridger 1999). Students with handicaps can become dysregulated by sensory input that is overwhelming, changes in routine and staff, inappropriate task demands related to the difficulty or duration of an activity, fragmented services, and disorganizing social and linguistic input. The use of transactional supports, such as nonverbal communication systems and visuals, plays an important role in efforts to help students with handicapping conditions (Prizant et al. 2003, p. 308). Common triggers and strategies for identifying them are shown in Fig. 11.4.

Goal Setting

Real-world stressors can significantly impair a student's ability to think flexibly. Emotions compete with other inputs for conscious processing (Lane and McRae 2004). Goal setting is extremely important. For some children, goals that are associated with reinforcements may be powerful enough to help them focus on what needs to be done.

Goals have to be set specifically for emotional control (Hromek 2004). This is no different from setting goals for reading or math or for decreasing aggressive behavior. Progress should be reviewed regularly. School psychologists have to solicit feedback about how the child is doing in other settings so that goals can be revised, new skills introduced, and practice expanded. Reinforcement is

---

Common Triggers and Strategies for Identifying Triggers

Triggers

Triggers are signals to which we react emotionally. They can bedescribed as 'hot buttons' (Richfield 2003). Triggers involve a mismatch between a student's desires and the outcomes that they expect (Harris 2000, p. 286).

Common Triggers

(Florida Department of Education 2001; Harris 2000)

- Disagreements over possessions or space (body space or play space).
- Physical contact with others (bumps, shoves, pushes, hits, etc.).
- Verbal statements (teasing, taunting, arguing, criticizing, annoying comments).
- Feeling disrespected (pride injuries to self-esteem).
- Rejection (being ignored by adults, left out by peers, chosen last, not chosen, told to get away).
- Compliance stress (others insisting on a standard that conflicts with what you want, frustration of desires, not getting what you want).
- Social stress (competition, others not doing what you expected, others taking advantage, being provoked).
- Internal (feeling angry or disappointed in oneself).

Strategies for Identifying Triggers

- Share your own triggers explaining that everyone has triggers.
- Observe the student to help him or her identify triggers.
- Interview parents, teachers and others who may be helpful in identifying personal triggers-work together (NASP 2002).
- Make a list of triggers with the student.
- Older students can keep a journal recording situations that caused the upset, thoughts, feelings, body signals, and behaviors.
- Groups can keep a list of triggers common to the group as well as a list of strategies for dealing with the triggers.

Emphasize 'calming down' strategies before problem solving

Fig. 11.4 Common triggers and strategies for identifying triggers

necessary at first, but should be phased out and replaced with self-reward. School psychologists should share the child's successes with staff and parents so that progress is noticed and acknowledged (Hromek 2004).

Planning for Generalization

An important goal of training emotion regulation is that young people will exhibit adequate social and emotional self-management skills in all environments. This is particularly critical for high school students who must deal with a number of different classes and teachers as well as the unstructured lunch-room, hallways, and locker rooms (Peterson, Young, Salzberg, West, and Hill 2006). Social skills instruction has not generalized well in the past partly because this service has been delivered by pulling students out of class and training them in offices or small treatment rooms, which did not ensure that they would use skills *where* or *when* they were needed (Elksnin and Elksnin 2000; Gresham, Sugai, and Horner 2001). Meta-analyses provide evidence for only limited, inconsistent, or modest effects on students' social behaviors (Leffert and Siperstein 2003). There is no reason to believe that training emotion regulation would have better outcomes if it were delivered in the same manner.

Teaching any type of social or management skill in a totally separate setting such as an office or empty classroom without planning for generalization and transfer of training reduces the likelihood of success. Davis, L. (2006) reminds us that insufficient generalization of skills is one of the consistent weaknesses of social skills training.

The list of reasons why generalization and transfer of training do not occur is a long one. It includes failure to: (a) identify whether a weakness is due to a skill or performance deficit; (b) identify very specific skill weaknesses before training begins; (c) integrate training across the whole school environment; (d) integrate training into the home environment; (e) insufficient amount of time dedicated to training; (f) collaborate between trainers and other school staff; and (g) provide feedback or sufficient reinforcement of new skills (Chen 2006; Davis, L. 2006; Mathur, Kavale, Quinn, Forness, and Rutherford 1998).

There are, however, a number of ways to improve generalization. Planning for generalization of training includes identifying *very specifically* the emotion regulation deficits that each student is exhibiting. If some students have not learned particular skills, these skills and strategies must be explicitly taught in a structured way. If students already know how to manage emotions but are not using the skills and strategies they know, reminding them to use strategies and rewarding their use would be more appropriate. Some of the students who know what to do but do not use strategies may need retraining and more practice before they master the use of emotion regulation strategies.

In order to increase the effectiveness of interventions, training has to extend over time. Time is a very important variable. Teachers are increasingly aware of the need for training, but school schedules need considerable tweaking to accommodate it. Teachers who are implementing general social skills training or a social-emotional learning curriculum in their classrooms may be more receptive to allowing additional time for training for specific students. Sufficient time also refers to the length of time that students will need targeted (training of specific skills) or intense training (individualized). The U.S. Department of Education recommends a training span of two years in order to effectively influence or change social-emotional behaviors in school-age children. In the U.S. Department of Education online continuing education training program for administrators, Lead and Manage MY School:

Identifying Prevention Priorities and Strategies for Success found on the ED.gov website, there is a list of critical student skills, including:

- Identifying emotions
- Empathy
- Anger management
- Impulse control
- Decision making
- Stress management
- Goal setting
- Problem solving

These are some of the skills related to emotion regulation. They need to be included in school-based interventions for all students and explicitly trained for with targeted and identified students.

Some students with identified disabilities may need training over a long period of time. For some it may have to be ongoing as the peer culture changes and new stresses present themselves at each grade level and with major transitions during the K–12 period. Students with Asperger syndrome, for example, may need training for some component of time during each grade level. These young people have difficulty learning new skills or changing skills already learned related to social interaction and emotion regulation without direct instruction. Moreover, they tend not to learn vicariously.

Training must be provided in a relevant context. It is important to teach students in the several places where they will be using the skills they are learning: in the classroom, on the playground, in the cafeteria, in the corridors of the school, in locker rooms and bathrooms, etc. These settings can be noisy, confusing, and stressful. Children may not be able to retrieve strategies easily under tumultuous or confusing environmental conditions. In addition to various settings, it is important to use a variety of models (adults and peers), to use natural language during training, to practice using emotion regulatory skills in a variety of situations, and to reinforce learning throughout the day. It is important to teach self-management skills including self-reinforcement, self-talk, self-monitoring, and self-recording (Gaylord, Quinn, McComas, and Lehr 2005; Stokes and Baer 1977).

Play and games are relevant contexts for elementary school students (Davis, L. 2006). For elementary school students these would be on the playground, in the cafeteria, in corridors, and in the classroom. School psychologists providing training in emotion regulation during a baseball game on the playground will find that strategies will generalize better and faster than providing practice in emotion control in their offices (Macklem 2006a). When initial skill and strategy instruction is provided in a separate setting, giving assignments to self-record and using adults to record use of strategies will help with the transfer of training to other settings.

Collaboration with parents and teachers can take place directly or through e-mail. When using e-mail, it is important to include instructions for reminding children to use skills that they are acquiring and instruction for providing appropriate reinforcement. Keep in mind that general e-mail instructions have to be sent without students' names attached to the message to ensure confidentiality. No information about individual observations or personal comments should be send via e-mail (Macklem 2006b).

Including reinforcement instruction is very important because many adults fail to reinforce new skills more than once or twice. It is important to make sure that familiar adults cue students to use skills in all school environments and at home. Parents, teachers, playground monitors, and teaching assistants have to be instructed to initially reinforce the use of skills and strategies, but not to reinforce every occurrence of behavior because reinforcements are infrequent in the real world (Macklem 2006a). This frequent communication serves several purposes. It builds a team around the child, keeps others interested and informed, helps others know exactly what to do to help, and expands the training significantly.

In addition, some children may need to be taught to solicit feedback in natural environments by asking, 'How did I do?' If training must temporarily be taught or practiced in environments that are not typically used by students, school psychologists should use the same cues that may be present in natural environments in training and guide practice using strategies under increasingly more stressful conditions. Reinforcement during training has to be gradually phased down, varied, and delayed so that children do not expect continual reinforcement. Initially, however, it may be important to remind teachers and aides in natural environments to provide the reinforcement needed until skills become well established (Macklem 2006a; Stokes and Baer 1977). Middle and secondary level students can provide some of the reinforcement they need for themselves and homework in the form of self-recording provides it, although some students will have to show their recordings to adults and receive the verbal reinforcement they need in this way.

Students have to be encouraged to join school-based clubs and teams so that they can practice and generalize self-regulatory skills in a semiprotected environment. School psychologists can volunteer to participate in one or more of the student activities in a supervisory capacity, which will give them an opportunity to cue their targeted students and allow them to observe when and how well skills are generalizing. This may be a particularly effective way to deliver emotion regulation training at the secondary level (Macklem 2006a).

Self-Recording and Self-Monitoring

One way to improve generalization and transfer of training into other environments is the use of self-regulation training. There are several forms of self-regulation: self-monitoring used alone, self-monitoring with reinforcement, self-reinforcement used alone, and self-management or self-evaluation (Reid, Trout and Schwaltz 2005). These are powerful generalization strategies.

Two types of self-monitoring that have been studied in some depth are self-monitoring of attention and self-monitoring of performance (Reid et al. 2005). Self-monitoring involves establishing goals, paying attention to what one is doing, and then recording one's behavior and thoughts. When recording negative thinking is important, students can be taught to record both their thoughts and more accurate or positive ways to look at the specific situation, as in Fig. 11.5.

Students are often taught to graph their behavior. Self-graphing provides visual feedback and graphing progress or accomplishments can be reinforcing. Graphing behavior is important and students should be taught to do it themselves.

Other self-monitoring methods include using checklists, keeping a journal, making audiotape recordings, or completing questionnaires. Self-recording use of the strategies that have already been taught gives the student an immediate feedback tool, which is a type of concrete running record. The thought record is the most frequently used method in cognitive therapy. It has three or more components, which become the headings for columns on a recording sheet (Freeman et al. 2004):

- What happened?
- How did I feel?
- What was I thinking?

The recording can be relatively simple as suggested here or quite complex. A more complex recording sheet would ask an adolescent to make notes about the situation, record the emotion or emotions that he or she experienced in the situation, record the 'automatic' thought that occurred connected with the emotion, and then record a more reasonable thought and resulting emotion.

When young people are being taught to self-record or self-monitor, they can be asked to role-play situations in which they might need emotion regulation

Identifying Negative Thoughts and Generating Counter Thoughts (Sample)	
Negative Thought	**Counter Thought**
No one likes me.	I have some good friends.
I can't do this.	I can do this if I calm down and take it one step at a time.
I'll never learn this.	If I put in time and effort, I'll do okay.
I can't handle this.	I can take a deep breath andwait until the anxiety passes.
I'm no good at this game	I can practice more often and be good enough.
I can't control my anger	I have a choice, I don'thave to let myself get so angry.

Fig. 11.5 Identifying Negative Thoughts and Generating Counter Thoughts (Sample)

strategies and record their use of strategies. Later, for homework, they will record how they used them in their daily lives. Parents and classroom teachers can be enlisted to cue students to use strategies and to record them. Students also have to learn to set reasonable goals for themselves and to practice working toward them. Planning and self-management helps them remain focused on those goals.

School psychologists always have the choice of developing tools for identifying skill weaknesses, for helping students learn to self-monitor, and/ or for outcome measurements. Ongoing data collection provides opportunities for comparing outcomes to preintervention behaviors. These are *informal* tools. The advantage of developing one's own tools is that they can be very specifically designed for the targeted student, focusing on the strategies that he or she is learning to master. A self-monitoring tool can be found in Fig. 11.6.

Self-recording has been demonstrated to be successful in increasing on-task behavior and improving task accuracy in children with learning disabilities or attention deficit disorders (Edwards, Salant, Howard, Brougher, and McLaughlin 1995; Reid, Trout, and Schartz 2005; Snider 1987). Additional self-recording information can be found in Fig. 11.7.

Teaching a student to self-record use of strategies combined with providing self-reinforcement should help strategies generalize beyond the teaching environment. Adults in other environments may have to cue children to use the strategies at first, as well as to cue them to self-record and self-reinforce, until a habit is formed.

Self-Monitoring Tool

Briefly describe what was upsetting. Record which strategy you used first. If this did not work and you needed a second strategy, record what you used. In the final column note if the strategy worked (+) or if it did not work (−).

Stress/Upset	Strategy Used	+ /−

Key

R — A strategy to help you relax (attending to your breathing, counting, other)

D — A strategy to help distract yourself (do something else, do something fun, try not to think about it, use a mantra)

C — A strategy to change your thinking (looking at the situation differently, thinking positively, telling yourself that everything will be okay)

PS — A problem-solving strategy (attempting to think positively, fixing the problem

N — Negative strategy (act out, over focus on the upset, worry too much, avoid dealing with the upset)

Fig. 11.6 Self-Monitoring Tool

Self-Recording

Self-recording and other self-regulation interventions are important interventions for use in schools. Self-monitoring interventions have involved both performance and attention to task as well as reduction of inappropriate behaviors (Reid et al. 2005).

Edwards, Salant, Howard, Brougher, and McLaughlin (1995) rewarded students with ADHD for recording whether or not they were attending to the task at hand when they heard a cue. Students were rewarded when they were on task a significant portion of the time, and their work was accurate as well. Middle school students effectively recorded whether or not teacher's behavioral expectancies were met (Clees 1994). Stecker (1996) demonstrated that students could reduce the amount of time spent outside of the class-room during required activities using self-recording procedures, and Minner (1990) showed that self-monitoring could decrease the time that students with behavior problems took to walk to special classes.

Researchers have increased the power of self-recording by requiring students to match their self-recordings of behavior with their teachers' recordings to improve accuracy of self-recording. Still others have explored the effects of having students' reward themselves should they improve their attention and academic task accuracy (Reid et al. 2005). The effect of various combinations of self-management techniques including self-recording and self-reinforcement is large (greater than one standard deviation) (Reid et al. 2005).

Fig. 11.7 Self-recording

Summary

If there is adequate planning ahead of time, interventions will be more success-ful. Careful identification of students and the skills and strategies that have to be addressed is necessary during the planning stage. Taking baseline data so that outcomes can be measured is particularly important given the reticence with which training is accepted in some schools and the importance of knowing whether or not an intervention is actually working. Selecting evidence-based interventions is a critical step, as is making appropriate adaptations to fit the training to the individual student. Identification of triggers is crucial when interventions involve emotion regulation. Goal setting, monitoring progress, and teaching self-regulatory skills all contribute to success. Moving training sessions to relevant settings and using relevant social contexts will reduce transfer-of-training problems, and clearly increase the likelihood that general-ization will take place.

Social skills training is commonly and frequently recommended in schools today. We cannot waste students' time or take them away from academics if we cannot improve outcomes. We know that young people have to be able to regulate their emotions in order to be successful interpersonally and to feel satisfied and successful. It is time to address these needs and to use the best knowledge and interventions we have available to do so.

References

Abela, J. R., Brozina, K., and Haigh, E. P. (2002). An examination of the response styles theory of depression in third- and seventh-grade children: A short-term longitudinal study. *Journal of Abnormal Child Psychology, 30(5)*, 515–527.

Aber, J. L., Brown, J. L., Roderick, T., and Lantieri, L. (2001). The Resolving Conflict Creatively Program: A school-based social and emotional learning program. *The CEIC Review, 10(6)*, 24–26.

Alexander, J. K., Hillier, A., Smith, R. M., Tivarus, M. E., and Beversdorf, D. Q. (2005). Noradrenergic modulation of cognitive flexibility during stress. Society for Neuroscience Annual Meeting, Washington, DC.

Amato-Zech, N. A., Hoff, K. E., and Doepke, K. J. (2006). Increasing on-task behavior in the classroom: Extension of self-monitoring strategies. *Psychology in the Schools, 43(2)*, 211–221.

Andersson, G., and Hägnebo, C. (2003). Hearing impairment, coping strategies, and anxiety sensitivity. *Journal of Clinical Psychology in Medical Settings, 10(1)*, 35–39.

Applegate, H., Kelley, M. L., Applegate, B. W., Jayasinghe, I. K., and Venters, C. L. (2003). Clinical case study: Pediatric residents' discussions of and interventions for children's behavioral and emotional problems. *Journal of Pediatric Psychology, 28(5)*, 315–321.

Apter, M. J. (2003). On a certain blindness in modern psychology. *The Psychologist, 16(9)*, 474–475.

Arseneault, L., Walsh, E., Trzesniewski, K., Newcombe, R., Caspi, A., and Moffitt, T. E. (2006). Bullying victimization uniquely contributes to adjustment problems in young children: A nationally representative cohort study. *Pediatrics, 118*, 130–138.

Attwood, T. (2000). Strategies for improving the social integration of children with Asperger Syndrome. *Autism, 4(1)*, 85–100.

Audrain-McGovern, J., Rodriguez, D., Tercyak, K. P., Neuner, G., and Moss, H. B. (2006). The impact of self-control indices on peer smoking and adolescent smoking progression. *Journal of Pediatric Psychology, 31(2)*, 130–151.

Austenfeld, J. L., and Stanton, A. L. (2004). Coping through emotional approach: A new look at emotion, coping, and health-related outcomes. *Journal of Personality, 72(6)*, 1335–1364.

Avery, A. W., Rider, K., and Haynes-Clements, L. A. (1981). Communication skills training for adolescents: A five-month follow-up. *Adolescence, 16(62)*, 289–298.

Bailey, V. (2001) Cognitive–behavioural therapies for children and adolescents. *Advances in Psychiatric Treatment, 7*, 224–232.

Barrett, L. F., Gross, J., Christensen, T. C., and Benvenuto, M. (2001). Knowing what you're feeling and knowing what to do about it: Mapping the relation between emotion differentiation and emotion regulation. *Cognition and Emotion, 15(6)*, 713–724.

Baumeister, R. F., Bratslavsky, E., Muraven, M. B., and Tice, D. M. (1998). Ego-depletion: Is the active self a limited resource? *Journal of Personality and Social Psychology, 74*, 1252–1265.

Baumeister, R. F., Dewall, C. N., Ciarocco, N. J., and Twenge, J. M. (2005). Social exclusion impairs self-regulation. *Journal of Personality and Social Psychology, 88*, 589–604.

Baumeister, R. F., Gailliot, M., Dewall, C. N., and Oaten, M. (2006). Self-regulation and personality: How interventions increase regulatory success, and how depletion moderates the effects of traits on behavior. *Journal of Personality, 74(6)*, 1773–1802.

Baumeister, R. F., Heatherton, T. F., and Tice, D. M. (1994). *Losing Control: How and Why People Fail at Self-Regulation*. San Diego: Academic Press.

Baumrind, D. (1989). Rearing competent children. In W. Damon (Ed.), *Child Development Today and Tomorrow* (pp. 349–378). San Francisco: Jossey-Bass.

Baumrind, D. (1991). The influence of parenting style on adolescent competence and substance use. *Journal of Early Adolescence, 11(1)*, 56–95.

Bear, G. G. (1998). School discipline in the United States: Prevention, correction, and long-term social development. *School Psychology Review, 27(1)*,14–32.

Bear, G. G., Manning, M. A., and Izard, C. E. (2003). Responsible behavior: The importance of social cognition and emotion. *School Psychology Quarterly, 18(2)*, 140–157.

Beauchaine T. P., Gatzke-Kopp, L., and Mead, H. K. (2006) Polyvagal theory and developmental psychopathology: Emotion dysregulation and conduct problems from preschool to adolescence. *Biological Psychology*, [Epub ahead of print]. Retrieved October 21, 2006, from http://www.ncbi.nlm.nih.gov/entrez/query.fcgi?db=pubmed & cmd=Search &itool=pubmed_AbstractPlus & term=%22Mead+HK%22%5BAuthor%5D

Beauregard, M. (2004). Introduction. In M. Beauregard (Ed.), *Consciousness, Emotional Self-Regulation and the Brain* (pp. IX–XII). New York: John Benjamin Publishing Company.

Beauregard, M., Lévesque, J., and Paquette, V. (2004). Neural basis of conscious and voluntary self-regulation of emotion. In M. Beauregard (Ed.), *Consciousness, Emotional Self- Regulation and the Brain* (pp. 163–194). Philadelphia: John Benjamins Publishing Company.

Behncke, L. (2002). Self-regulation: A brief review. *Athletic Insight: The Online Journal of Sport Psychology, 4(1)*. Retrieved February 22, 2006, from http://www.athleticinsight. com/Vol4Iss1/SelfRegulation.htm

Behncke, L. (2005). Mental skills training for sports: A brief review. *Athletic Insight: The Online Journal of Sport Psychology, 7(3)*. Retrieved February 22, 2006, from http://www. athleticinsight.com/Vol6Iss1/MentalSkillsReview.htm

Bell, M., and Wolfe, D. (2004) Emotion and cognition: An intricately bound developmental process. *Child Development, 75(2)*, 366–370.

Bennett, D., and Gibbons, T. (2000). Efficacy of child cognitive behavioral-interventions for antisocial behavior: A meta-analysis. *Child and Family Behavior Therapy, 22(1)*, 1–15.

Bernstein, G. A., Layne, A. E., Egan, E. A., and Tennison, D. M. (2005). School-based interventions for anxious children. *Journal of the American Academy of Child and Adolescent Psychiatry, 44(11)*, 1118–1127.

Besley, K. R. (1999). Anger management: Immediate intervention by counselor coach. *Professional School Counseling, 3(2)*, 81–90.

Birch, S. H., and Ladd, G. W. (1997). The teacher-child relationship and children's early school adjustment. *Journal of School Psychology, 35(1)*, 61–79.

Black, S. (2005). Test anxiety. *American School Board Journal*, 42–44.

Blair, C. (2002). School readiness: Integrating cognition and emotion in a neurobiological conceptualization of children's functioning at school entry. *American Psychologist, 57(2)*, 111–127.

Blair, C. (2003). Self-regulation and school readiness. *ERIC Digest* (ED477640). Retrieved July 17, 2006, from http://www.ericdigests.org/2004-1/self.htm

Blanc, R., Adrien, J. L., Roux, S., and Barthelemy, C. (2005). Dysregulation of pretend play and communication development in children with autism. *Autism, 9(3)*, 229–245.

Bloodworth, M. R., Weissberg, R. P., Zins, J. E., and Walberg, H. J. (2001). Implications of social and emotional research for education evidence linking social skills and academic outcomes. *The CEIC Review, 10(6)*, 4–5, 27.

Bloomquist, M. L., August, G. J., and Ostrander, R. (1991). Effects of a school-based cognitive-behavioral intervention for ADHD children. *Journal of Abnormal Child Psychology, 19(5)*, 591–605.

Blumberg, S. H., and Izard, C. E. (1986). Discriminating patterns of emotions in 10 and 11 year old children's anxiety and depression. *Journal of Personality and Social Psychology, 51*, 852–857.

Boo, G. M., and Wicherts, J. M. (2007). Assessing cognitive and behavioral coping strategies in children. *Cognitive Therapy and Research.* Retrieved May 22, 2007, from http://www.springerlink.com/content/rm64411358433415/?p = 9dbe76c22bb14871b7bc37c3cd9798cd & pi = 8

Boone, E. M., and Ledbeater, B. J. (2006). Game on: Diminishing risks for depressive symptoms in early adolescence through positive involvement in team sports. *Journal of Research on Adolescence, 16(1)*, 79–90.

Bormann, J., Oman, D., Kemppainen, J. K., Becker, S., Gershwin, M., and Kelly, A. (2006). Mantram repetition for stress management in veterans and employees: A critical incident study. *Journal of Advanced Nursing, 53(6)*, 502–512.

Bowker, A., Bukowski, W. M., Hymel, S., and Sippola, L. K. (2000). Coping with daily hassles in the peer group during early adolescence: Variations as a function of peer experience. *Journal of Research on Adolescence, 10*, 211–243.

Boxer, P., Musher-Eizenman, D., Dubrow, E. F., Danner, S., and Heretick, D. M. (2006). Assessing teachers' perceptions for school-based aggression prevention programs: Applying a cognitive-ecological framework. *School Psychology Review, 43(3)*, 331–344.

Boyer, M., Compas, B. E., Stanger, C., Colletti, R. B., Konik, B. S., Morrow, S. B., and Thomsen, A. H. (2005). Attentional biases to pain and social threat in children with recurrent abdominal pain. *Journal of Pediatric Psychology, 31(2)*, 209–220.

Boyle, J., Hunter, S., and Turner, S. (2005, September). Bullying: Research into practice. Paper presented at the Annual Conference for Educational Psychologists in Scotland, Heriot-Watt University, Edinburgh.

Bradley, J., Ama, S., Gettman, M., Brennan, E., and Kibera. P. (2004). Promoting inclusion in child care centers: Learning from success. *Focal Point. A National Bulletin on Family Support and Children's Mental Health: Partnering with Families, 18(1)*, 11–14.

Bridges, L. J., Denham, S. A., and Ganiban, J. M. (2004). Definitional issues in emotion regulation research. *Child Development, 75(2)*, 340–346.

Bridges, L. J., Margie, N. G., and Zaff, F. J. (2001). *Background for community-level work on emotional well-being in adolescence: Reviewing the literature on contributing factors.* Child Trends Research Brief. Washington, DC: John S. and James L. Knight Foundation.

Brigman, G., and Campbell, C. (2003). Helping students improve academic achievement and school success behavior. *Professional School Counseling, 7*, 91–98.

British Psychological Society (2004). Surviving the bully. *Counselling and Psychotherapy Journal, 15(4)*, 9.

Broderick, P. (2005). Mindfulness and coping with dysphoric mood: Contrasts with rumination and distraction. *Cognitive Therapy and Research, 29(5)*, 501–510.

Bronson, M. (2000). *Self-Regulation in Early Childhood: Nature and Nurture.* New York: The Guilford Press.

Bronte-Tinkew, J., Moore, K. A., and Carrano, J. (2006). The father-child relationship, parenting styles, and adolescent risk behaviors in intact families. *Journal of Family Issues, 27(6)*, 850–881.

Brown, K., Atkins, M. S., Osborne, M. L., and Milnamow, M. (1996). A revised teacher rating scale for reactive and proactive aggression. *Journal of Abnormal Child Psychology*, *24(4)*, 473–480.

Brown, J. R., and Dunn, J. (1996). Continuities in emotion understanding from three to six years. *Child Development*, *67(3)*, 789–802.

Bryson, S. E., Landry, R., Czapinski, P., McConnell, B., Rombough, V., and Wainwright, A. (2004). Autistic Spectrum Disorders: Causal mechanisms and recent findings on attention and emotion. *International Journal of Special Education*, *19(1)*, 14–22.

Buckley, M., and Saarni, C. (2006). Skills of emotional competence: Developmental implications. In J. Ciarrochi and J. D. Meyer (Eds.), *Emotional Intelligence in Everyday Life* (pp. 51–76). New York: Psychology Press.

Buckley, M., Storino, M., and Saarni, C. (2003). Promoting emotional competence in children and adolescents: Implications for school psychologists. *School Psychology Quarterly*, *18(2)*, 177–191.

Buhs, E. S., Ladd, G. W., and Herald, S. L. (2006). Peer exclusion and victimization: Processes that mediate the relation between peer group rejection and children's classroom engagement and achievement. *Journal of Educational Psychology*, *98(1)*, 1–13.

Burg, J. E. (2004). The emotions thermometer: An intervention for the scaling and psychoeducation of intense emotions. *British Dental Journal*, *193(8)*, 447–450.

Bushman, B. J. (2002). Does venting anger feed or extinguish the flame? Catharsis, rumination, distraction, anger, and aggressive responding. *Personality and Social Psychology Bulletin*, *28(6)*, 724–731.

Bushman, B. J., Bonacci, A. M., Pedersen, W. C., Vasquez, E. A., and Miller, N. (2005). Chewing on it can chew you up: Effects of rumination on triggered displaced aggression. *Journal of Personality and Social Psychology*, *88(6)*, 969–983.

Calkins, S. (2004). Temperament and emotional regulation: Multiple models of early development. In M. Beauregard (Ed.), *Consciousness, Emotional Self-Regulation and the Brain* (pp. 35–60). Philadelphia: John Benjamins Publishing Company.

Calkins, S. D., and Dedmon, S. E. (2000). Physiological and behavioral regulation in two-year old children with aggressive/destructive behavior problems. *Journal of Abnormal Child Psychology*, *28(2)*, 103–118.

Calkins, S. D., Gill, K. L., Johnson, M. C., and Smith, C. L. (1999). Emotional reactivity and emotional regulation strategies as predictors of social behavior with peers during toddlerhood. *Social Development 8(3)*, 310–334.

Camp, B., and Bash, M. (1985). *Think Aloud: Increasing Social and Cognitive Skills – A Problem-Solving Programme for Children*. Champaign, IL: Research Press.

Card, N. A., and Little, T. D. (2006). Proactive and reactive aggression in childhood and adolescence: A meta-analysis of differential relations with psychosocial adjustment. *International Journal of Behavioral Development*, *30(5)*, 466–480.

Cartwright-Hatton. S., Roberts, C., Chitsabesan, P., Fothergill, C., and Harrington, R. (2004). Systematic review of the efficacy of cognitive behaviour therapies for childhood and adolescent anxiety disorders. *British Journal of Clinical Psychology*, *43(4)*, 421–436.

Cartwright-Hatton, S., Tschernitz, N., and Gomersall, H. (2005). Social anxiety in children: Social skills deficit, or cognitive distortion? *Behavior Research and Therapy*, *43(1)*, 131–141.

Carver, C. S. (2006). Approach, avoidance, and self-regulation of affect and action. *Motivation and Emotion*, *30(2)*, 105–110.

Carver, C. S., Scheier, M. F., and Weintraub, J. K. (1989). Assessing coping strategies: A theoretically based approach. *Journal of Personality and Social Psychology*, *56*, 267–283.

Casey, B. J., and Durston, S. (2006). From behavior to cognition to the brain and back: What have we learned from functional imaging studies of Attention Deficit Hyperactivity Disorder? *American Journal of Psychiatry*, *163(6)*, 957–960.

Cates, G. L., and Rhymer, K. N. (2003). Examining the relationship between mathematics anxiety and mathematics performance: An instructional hierarchy perspective. *Journal of Behavioral Education, 12(1)*, 23–34.

Center for Educational Research and Innovation (2003). A report of the brain research and learning sciences. Emotions and Learning Planning Symposium. Organization for Economic Cooperation and Development, Centre for Educational Research and Innovation, Germany. Retrieved January 8, 2007, from http://web.sfn.org/index.cfm?pagename = brainBriefings_stressAndTheBrain & print = on

Chafouleas, S. M., Riley-Tillman, T. C., and McDougal, J. L. (2002). Good, bad, or in-between: How does the daily behavior report card rate? *Psychology in the Schools, 39(2)*, 157–169.

Chambless, D. L., and Hollon, S. D. (1998). Defining empirically supported therapies. *Journal of Consulting and Clinical Psychology, 66*, 7–18.

Chapman, H. R., and Kirby-Turner, N. (2002). Visual/verbal analogue scales: Examples of brief assessment methods to aid management of child and adult patients in clinical practice. *The British Dental Journal, 193(8)*, 447–450.

Chen, K. (2006). Social skills intervention for students with emotional/behavioral disorders: A literature review from the American perspective. *Educational Research and Reviews, 1(3)*, 143–149.

Chen, W., and Taylor, E. (2005). Resilience and self-control impairment. In S. Goldstein and R. B. Brooks, *Handbook of Resilience in Children* (pp. 257–278) . New York: Springer Science and Business Media, Inc.

Chowdhuy, U., Caulfield, C., and Heyman, I. (2003). A group for children and adolescents with obsessive-compulsive disorder. *Psychiatric Bulletin, 27*, 187–189.

Christensen, M. V., and Kessing, L. V. (2005). Clinical use of coping in affective disorder: A critical review of the literature. *Clinical Practice and Epidemiology in Mental Health, 1(20)*, 1–20.

Ciarochi, J. (2006). The current state of emotional intelligence research: Answers to some old questions and the discovery of some new ones. In J. Ciarrochi and J. D. Meyer (Eds.), *Emotional Intelligence in Everyday Life* (pp. 251–260). New York: Psychology Press.

Cicchetti, D., Ganiban, J., and Barnett, D. (1991). Contributions from the study of high-risk populations to understanding the development of emotion regulation. In J. Garber and K. Dodge (Eds.), *The Development of Emotion Regulation and Dysregulation* (pp. 15–42). New York: Cambridge University Press.

Clarke, G. N., Hawkins, W., Murphy, M., Sheeber, L., Lewinsohn, P. M., and Seeley, J. R. (1995). Targeted prevention of unipolar depressive disorder in an at-risk sample of high school adolescents: A randomized trial of a group cognitive intervention. *Journal of the American Academy of Child and Adolescent Psychiatry, 34*, 312–321.

Clarke, G. N., Hornbrook, M. C., Lynch, F., Polen, M., Gale, J., and Beardslee, W. et al. (2001). A randomized trial of a group cognitive intervention for preventing depression in adolescent offspring of depressed parents. *Archives of General Psychiatry, 58(12)*, 1127–1134.

Clarke, G. N., Rohde, P., Lewinsohn, P. M., Hops, H., and Seeley, J. R. (1999). Cognitive-behavioral treatment of adolescent depression: Efficacy of acute group treatment and booster sessions. *Journal of the American Academy of Child and Adolescent Psychiatry, 38*, 272–279.

Cleary, T. J. (2006, March) Reliability and validity of the Self-Regulation Strategy Inventory (SRSI-SR). Poster presented at the Annual Convention of the National Association of School Psychologists. Anaheim, CA.

Clees, T. J. (1994). Self-recording of students' daily schedules of teachers' expectancies: Perspectives on reactivity, stimulus control, and generalization. *Exceptionality, 5(3)*, 113–129.

Cole, P. M., and Dennis, T. A. (1998). Variations on a theme: Culture and the meaning of socialization practices and child competence. *Psychological Review, 9*, 276–278.

Cole, P. M., Dennis, T. A., and Cohen, L. H. (2001, April). Emotion regulation and understanding in 3- and 4-year-olds. Poster session presented at the biennial meeting of the Society for Research in Child Development, Minneapolis, MN.

Cole, P. M., Dennis, T. A., and Martin, S. A. (2004, July). Emotion regulation: A scientific conundrum. Poster session presented at the annual meeting of the International Society for the Study of Behavioural Development, Ghent, Belgium. Retrieved January 21, 2007, from http://urban.hunter.cuny.edu/~tdennis/publications_posters.html

Cole, P., Martin, S., and Dennis, T. (2004) Emotion regulation as a scientific construct: Methodological challenges and directions for child development research. *Child Development, 75(2)*, 317–333.

Cole, P., Michel, M., and Teli, L. (1994). The development of emotion regulation and dysregulation: A clinical perspective. Monographs of the Society for Research in Child Development, *59(2–3)*, 73–100.

Cole, P. M., Teti, L. O., and Zahn-Waxler, C. (2003). Mutual emotion regulation and the stability of conduct problems between preschool and early school age. *Development and Psychopathology, 15*, 1–18.

Cole, S. F., O'Brien, J. G., Gadd, M. G., Ristuccia, J., Wallace, D. L., and Gregory, M. (2005). *Helping traumatized children learn: Supportive school environments for children traumatized by family violence.* Massachusetts Advocates for Children, Boston.

Collaborative for Academic, Social, and Emotional Learning (2003). Safe and sound: An educational leader's guide to evidence-based social and emotional learning (SEL) programs. Retrieved January 7, 2007, from http://www.casel.org/downloads/Safe%20-and%20Sound/1A_Safe_&_Sound.pdf

Conte, R., and Paolucci, M. (2001). Intelligent social learning. *Journal of Artificial Societies and Social Simulation, 4(1)*. Retrieved February 25, 2007, from http://jasss.soc.surrey.ac.uk/4/1/3.html

Corkum, P. V., Mullane, J. C., and McKinnon, M. M. (2005). The effect of involving classroom teachers in a parent training program for families of children with ADHD. *Child and Family Behavior Therapy, 27(4)*, 29–49.

Crick, N. R., Murray-Close, D., and Woods, K. (2005). Borderline personality features in childhood: A short-term longitudinal study. *Development and Psychopathology, 17(4)*,1051–1070.

Crisp, H. L., Gudmundsen, G. R., and Shirk, S. R. (2006). Transporting evidence-based therapy for adolescent depression to the school setting. *Education and Treatment of Children, 29(2)*, 287–309.

Crothers, L. (2007). Bullying of sexually diverse children and adolescents. *Communiqué, 35(5)*, 28–30.

Crundwell, R. M. (2006, March). Differentiating the bad brake disorders. Annual Convention of the National Association of School Psychologists. Anaheim, California.

Cumberland-Li, A., Eisenberg, N., Champion, C., Gershoff, E., and Fabes, R. A. (2003). The relation of parental emotionality and related dispositional traits to parental expression of emotion and children's social functioning. *Motivation and Emotion, 27(1)*, 27–56.

Cunningham, M., Rapee R., and Lyneham, H. (2006). Feedback to a prototype self-help computer program for anxiety disorders in adolescents. *Australian e-Journal for the Advancement of Mental Health, 5(3)*. Retrieved May 6, 2007, from http://www.auseinet.com/journal/vol5iss3/cunningham.p

Dadds, M. R., Holland, D., Barrett, P. M., Laurens, K., and Spence, S. (1999). Early intervention and prevention of anxiety disorders in children: Results at 2-year follow-up. *Journal of Consulting and Clinical Psychology, 67*, 145–150.

Dadds, M. R., Spence, S. H., Holland, D. E., and Barrett, P. M. (1997). Prevention and early intervention for anxiety disorders: A controlled trial. *Journal of Consulting and Clinical Psychology, 65*, 627–635.

Dahl, R. E. (2001). Affect regulation, brain development, and behavioral/emotional health in adolescence. *CNS Spectrums, 6(1)*, 60–72.

Dansei, M. (1994). *Cool: The Signs and Meanings of Adolescence.* Toronto: University of Toronto Press, pp. 37–38.

Darling, N. (1999). Parenting style and its correlates. *ERIC Digest* (ED427896). ERIC Clearinghouse on Elementary and Early Childhood Education, Champaign, IL. Retrieved January 11, 2006, from http://www.ericdigests.org/1999-4/parenting.htm

Darwish, D., Esquivel, G. B., Houtz, J. C., and Alfonso, V. C. (2001). Play and social skills in maltreated and non-maltreated preschoolers during peer interactions. *Child Abuse and Neglect, 25(1)*, 13–31.

Davidov, M., and Grusec, J. E. (2006). Untangling the links of parental responsiveness to distress and warmth to child outcomes. *Child Development, 77(1)*, 44–58.

Davidson, R. J. (1998). Affective style and affective disorders: Perspectives from affective neuroscience. *Cognition and Emotion, 12(30)*, 307–330.

Davidson, R. J. (2000). Affective neuroscience and psychophysiology: Toward a synthesis. Presidential Address 2000, The Society for Psychophysiological Research, Thirty-Sixth Annual. Retrieved July 6, 2006, from http://www. sprweb.org/~spr/archive/past_mtng/1996/96program.html

Davidson, R. J. (2001). Toward a biology of personality and emotion. *Annals of the New York Academy of Sciences, 935*, 191–207.

Davidson, R. J., Jackson, D. C., and Kalin, N. H. (2000). Emotion, plasticity, context and regulation: Perspectives from affective neuroscience. *Psychological Bulletin, 126*, 890–906.

Davidson, R. J., Putnam, K. M., and Larson, C. L. (2000). Dysfunction in the neural circuitry of emotion regulation - A possible prelude to violence. Violence review. *Science, 289*, 591–594.

Davidson, R. J., and Rickman, M. (1999) Behavioral inhibition and the emotional circuitry of the brain: Stability and plasticity during the early childhood years. In L. A. Schmidt and J. Schulkin (Eds.), *Extreme Fear, Shyness, and Social Phobia: Origins, Biological Mechanisms, and Clinical Outcomes* NY: Oxford University Press, pp. 67–87.

Davidson, R. J., Scherer, K. R., and Goldsmith, H. H. (2003) *Handbook of Affective Sciences.* New York: Oxford University Press.

Davis, A.S. (2006). The neuropsychological basis of childhood psychopathology. *Psychology in the Schools, 43(4)*, 503–512.

Davis, H. A. (2006). Exploring the contexts of relationship quality between middle school students and teachers. *The Elementary School Journal, 106(3)*, 193–223.

Davis, L. E. (2006). Effects of social skills role play for emotional and behavior disordered students. *Instructional Technology Monographs, 3(2)*. Retrieved May 24, 2007, from http://projects.coe.uga.edu/itm/archives/fall2006/ldavis.htm.

Dearing, K. F., Hubbard, J. A., Ramsden, S. R., Parker, E. H., Relyea, N., and Smithmyer, C. M. (2002). Children's self-reports about anger regulation: Direct and indirect links to social preference and aggression. *Merrill-Palmer Quarterly, 48(30)*, 308–336.

De Castro, B. O., Bosch, J. D., Veerman, J. W., and Koops, W. (2003). The effects of emotion regulation, attribution, and delay prompts on aggressive boys' social problem solving. *Cognitive Therapy and Research, 27(2)*, 153–166.

DeGangi, G. A., Breinbauer, C., Roosevelt, J. D., Porges, S., and Greenspan, S. (2000). Prediction of childhood problems at three years in children experiencing disorders of regulation during infancy. *Infant Mental Health Journal, 21(3)*, 156–175.

Delaney, K. R. (2006). Top 10 milieu interventions for inpatient child/adolescent treatment. *Journal of Child and Adolescent Psychiatric Nursing, 19(4)*, 203–214.

Denham, S. A., and Burton, R. (2003). *Social and Emotional Prevention and Intervention Programming for Preschoolers.* New York: Kluwer Academic/Plenum Publishers.

Denham, S. A., and Grout, L. (1993). Socialization of emotion: Pathway to preschoolers' emotional and social competence. *Journal of Nonverbal Behavior, 17*, 205–227.

Denham, S., Salisch, M. von, Olthof, T., Kochanoff, A., and Caverly, S. (2002) Emotional and social development in childhood. In P.K. Smith and C. H. Hart (Eds.), *Blackwell Handbook of Childhood Social Development*. Malden, MA: Blackwell Publishing.

Dennis, T.A. (2003, April). Motivation and the socialization of self-regulation. Poster session presented at the biennial meeting of the Society for Research in Child Development, Tampa.

Dennis, T.A. (2006). Emotional self regulation in preschoolers: The interplay of temperamental approach reactivity and control processes. *Developmental Psychology*, *42*, 84–97.

Dennis, T.A., and Brotman, L. M. (2003a). Effortful control, attention, and aggressive behavior in preschoolers at risk for conduct problems. In J. A. King, C. F. Ferris, and I. I. Lederhendler (Eds.), *Annals of the New York Academy of Science: Roots of Mental Illness in Children*, 1008, pp. 252–255.

Dennis, T. A., and Brotman, L. M. (2003b, March). Effortful control: Linkages with attention and conduct problems. Poster presented at the New York Academy of Sciences, Roots of Mental Illness in Children. New York.

Dennis, T.A., and Gonzalez, N. (2005, April). Emotional self-regulation in preschoolers: The interplay between approach reactivity and control processes. Poster presented at the biennial meeting of the Society for Research in Child Development, Atlanta.

Dennis, T.A., and Kelemen, D. (1999, April). Can I feel happy when I feel bad? Children's understanding of the intentional control of emotion. Poster session presented at the biennial meeting of the Society for Research in Child Development, Washington, DC.

Dennis, M., Lockyer, L., and Lazenby, A. L. (2000). How high-functioning children with autism understand real and deceptive emotion. *Autism*, *4(4)*, 370–381.

DeWall, C. N., Baumeister, R. F., Stillman, T. F., and Gailliot, M. T. (2006). Violence restrained: Effects of self-regulatory capacity and its depletion on aggressive behavior. *Journal of Experimental Social Psychology*. Retrieved October 26, 2006, from http://www.psy.fsu.edu/~baumeistertice/pubs.html

Diamond, L. M., and Aspinwall, L. G. (2003). Emotion regulation across the life span: An integrative perspective emphasizing self-regulation, positive affect, and dyadic processes. *Motivation and Emotion*, *27(2)*, 125–156.

Dimidjian, S., and Linehan, M. M. (2003). Defining an agenda for future research on the clinical application of mindfulness practice. *Clinical Psychology: Science and Practice* , *10(2)*, 166–171.

Dixon, W. E., and Smith, P. H. (2000). Links between early temperament and language acquisition. *Merrill-Palmer Quarterly*, *46*, 417–440.

Dodge, K.A., and Garber, J. (1991). Domains of emotion regulation. In J. Garber and K.A. Dodge (Eds.), *The Development of Emotion Regulation and Dysregulation* (pp. 3–10). New York: Cambridge University Press.

Downer, J. T., and Mendez, J. L. (2005). African American father involvement and preschool children's school readiness. *Early Education and Development*, *16(3)*, 317–340.

Ebata, A. T., and Moos, R. H. (1991). Coping and adjustment in distressed and healthy adolescents. *Journal of Applied Developmental Psychology*, *12(1)*, 33–54.

Edwards, L., Salant, V., Howard, V. F., Brougher, J., and McLaughlin, T. F. (1995). Effectiveness of self-management on attentional behavior and reading comprehension for children with Attention Deficit Disorder. *Child and Family Behavior Therapy*, *17(2)*, 1–17.

Eisenberg, N., and Fabes, R. A. (1999). Emotion, emotion-related regulation, and quality of socioemotional functioning. In L. Balter and C. S. Tamis-LeMonda (Eds.), *Child Psychology: A Handbook of Contemporary Issues* (pp. 318–335). Philadelphia: Psychology Press/ Taylor & Francis.

Eisenberg, N., Champion, C., and Ma, Y. (2004). Emotion-related regulation: An emerging construct. *Merrill-Palmer Quarterly*, *50*, 236–259.

Eisenberg, N., Fabes, R.A., and Murphy, B.C. (1996). Parents' reactions to children's negative emotions: Relations to children's social competence and comforting behavior. *Child Development, 67*, 2227–2247.

Eisenberg, N., Fabes, R. A., Shepard, S. A., Guthrie, I. K., Murphy, B. C., and Reiser, M. (1999). Parental reactions to children's negative emotions: Longitudinal relations to quality of children's social functioning. *Child Development, 70(2)*, 513–534.

Eisenberg, N., Sadovsky, A., and Spinrad, T. L. (2005). Associations of emotion-related regulation with language skills, emotion knowledge, and academic outcomes. *New Directions for Child and Adolescent Development, 109*, 109–118.

Eisenberg, N., Sadovsky, A., Spinrad, T., Fabes, R., Losoya, S., and Valiente, C. et al. (2005). The relations of problem behavior status to children's negative emotionality, effortful control, and impulsivity: Concurrent relations and prediction of change. *Developmental Psychology, 41(1)*, 193–211.

Eisenberg, N., Smith, C. L., Sadovsky, A., and Spinrad, T. L. (2004). Effortful control: Relations with emotion regulation, adjustment, and socialization in childhood. In R. F. Baumeister and K. D. Vohs (Eds.), *Handbook of Self-regulation: Research, Theory, and Applications* (pp. 259–282). New York: Guilford Press.

Eisenberg, N., and Spinrad, T. (2004). Emotional-related regulation: Sharpening the definition. *Child Development, 75(2)*, 317–333.

Eisenberg, N., Wentzel, N. M., and Harris, J. D. (1998). The roles of emotionality and regulation in empathy-related responding. *School Psychology Review, 27(4)*, 506–521.

Eisenberg, N., Zhou, Q., Spinrad, T. L., Valiente, C., Fabes, R. A., and Liew, J. (2005). Relations among positive parenting, children's effortful control, and externalizing problems: A three-wave longitudinal study. *Child Development, 76(5)*, 1055–1071.

Eley, T. C., Stirling, L. Ehlers, A., Gregory, A. M., and Clark, D. M (2004). Heart-beat perception, panic/somatic symptoms and anxiety sensitivity in children. *Behaviour Research and Therapy, 42*, 439–44.

Ellis, A., and Bernard, M. E. (2006). *Emotional Resilience in Children and Adolescence: Implications for Rational-Emotive Behavior Therapy. Rational Emotive Behavioral Approaches to Childhood Disorders, Part 1.* New York: Springer Science + Business Media, Inc., pp. 156–174.

Elias, M. J.(1983) Improving coping skills of emotionally disturbed boys through television-based social problem solving. *American Journal of Orthopsychiatry, 53(1)*, 61–72.

Elias, M. J. (2001). How social and emotional learning is infused into academics in the Social Decision Making/Social Problem Solving Program. *The CEIC Review, 10(6)*, 16–17.

Elias, M. J., Gara, M., Ubriaco, M., Rothbaum, P. A., Clabby, J. F., and Schuyler, T. (1986). Impact of a preventive social problem solving intervention on children's coping with middle-school stressors. *American Journal of Community Psychology, 14(3)*, 259–275.

Elias, M. J., Kress, J. S., and Hunter, L. (2006). Emotional intelligence and the crisis in schools. In J. Ciarrochi and J. D. Meyer (Eds.), *Emotional Intelligence in Everyday Life* (pp. 166–186). New York: Psychology Press.

Elias, M. J., Parker, J., and Rosenblatt, J. L. (2005). Building educational opportunity. In S. Goldstein and R. B. Brooks, *Handbook of Resilience in Children* (pp. 325–336). New York: Springer Science + Business Media, Inc.

Elias, M. J., and Tobias, S. E. (1990). *Problem solving/decision making for social and academic success*, National Education Association, Washington, DC.

Elksnin, L. K., and Elksnin, N. (2000). Teaching parents to teach their children to be prosocial. *Intervention in School and Clinic, 36*, 27–35.

Ellett, J. A. (n.d.). Neuropsychological dysfunction in children with Borderline Personality Disorder features. Dissertation. University of Colorado. Retrieved October 20, 2006, from http://www.web.uccs.edu/jules/newpage21.htm.

Elliott, S. N., and Gresham, F. M. (1987). Children's social skills: Assessment and classification practices. *Journal of Counseling and Development, 66*, 96–99.

Emerson, R. W. (1903) *The Complete Works of Ralph Waldo Emerson*. Volume VII - Society and Solitude (1870). Boston: Houghton Mifflin and Company, Chapter IV, Eloquence. Retrieved January 9, 2006, from http://www.rwe.org/comm/index.php?option = com_content & task = view & id = 34 & Itemid = 42

Erismana, S. M., Salters-Pedneaultb, K., and Roemera, L. (2005). Emotion regulation and mindfulness. Retrieved January 10, 2007, from http://psych.umb.edu/faculty/roemer/(AABT%202005)%20ER%20 & 20Mindfulness%20Poster%20Hanout%203.pdf

Erwin, B. A., Heimberg, R. G., Schneier, F. R., and Liebowitz, M. R. (2003). Anger experience and expression in Social Anxiety Disorder: Pretreatment profile and predictors of attrition and response to Cognitive-Behavioral Treatment. *Behavior Therapy, 34(3)*, 331–350.

Etkin, A., Egner, T., Peraza, D. M., Kandel, E. R., and Hirsch, J. (2006). Resolving emotional conflict: A role for the rostral anterior cingulate cortex in modulating activity in the amygdala. *Neuron, 51*, 1–12.

Etscheidt, S. (1991). Reducing aggressive behavior and increasing self control. A cognitive behavioral training program for behaviorally disordered adolescents. *Behavioral Disorders, 16*, 107–115.

Eynde, P. O., and Turner, J. E. (2006). Focusing on the complexity of emotion issues in academic learning: A dynamical component systems approach. *Educational Psychology Review, 18(4)*, 361–376.

Fabes, R. A., Hanish, L. D., Martin, C. L., and Eisenberg, N. (2002). Young children's negative emotionality and social isolation: A latent growth curve analysis. *Merrill-Palmer Quarterly, 43(3)*, 284–307.

Fabes, R. A., Leonard, S. A., Kupanoff, K., and Martin, C. L. (2001). Parental coping with children's negative emotions: Relations with children's emotional and social responding. *Child Development, 72(3)*, 907–920.

Fabes, R., Martin, C., Hanish, L., Anders, M., and Madden-Derdich, D. (2003). Early school competence: The roles of sex-segregated play and effortful control. *Developmental Psychology, 39(5)*, 848–858.

Fainsilber, K., and Windecker-Nelson, B. (2004). Parental meta-emotion philosophy in families with conduct-problem children: Links with peer relations. *Journal of Abnormal Child Psychology*, Retrieved August 21, 2006, from http://www.findarticles.com/p/articles/mi_m0902/is_4_32/ai_n6135647

Faith, M. S., Leone, M. A., Ayers, T. S. Heo, M., and Pietrobelli, A. (2002). Weight criticism during physical activity, coping skills, and reported physical activity in children. *Pediatrics, 110(2)*, e23-e23.

Family and Community Services. (2004). *Part A: Parenting and the factors that influence it. Parenting Information Project*. (Vol. 2). Commonwealth of Australia. Retrieved July 30, 2005, from http://www.facs.gov.au/family/early_childhood_pip/volume2/sec2.htm

Fantuzzo, J., Sekino, Y., and Cohen, H. (2004). An examination of the contributions of interactive peer play to salient classroom competencies for urban head start children. *Psychology in the Schools, 41(3)*, 323–336.

Fazio R. H. (2001). On the automatic activation of associated evaluations: An overview. *Cognition and Emotion, 15(2)*, 115–141.

Feindler, E. L., and Ecton, R.B. (1986). *Adolescent Anger Control: Cognitive-Behavioral Techniques*. New York: Pergamon Press.

Feshbach, S., and Feshbach, N. (2004, November). Reducing social prejudice and fostering social understanding: A cognitive-affective curriculum approach. The Civil Rights Project, Roundtable, "Positive Interracial Outcomes in the Classroom," Harvard Law School in Cambridge. Retrieved January 21, 2007, fromhttp://www.civilrightsproject.harvard.edu/convenings/positive/papers/abs_Feshbach.pdf.

Finley-Belgrad, E., and Davies, J. (2006). Personality Disorder: Borderline. EMedicine. *Instant Access to the Minds of Medicine.* Retrieved April 12, 2006, from http://www.emedicine.com/PED/topic270.htm#section~author_information

Fitea, P. J., Colder, C. R., Lochman, J. E., and Wells, K. C. (2006). The mutual influence of parenting and boys' externalizing behavior problems. *Journal of Applied Developmental Psychology, 27(2),* 151–16.

Fivush, R., Brotman, M. A., Buckner, J. P., and Goodman, S. H. (2000). Gender differences in parent-child emotion narratives. *Sex Roles: A Journal of Research.* Retrieved February 16, 2007, from http://www.findarticles.com/p/articles/mi_m2294/is_2000_Feb/ai_63787373

Flannery-Schroeder, E. C., and Kendall, P. C. (1996). *Cognitive-Behavioral Therapy for Anxious Children: Therapist Manual for Group Treatment.* Ardmore, PA: Workbook Publishing.

Fleener, P. (1999). Borderline Personality Disorder: Proposal to include a supplementary name in the DSM-IV text revision. Retrieved April 12, 2006, from http://www.borderlinepersonalitytoday.com/main/name_change.htm

Florida Department of Education (2001). Anger management and schools. *SDDFS Notes, 4(3),* 1–11.

Fogt, J. B., and Piripavel, C. M. (2002). Positive school-wide interventions for eliminating physical restraint and exclusion. *Reclaiming Children and Youth, 10(4),* 227–232.

Folkman, S., Lazarus, R. S., Dunkel-Schetter, C., DeLongis, A., and Gruen, R. J. (1986). Dynamics of a stressful encounter: Cognitive appraisal, coping, and encounter outcomes. *Journal of Personality and Social Psychology, 50,* 992–1003.

Fonagy, P., Twemlow, S. W., Vernberg, E., Sacco, F. C., and Little, T. D. (2005). Creating a peaceful school learning environment: The impact of an antibullying program on educational attainment in elementary schools. *Medical Science Monitor, 11(7),* 317–325.

Forbes, E. E. (2003). Children's emotion regulation: Frontal EEG asymmetry and behavior during a disappointment. Submitted to the Graduate Faculty of Arts and Sciences in partial fulfillment of the requirements for the degree of Doctor of Philosophy. University of Pittsburgh.

Forgas, J. P., and Wyland, C. L. (2006). Affective intelligence: Understanding the role of affect in everyday social behavior. In J. Ciarrochi and J. D. Meyer (Eds.), *Emotional Intelligence in Everyday Life* (pp. 77–99). New York: Psychology Press.

Forrest, W., and Hay, C. (2006, October 5). The development of self control: Examining self control theory's stability thesis. Paper presented at the annual meeting of the American Society of Criminology (ASC). Retrieved May 24, 2007, from http://www.allacademic.com/meta/p121508_index.html

Fox, N. (1998). Temperament and regulation of emotion in the first years of life. *Pediatrics, 5,* 1230–1235.

Fox, N. A., and Calkins, S. D. (2003). The development of self-control of emotion: Intrinsic and extrinsic influences. *Motivation and Emotion, 27(1),* 7–26.

Fraser, M. W. (2006, October). Conceptualizing and designing of social interventions. A presentation at the Graduate School of Social Work, University of Denver. Retrieved February 27, 2007, from http://ssw.unc.edu/jif/makingchoices/Presentations/Conceptualizing%20and%20Designing%20Interventions.ppt.

Fraser, M. W., Galinsky, M. J., Smokowski, P. R., Day, S. H., Rose, R. A., Terzian, M. A. et al. (2005, January). Outcomes from a quasi-experimental study of the effectiveness of school-based social skills training to prevent conduct problems in childhood. Paper presented at the Society for Social Work and Research, Miami.

Fraser, M. W., Nash, J. K., Galinsky, M. J., and Darwin, K. M. (2000). *Making Choices: Social Problem-Solving Skills for Children.* Washington, DC: NASW Press.

Freeman, T. M., and Anderman, L. H. (2005, February 4). Changes in mastery goals in urban and rural middle school students. *Journal of Research in Rural Education, 20(1)*. Retrieved May 3, 2007, from http://www.umaine.edu/jrre/20-1.htm

Freeman, A., Pretzer, J., Fleming, B., and Simon, K. M. (2004). *Clinical Applications of Cognitive Therapy* (2nd Ed.) (pp. 341–389). New York: Kluwer Academic/Plenum Publishers.

Fresco, D., Wolfson, S., Crowther, J., and Docherty, N. (2002). Distinct and overlapping patterns of emotion regulation in the comorbidity of generalized anxiety disorder and the eating disorders. Poster presented at the Annual Meeting of the Society for Research in Psychopathology. San Francisco.

Frey, K., Edstrom, L. V., and Hirschstein, M. (2005). The Steps to Respect Program uses a multilevel approach to reduce playground bullying and destructive bystander behaviors. Persistently Safe Schools. The National Conference of the Hamilton Fish Institute on School and Community Violence.

Furlong, M., and Smith, D. (1998, April). Angry children: Anger subtypes: A prescriptive intervention program for hostile and aggressive youth. Paper presented at the Annual Conference of the National Association of School Psychologists, Orlando.

Furner, J. M. and Berman, B. T. (2003) Math anxiety: Overcoming a major obstacle to the improvement of student math performance. *Journal of Research on Childhood Education, 79 (3)*, p. 170–174.

Gagnon, E. (2001). *Power Cards: Using Special Interests to Motivate Children and Youth with Asperger Syndrome and Autism*. Shawnee Mission, KS: Autism Asperger Publishing Co.

Gailliot, M. T., Baumeister, R. F., DeWall, C. N., Maner, J. K., Plant, E. A. Tice, D.M. et al. (2007). Self-control relies on glucose as a limited energy source: Willpower is more than a metaphor. *Journal of Personality and Social Psychology, 92(2)*, 325–336.

Garber, J., Braafladt, N., and Zeman, J. (1991). The regulation of sad affect: An information-processing perspective. In J. Garber and K. Dodge. *The Development of Emotion Regulation and Dysregulation* (pp. 208–238). New York: Cambridge University Press.

Garnefski, N., Kraaij, V., and Spinhoven, P. (2001). Negative life events, cognitive emotion regulation and emotional problems. *Personality and Individual Differences, 30(8)*, 1311–1327.

Garnefski, N., Teerds, J., Kraaij, V., Legerstee, J., and Kommer, T. van den (2004). Cognitive emotion regulation strategies and depressive symptoms: Differences between males and females. *Personality and Individual Differences, 36*, 267–276.

Garnefski, N., Kommer, T. van den, Kraaij, V., Teerds, J., Legerstee, J., and Onstein, E. (2002). The relationship between cognitive emotion regulation strategies and emotional problems: Comparison between a clinical and a non-clinical sample. *European Journal of Personality, 16(5)*, 403–420.

Garner, P. W. (1999). Continuity in emotion knowledge from preschool to middle-childhood and relation to emotion socialization. *Motivation and Emotion, 23(4)*, 247–266.

Garrison Institute Report (2005). *Contemplation and education: Current status of programs using contemplative techniques in K-12 educational settings. A mapping report*. Garrison, NY. Retrieved October 29, 2006, from, http://projectrenewal-tidescenter.org/pdfs/contemplation.pdf

Garside, R.B., and Klimes-Dougan, B. (2002). Socialization of discrete negative emotions: Gender differences and links with psychological distress. *Sex Roles, 47(3–4)*, 115–128.

Gaylord, V., Quinn, M., McComas, J., and Lehr, C. (Eds.) (2005). *Impact: Feature Issue on Fostering Success in School and Beyond for Students with Emotional/Behavioral Disorders 18*(2). Minneapolis: University of Minnesota, Institute on Community Integration.

Gazelle, H. (2006). Class climate moderates peer relations and emotional adjustment in children with an early history of anxious solitude: A child X environment model. *Developmental Psychology, 42(6)*, 1179–1192.

Gillham, J. E., Reivich, K. J., Freres, D. R., Lascher, M., Litzinger, S., Shatté, A. et al. (2006). School-based prevention of depression and anxiety symptoms in early adolescence: A pilot of a parent intervention component. *School Psychology Quarterly, 21(3)*, 323–348.

Gillham, J. E ., Reivich, K. J., Jaycox, L. H., and Seligman, M. E. P. (1995). Preventing depressive symptoms in school children: Two year follow-up. *Psychological Science, 6*, 343–351.

Gimpel, G. A., and Holland, M. L. (2003). *Emotional and Behavioral Problems of Young Children*. New York: The Guilford Press.

Gioia, G. A., and Isquith, P. K. (2004) Ecological assessment of executive function in traumatic brain injury. *Developmental Neuropsychology, 25*, 135–158.

Gioia, G. A., Isquith, P. K., Guy, S. C., and Kenworthy, L. (2000). *Behavior Rating Inventory of Executive Functions*. Odessa, FL: Psychological Assessment Resources.

Gioia, G. A., Isquith, P. K., Retzlaff, P. D., and Espy, K. A. (2002). Confirmatory factor analysis of the Behavior Rating Inventory of Executive Function (BRIEF) in a clinical sample. *Child Neuropsychology, 8(4)*, 249–257.

Giota, J. (2006). Why am I in school? Relationships between adolescents' goal orientation, academic achievement and self-evaluation. *Scandinavian Journal of Educational Research, 50(4)*, 441–461.

Gjone, H., and Stevenson, J. (1997). The association between internalizing and externalizing behavior in childhood and early adolescence: Genetic or environmental common influences? *Journal of Abnormal Child Psychology, 25(4)*, 277–286.

Goetz, T., Pekrun, R., Hall, N., and Haag. L. (2006). Academic emotions from a social-cognitive perspective: Antecedents and domain specificity on students' affect in the context of Latin instruction. *British Journal of Educational Psychology, 76(Pt. 2)*, 289–308.

Goldsmith, H. H., and Rothbart, M. K. (1991) Contemporary instruments for assessing early temperament by questionnaire and in the laboratory. In A. Angleitner and J. Strelau (Eds.), *Explorations in Temperament: International Perspectives on Theory and Measurement* (pp. 249–271). New York: Plenum.

Goldstein, A. P. (1999). *The PREPARE Curriculum: Teaching Prosocial Competencies* (Rev. Ed.). Champaign, IL: Research Press.

Goldstein, A. P., and Glick, B. (1987). *Aggression Replacement Training: A Comprehensive Intervention for Aggressive Youth*. Champaign, IL: Research Press.

Goldstein, S., and Brooks, R. B. (2005). Why study resilience? In S. Goldstein and R. B. Brooks, *Handbook of Resilience in Children* (pp. 3–15). New York: Springer Science + Business Media, Inc.

Goleman, D. (2006). The socially intelligent leader. *Educational Leadership, 64(1)*, 76–81.

Good, C. & Dweck, C. (2003a). *How teachers inadvertently send messages about the nature of intelligence*. Unpublished manuscript, Columbia University.

Good, C. & Dweck, C. (2003b). *The effects of stereotypes and fixed-views of intelligence on students' sense of belonging to math*. Unpublished manuscript, Columbia University.

Goodenow, C. (1993) Classroom belonging among early adolescent students: Relationships to motivation and achievement. *The Journal of Early Adolescence, 13(1)*, 21–43.

Goodvin, R., and Torquati, J. (2006). The role of child emotional responsiveness and maternal negative emotion expression in children's coping strategy use. *Social Development, 15(4)*, 591–611.

Gosch, E. A., Flannery-Schroeder, E., Mauro, C. F., and Compton, S. N. (2006). Principles of cognitive-behavioral therapy for anxiety disorders in children. *Journal of Cognitive Psychotherapy: An International Quarterly, 20(3)*, 247–262.

Gray, C. (1993). Social stories: Improving responses of students with autism with accurate social information. *Focus on Autistic Behavior, 8*, 1–10.

Gray, C. (1995a). *Social Stories and Comic Strip Conversations: Unique Methods to Improve Social Understanding*. Jenison, MI: Jenison Public Schools.

Gray, C. (1995b). *Social Stories Unlimited: Social Stories and Comic Strip Conversations.* Jenison, MI: Jenison Public Schools.

Gray, C. (1996a). Social assistance. In A. Fullerton (Ed.), *Higher Functioning Adolescents and Young People with Autism* (pp. 71–89). Austin, TX: Pro Ed Inc.

Gray, C. (1996b). Teaching children with autism to "read" social situations. In K. Quill (Ed.), *Teaching Students with Autism: Methods to Enhance Learning, Communication, and Socialization* (pp. 219–242). New York: Delmar Publishers.

Greenberg, L. (2006). Emotion-focused therapy: A synopsis. *Journal of Contemporary Psychotherapy, 36(2)*, 87–93.

Greenberg, M. T., Kusché, C., and Mihalic, S. F. (1998). *Blueprints for Violence Prevention, Book Ten: Promoting Alternative Thinking Strategies (PATHS).* Boulder, CO: Center for the Study and Prevention of Violence.

Greenberg, M. T., Kusché, C. A., and Riggs, N. (2001). The P(romoting) A(lternative) TH(inking)S(trategies) curriculum theory and research on neurocognitive and academic development. *The CEIC Review, 10(6)*, 22–23, 26.

Gresham, F., Sugai, G., and Horner, R. (2001). Interpreting outcomes of social skills training for students with high-incidence disabilities. *The Council for Exceptional Children, 67(3)*, 331–344.

Gross, J. J. (1998a). Sharpening the focus: Emotion regulation, arousal, and social competence. *Psychological Inquiry, 9(4)*, 287–290.

Gross, J. J. (1998b). The emerging field of emotion regulation: An integrative review. *Review of General Psychology, 2(3)*, 271–299.

Gross, J. J. (2002). Emotion regulation: Affective, cognitive, and social consequences. *Psychophysiology, 39(3)*, Development of an anxiety hierarchy, pp. 281–291.

Gross, J. J., and John, O. P. (2003). Individual differences in two emotion regulation processes: Implications for affect, relationships, and well-being. *Journal of Personality and Social Psychology, 85*, 348–362.

Gross, J. J., Richards, J. M., and John, O. P. (2006). Emotion regulation in everyday life. In D. K. Snyder, J. A. Simpson, and J. N. Hughes (Eds.), *Emotion Regulation in Families: Pathways to Dysfunction and Health.* Washington, DC: American Psychological Association.

Gross, J. J., and Thompson, R. A. (2007). Emotion regulation: Conceptual foundations. In: J. J. Gross (Ed.), *Handbook of Emotion Regulation* (pp. 3–26). New York: Guilford Press.

Gumora, G., and Arsenio, W. F. (2002). Emotionality, emotion regulation, and school performance in middle school children. *Journal of School Psychology, 40(5)*, 395–413.

Guyer, A. E., Nelson, E. E., Perez-Edgar, K., Hardin, M. G., Roberson-Nay, R., Monk, C. S. et al. (2006). Striatal functional alteration in adolescents characterized by early childhood behavioral inhibition. *Journal of Neuroscience, 26(24)*, 6399–6405.

Hagekull, B., and Bohlin, G. (2004). Predictors of middle childhood psychosomatic problems: An emotion regulation approach. *Infant and Child Development, 13(5)*, 389–405.

Hair, E. C., Jager, J., and Garrett, S. (2001). *Background for community-level work on social competency in adolescence: Reviewing the literature on contributing factors.* Prepared for the John S. and James L. Knight Foundation. Retrieved January 2, 2007, from http://www.childtrends.org/what_works/youth_development/social_comp/t12whatworks3.asp

Hampel, P., and Petermann, F. (2005). Age and gender effects on coping in children and adolescents. *Journal of Youth and Adolescence, 34(2)*, 73–83.

Hamre, B., and Pianta R. (2005). Can instructional and emotional support in the first-grade classroom make a difference for children at risk of school failure? *Child Development, 76(5)*, 949–967.

Hargreaves, A. (2000). Mixed emotions: Teacher's perceptions of their interactions with students. *Teaching and Teacher Education, 16*, 811–826.

Hariri, A. R., and Holmes, A. (2006). Genetics of emotional regulation: The role of the serotonin transporter in neural function. *TRENDS in Cognitive Sciences, 10(4)*, 182–191.

Harned, M. S., Banawan, S. F., and Lynch, T. R. (2006). Dialectical behavior therapy: An emotion-focused treatment for Borderline Personality Disorder. *Journal of Contemporary Psychotherapy, 36(2)*, 67–76.

Harrington, D. (2005). "I'm mad at you!" Why even the nicest kids get angry- and how to know what's normal, what's not. *Parenting*, 146–148.

Harris, P. L. (2000) Understanding emotion. In M. Lewis and J. M. Haviland (Eds.), *Handbook of Emotions* (2nd Ed.) (pp. 281–292). New York: Guilford Press.

Hawkins, J. D., Catalano, R. F., Morrison, D. M., O'Donnell, J., Abbott, R. D., and Day, L. E. (1992). The Seattle Social Development Project: Effects of the first four years on protective factors and problem behaviors. In J. McCord and R. Tremblay (Eds.), *The Prevention of Antisocial Behavior in Children* (pp. 139–161). New York: Guilford Publications.

Hawkins, J. D., Smith, B. H., and Catalano, R. F. (2001). Social development and social and emotional learning: The Seattle Social Development Project. *The CEIC Review, 10(6)*, 18–19, 27.

Hayes, S. C., Luoma, J., Bond, F., Masuda, A., and Lillis, J. (2006). Acceptance and Commitment Therapy: Model, processes, and outcomes. *Behaviour Research and Therapy, 44*, 1–25.

Heffner, M., Greco, L. A., and Eifert, G. H. (2003). Pretend you are a turtle: Children's responses to metaphorical versus literal relaxation instructions. *Child and Family Behavior Therapy, 25(1)*, 19–35.

Helms, B. J., and Gable, R. K. (1989) *School Situation Survey: Manual*. Palo Alto: Consulting Psychologists Press.

Herman, K. C., Merrell, K. W., Reinke, W. M., and Tucker, C. M. (2004). The roles of school psychology in preventing depression. *Psychology in the Schools, 41(7)*, 763–775.

Hill. L. G., and Werner, N. E. (2006). Affiliative motivation, school attachment, and aggression in school. *Psychology in the Schools, 43(2)*, 231–246.

Hoeksma, J., Oosterlaan, J., and Shipper, E. (2004). Emotion regulation and the dynamics of feelings: A conceptual and methodological framework. *Child Development, 75(2)*, 354–360.

Hogan, E. K. (2003). Anger management 3: Structured programs and interventions. *ERIC Digest* (ED482768). ERIC Clearinghouse on Counseling and Student Services. Retrieved January 24, 2007, from http://www.ericdigests.org/2004-3/anger-3.html

Holahan, C. J., and Moos, R. H. (1987). Risk, resistance, and psychological distress: A longitudinal analysis with adults and children. *Journal of Abnormal Psychology, 96*, 3–13.

Holloway, J. D. (2003) Advances in anger management. *Monitor on Psychology, 34(3)*, p. 54. Retrieved March 4, 2006, from http://www.apa.org/monitor/mar03/advances.html

Holodynski M., and Friedlmeier, W. (2006) *Development of emotions and emotion regulation*. Springer Science + Business Media, Inc.

Howes, C. (2000). Social-emotional classroom climate in child care, child-teacher relationships and children's second grade peer relations. *Social Development, 9(2)*, 191–204.

Hromek, R. (2004). Emotional coaching: Featuring emotional first aid and the Life Space Interview. Paper presented at the National Conference of the Australian Association of Special Education. Retrieved November 5, 2006, from http://www.aase.edu.au/2005_AASE_2004_Nat_Conf_Papers.htm

Huan, U. S., Yeo, L. S., Ang R. P., and Chong, W. H. (2006). The influence of dispositional optimism and gender on adolescents perception of academic stress. *Adolescence, 41(163)*, 533–546.

Hubbard, J. A., and Coie, J. D. (1994). Emotional correlates of social competence in children's peer relationships. *Merrill-Palmer Quarterly, 40(11)*, 1–20.

Hughes, J. N., and Cavell, T. A. (1999). Influence of the teacher-student relationship in childhood conduct problems: A prospective study. *Journal of Clinical Child Psychology, 28(2)*, 173–184.

Huizinga, M., Dolan, C., and Molen, M. van der (2006). Age-related change in executive function: Developmental trends and a latent variable analysis. *Neuropsychologia, 44(11)*, 2017–2036.

Hunter, S. C., and Boyle, J. M. E. (2004). Coping and appraisal in victims of school bullying. *British Journal of Educational Psychology, 74(1)*, 83–107.

Hunter, S. C., Boyle, J. M., and Warden, D. (2004). Help seeking amongst child and adolescent victims of peer-aggression and bullying: The influence of school-stage, gender, victimisation, appraisal, and emotion. *British Journal of Educational Psychology, 74(Pt 3)*, 375–390.

Hutchins, T. L., and Prelock, P. A. (2006). Using social stories and comic strip conversations to promote socially valid outcomes for children with autism. *Seminars in Speech and Language, 27*, 47–59.

Huttenlocher, P. R. (1990). Morphometric study of human cerebral cortex development. *Neuropsychologia, 28(6)*, 517–527.

Jahnke, K. (1998, April). Anger management programs for children and teens: A review of eleven anger management programs. Paper presented at the Annual Meeting of the National Association of School Psychologists, Orlando.

Jellinek, M. S., Murphy, J. M., Little, M., Pagano, M. E., Comer, D. M., and Kelleher, K. J. (1999). Use of the Pediatric Symptom Checklist to screen for psychosocial problems in pediatric primary care: A national feasibility study. Archives of Pediatric & Adolescent Medicine, *153(3)*, 254–260.

John, O. P., and Gross, J. A. (2004). Healthy and unhealthy emotion regulation: Personality Processes, individual differences, and life span development. *Journal of Personality, 72(6)*, 1301–1334.

Joiner, T. E., Schmidt, N. B., Schmidt, K. L., Laurent, J., Catanzaro, S. J., Perez, M., and Pettit, J. W. (2002). Anxiety sensitivity as a specific and unique marker of anxious symptoms in youth psychiatric inpatients. *Journal of Abnormal Child Psychology, 30(2)*, 167–175.

Jones, S., Eisenberg, N., Fabes, R. A., and MacKinnon, D. P. (2002). Parents' reactions to elementary school children's negative emotions: Relations to social and emotional functioning at school. *Merrill-Palmer Quarterly, 48(2)*, 133–159.

Jorm, A. F., Allen, N. B., O'Donnell, C. P., Parslow, R. A., Purcell. R., and Morgan, A. J. (2006). Effectiveness of complementary and self-help treatments for depression in children and adolescents. *The Medical Journal of Australia, 185(7)*, 368–372.

Joseph, G., and Strain, P. (2003a). Comprehensive evidence-based social–emotional curricula for young children: An analysis of efficacious adoption potential. *TECSE, 23(2)*, 65–76.

Joseph, G., and Strain. P. (Revised 11/03b). Enhancing emotional vocabulary in young children. The Center on the Social and Emotional Foundations for Early Learning, Module 2, Handout 2.4 Social Emotional Teaching Strategies. Retrieved February 14, 2006, from http://csefel.uiuc.edu/modules/module2/handouts/4.pdf

Joseph, G., and Strain, P. (revised 11/03c). Helping children control anger and handle disappointment. Center on the Social and Emotional Foundations for Early Learning. Training Modules. Module 2: Handout 2.6. Retrieved January 1, 2006, from http://www.csefel.uiuc.edu/modules/module2/handouts/6.html - 32k

Kagan, J. (1994). *Galen's Prophecy: Temperament in Human Nature*. New York: Basic Books.

Kagan, J., and Snidman, N. (2004). *The Long Shadow of Temperament*. Boston: The Belknap Press of Harvard University Press.

Kalpidou, M. D., Power, T. G., Cherry, K. E., and Gottfried, N. W. (2004). Regulation of emotion and behavior among 3- and 5-year-olds. *Journal of General Psychology, 131(2)*, 159–178.

Kariv, D., and Heiman. T. (2005). Task-oriented versus emotion-oriented coping strategies: The case of college students. *College Student Journal*. Retrieved October 22, 2006, from http://www.findarticles.com/p/articles/mi_m0FCR/is_1_39/ai_n13603935

Kashdan, T. B., Barrios, V., Forsyth, J. P., and Steger, M. F. (2006). Experiential avoidance as a generalized psychological vulnerability: Comparisons with coping and emotion regulation strategies. *Behaviour Research and Therapy, 44(9)*, 1301–1320.

Kaswer, C. H. (2005). Series on Highly Effective Practices—Social Problem Solving. (7. Teaching Social Problem Solving to Students). Old Dominion University, The Department of Early Childhood, Speech-Language Pathology and Special Education. Retrieved January 12, 2007, fromhttp://education.odu.edu/esse/research/series/social.shtml

Katz, L. F., and Windecker-Nelson, B. (2004). Parental meta-emotion philosophy in families with conduct-problem children: Links with peer relations. *Journal of Abnormal Child Psychology, 14*, 385–398.

Katz, L. F., and Windecker-Nelson, B. (2006). Domestic violence, emotion coaching, and child adjustment. *Journal of Family Psychology, 20*, 56–67.

Kavushansky A., Vouimba, R. M., Cohen, H., and Richter-Levin, G. (2006). Activity and plasticity in the CA1, the dentate gyrus, and the amygdala following controllable vs. uncontrollable water stress. *Hippocampus, 16(1)*, 35–42.

Kazdin, A., interviewed by Souter, C. R. (May 2006). Insights offered on parent management training. *New England Psychologist, 14(4)*, p. 3.

Keith, P. B., and Christensen, S. L. (1997). Parenting Styles. In G. G. Bear, K. M. Minke and A. Thomas (Eds.), *Children's Needs II: Development, Problems and Alternatives* (pp. 559–574). Bethesda, MD: National Association of School Psychologists.

Kelley, G. (1955). *The Psychology of Personal Constructs*. New York: Norton.

Kellner, M. (1999). Children can learn to manage anger. *Behavioral Healthcare, Inc.* Retrieved September 2004, from http://www.healthlinks.net/archieve/mill1.htm

Kellner, M. H., and Tutin, J. (1995). A school-based anger management program for developmentally and emotionally disabled high school students, in adolescence. *Adolescence, 30(120)*, 813–825.

Kempes, M., Matthys, W., de Vries, H., and Engeland, H. van (2005). Reactive and proactive aggression in children: A review of theory, findings and the relevance for child and adolescent psychiatry. *European Child & Adolescent Psychiatry, 14(10)*, 11–19.

Kendall, P. (1994). *Coping Cat Workbook and Notebook*. Ardmore, PA: Workbook Publishing.

Kendall, P.C. (2000). *Cognitive-Behavioral Therapy for Anxious Children, Therapist Manual*, 2nd Ed.. Ardmore, PA: Workbook Publishing.

Kendall, P., and Southam-Gerow, M. (1996). Long-term follow up of a cognitive behavioural therapy for anxiety disordered youth. *Journal of Consulting and Clinical Psychology, 64*, 724–730.

Kernberg, P., Weiner, A., and Bardenstein, K. (2000). *Personality Disorders in Children and Adolescents*. New York: Basic Books.

Kerr, S., and Durkin, K. (2004). Understanding of thought bubbles as mental representations in children with autism: Implications for theory of mind. *Journal of Autism and Developmental Disorders, 34(6)*, 637–648.

Keyes, A. W. (2004). The enhanced effectiveness of parent education with an emotion socialization component. A Dissertation Submitted to the Graduate Faculty of the University of New Orleans in partial fulfillment of the requirements for the degree of Doctor of Philosophy in Applied Developmental Psychology. Retrieved January 25, 2007, from http://etd-db.uno.edu/theses/available/etd-12032004-143128/unrestricted/2004_PhD_keyes_angela.pdf.

King, N., Cranstoun, F., and Josephs, A. (1989). Emotive imagery and children's night-time fears: A multiple baseline design evaluation. *Journal of Behavior Therapy and Experimental Psychiatry, 20(2)*, 125–135.

King, N. J., Heyne, D., Gullone, E., and Molloy, G. N. (2001). Usefulness of emotive imagery in the treatment of childhood phobias: Clinical guidelines, case examples and issues. *Counseling Psychology Quarterly, 14(2)*, 95–101.

Kleinke, C. L., Peterson, T. R., and Rutledge, T.R. (1998). Effects of self-generated facial expressions on mood. *Journal of Personality and Social Psychology, 74*, 272–279.

Koch, E. (2003). Reflections on a study of temper tantrums in older children. *Psychoanalytic Psychology, 20*, 456–471.

Kochanska, G., and Aksan, N. (2004). Conscience in childhood: Past, present, and future. *Merrill Palmer Quarterly, 50*, 299–310.

Kochenderfer-Ladd, B. (2004). Peer victimization: The role of emotions in adaptive and maladaptive coping. *Social Development, 13*, 329–249.

Knoll, M., and Patti, J. (2003). Social-emotional learning and academic achievement. In M. J. Elias, H. Arnold and C. S. Hussey (Eds.), *EQ + IQ = Best Leadership Practices for Caring and Successful Schools* (p. 133). Thousand Oaks, CA: Corwin Press, Inc.

Knox, S. S., McHale, S. M., and Windon, C. P. (2004, October). (Co-chairs) National Children's Study Workshop: Measuring Parenting from an Epidemiological Perspective. Washington, DC.

Kostiuk, L. M., and Fouts, G. T. (2002). Understanding of emotions and emotion regulation in adolescent females with conduct problems. *The Qualitative Report, 7(1)*, Retrieved August 30, 2005, from http://www.nove.edu/ssss/QR/QR7-1/kistiuk.html

Kovacs, M., Sherrill, J., George, C. J., Pollock, M., Tumuluru, R. V., and Ho, V. (2006). Contextual emotion-regulation therapy for childhood depression: Description and pilot testing of a new intervention. *Journal of the American Academy of Child & Adolescent Psychiatry, 45(8)*, 892–903.

Kruczek, T., and Salsman, J. (2006). Prevention and treatment of posttraumatic stress disorder in the school setting. *Psychology in the Schools, 43(4)*, 461–470.

Ladouceur, C. D., Dahl, R. E., Williamson, D. E., Birmaher, B., Ryan, N. D., and Casey, B. J. (2005). Altered emotional processing in pediatric anxiety, depression, and comorbid anxiety-depression. *Journal of Abnormal Child Psychology, 33(2)*, 165–177.

Lagattuta, K. H., and Wellman, H. M. (2002). Differences in early parent-child conversations about negative versus positive emotions: Implications for the development of psychological understanding. *Developmental Psychology, 38*, 564–580.

Laible, D. J. (2004). Mother-child discourse surrounding a child's past behavior at 30 months: Links to emotional understanding and early conscience development at 36 months. *Merrill-Palmer Quarterly, 50*, 159–180.

Lakes, K. D., and Hoyt, W. T. (2004). Promoting self-regulation through school-based martial arts training. *Journal of Applied Developmental Psychology, 25(3)*, 283–302.

Lance, J. (2003). *Emotional regulation*. Retrieved February 25, 2005 from http://www.therapyinla.com/articles/article0903.html

Lane, K. L., Pierson, M. R., and Givner, C. C. (2004). Secondary teacher's views on social competence: Skills essential for success. *The Journal of Special Education, 38(3)*, 174–186.

Lane, R., and McRae, K. (2004). Neural substrates of conscious emotional experience: A cognitive neuroscientific perspective. In M. Beauregard, *Consciousness, Emotional Self-regulation and the Brain* (pp. 87–122). Philadelphia: John Benjamins Publishing Company.

Larson, J. D. (1992). Anger and aggression management techniques through the Think First Curriculum. *Journal of Offender Rehabilitation, 18(1/2)*, 101–118.

Lavoie, R. (2005) *It's So Much Work to be Your Friend: Helping the Child with Learning Disabilities Find Social Success*. NY: Simon and Schuster.

Law, B. M. (2005). Probing the depression-rumination cycle: Why chewing on problems just makes them harder to swallow. *Monitor on Psychology, 36(10)*. Retrieved May 5, 2007, from http://www.apa.org/monitor/nov05/cycle.html

Leahy, R. L., and Holland, S. J. (2000). *Treatment Plans and Interventions for Depression and Anxiety Disorders*. New York: The Guilford Press, pp. 89–91.

Leary, A., and Katz, L. (2005). Observations of aggressive children during peer provocation and with a best friend. *Developmental Psychology, 41(1)*, 124–134.

Lee, S. M., Daniels, M. H., and Kissinger, D. B. (2006). Parental influences on adolescent adjustment: Parenting styles versus parenting practices. *The Family Journal, 14(3)*, 253–259.

Leffert, J., and Siperstein, G. (2003). A focus on social skills instruction for students with learning disabilities. *Current Practice Alerts, 9.* Retrieved January 9, 2006, from http://www.didcec.org/alert9_03.pdf

Lengua, L. J., and Kovacs, E. A. (2005). Bidirectional associations between temperament and parenting and the prediction of adjustment problems in middle childhood. *Journal of Applied Developmental Psychology, 26(1)*, 21–38.

Lengua, L. J., Sandler, I. N., West, S. G., Wolchik, S. A., and Curran, P. J. (1999). Emotionality and self-regulation, threat appraisal and coping in children of divorce. *Development and Psychopathology, 11*, 15–37.

Leventhal, A. (2003). Reactions to Segal, Williams, and Teasdale's mindfulness-based cognitive therapy for depression. *Psychotherapy Bulletin, 18(2)*, 27–28.

Lévesque, J., Eugène, F., Joanette, Y., Paquette, V. Mensour, B. Beaudoin, G. et al. (2003). Neural circuitry underlying voluntary suppression of sadness. *Biological Psychiatry, 53*, 502–510.

Lévesque, J., Joanette, Y, Mensour, B., Beaudoin, F., Leroux, J. M., Bourgouin, R. et al. (2004). Neural basis of emotional self-regulation in childhood. *Neuroscience, 129*, 361–369.

Levine, J. (2005). Getting in good. In R. Lavoie, *It's So Much Work to be Your Friend: Helping the Child with Learning Disabilities Find Social Success.* New York: Simon & Schuster.

Lewis, M. D., and Stieben, J (2004) Emotion regulation in the brain: Conceptual issues and directions for developmental research. *Child Development, 75(2)*, 371–376.

Linnenbrink, E. A. (2006). Emotion research in education: Theoretical and methodological perspectives on the integration of affect, motivation, and cognition. *Educational Psychology Review, 18(4)*, 307–314.

Livneh. H. (2000). Psychosocial adaptation to cancer: The role of coping strategies. *Journal of Rehabilitation.* Retrieved October 20, 2006, from http://www.findarticles.com/p/articles/mi_m0825/is_2_66/ai_62980227

Lochman, J. E. (1992). Cognitive-behavioral intervention with aggressive boys: Three-year follow-up and preventive effects. *Journal of Consulting and Clinical Psychology, 60(3)*, 426–432.

Lochman, J. E., Dunn, S. E., and Wagner, E. E. (1997). Anger. In G. Bear, K. Minke and A. Thomas (Eds.), *Children's Needs II: Development, Problems and Alternatives* (pp. 149–160). Bethesda, MD: National Association of School Psychologists.

Locker, J., and Cropley, M. (2004). Anxiety, depression and self-esteem in secondary school children: An investigation into the impact of standard assessment tests (SATs) and other important school examinations. *School Psychology International, 25(3)*, 333–345.

Lopez, D. F., Little, T. D., Oettingen, G., and Baltes, P. B. (1998). Self-regulation and school performance: Is there an optimal level of action-control? *Journal of Experimental Child Psychology 70*, 54–74.

Loveland, K. A. (2005). Social-emotional impairment and self–regulation in autism spectrum disorders. In: D. M. Nadel and D. Muir (Eds.), *Emotional Development: Recent Research Advances* NY: Oxford University Press, pp. 365–384.

Lubit, R., Rovine, D., Defrancisci, L., and Spencer, E. (2003). Impact of trauma on children. *Journal of Psychiatric Practice, 9(2)*,128–138.

Lunkenheimer, E. S., Shields, A. M., and Cortina, K. S. (2007). Parental emotion coaching and dismissing in family interaction social development. *Social Development, 16(2)*, 232–248.

Lyubomirsky, S., Kasri, F., and Zehm, K. (2003). Dysphoric rumination impairs concentration on academic tasks. *Cognitive Therapy and Research, 27(3)*, 309–330.

Maccoby, E. E., and Martin, J. A. (1983). Socialization in the context of the family: Parent–child interaction. In P. H. Mussen (Ed.) and E. M. Hetherington (Vol. Ed.), *Handbook of Child Psychology: Vol. 4. Socialization, Personality, and Social Development* (4th Ed.) (pp. 1–101). New York: Wiley.

Macklem, G. L. (2003). *Bullying and Teasing: Social Power in Children's Groups*. Boston: Kluwer Academic/Plenus Publishers, pp. 75–83.

Macklem, G. L. (2006a). Strengthening the effect of social skills training. *Massachusetts School Psychologists Association Newsletter, 25(1)*, 1–2, 4, 6.

Macklem, G. (2006b). Technology 101: Safety, security, profession responsibility and common sense. Paper presented at Massachusetts School Psychologists Association Fall Conference, Woburn, MA.

Macklem, G. L., and Pluymert, K. (1998). Developing a parenting skills workshop: A menu of ideas for school psychologists. *Communiqué, 27(1)*, Insert, 2–4.

MacPhee, A. R., and Andrews, J. J. (2006). Risk factors for depression in early adolescence. *Adolescence, 41(163)*, 435–466.

Maedgen, J. W., and Carlson, C. L. (2000). Social functioning and emotional regulation in the Attention Deficit Hyperactivity Disorder subtypes. *Journal of Clinical Child Psychology, 29(1)*, 30–42.

Mamorstein, N. R. (2007). Relationships between anxiety and externalizing disorders in youth: The influences of age and gender. *Journal of Anxiety Disorders, 21(3)*, 420–432.

Marion, M. (1997). Helping young children deal with anger. (EDO-PS-97-24) *ERIC Digest* (Online). Retrieved October 10, 2004, from http://ericeece.org/pubs/digests/1997/marion97.html

Marsiglia, C. S., Walczyk, J. J., Buboltz, W. C., and Griffith-Ross, D. A. (2006). Impact of parenting styles and locus of control on emerging adults' psychosocial success. *Journal of Educational and Human Development, 1(1)*. Retrieved January 11, 2007, from http://www.scientificjournals.org/articles/1031.htm

Martell, C. R., Safren, S. A., and Prince, S. E. (2004). Cognitive-behavioral therapies with lesbian, gay and bisexual clients (p. 96). New York: Guilford Press.

Martin, K. (2003). Substance-abusing adolescents show ethnic and gender differences in psychiatric disorders. *NADA Notes, 18(1)*. Retrieved February 11, 2007, from http://www.nida.nih.gov/NIDA_Notes/NNVol18N1/Substance.html

Martin, R. P., and Bridger, R. C. (1999). Temperament assessment battery for children-revised: A tool for the assessment of temperamental traits and types of young children. Unpublished.

Masia-Warner, C., Fisher, P. H., Shrout, P. E., Rathor, S., and Klein, R. G. (2007, Mar. 21). Treating adolescents with social anxiety disorder in school: an attention control trial. *Journal of Child Psychology and Psychiatry*. Online Early Articles. doi:10.1111/j.1469-7610.2007.01737.x

Masten, A. S., and Coatsworth, J. D. (1998). The development of competence in favorable and unfavorable environments: Lessons from research on successful children. *American Psychologist, 53*, 205–220.

Masters, J. (1991). Strategies and mechanisms for the personal and social control of emotion. In J. Garber and K. Dodge (Eds.), *The Development of Emotion Regulation and Dysregulation* (pp. 182–205). New York: Cambridge University Press.

Masters, J. C., Ford, M. E., and Arend, R. A.(2005). Children's strategies for controlling affective responses to aversive social experience. *Motivation and Emotion, 7(1)*, 103–116.

Matheson, K., and Anisman, H. (2003). Systems of coping associated with dysphoria, anxiety, and depressive illness: A multivariate profile perspective. *Stress, 6(3)*, 223–234.

Mathur, S. R., Kavale, K. A., Quinn, M. M., Forness, S. R., and Rutherford, R. B. (1998). Social skills interventions with students with emotional and behavioral problems: A quantitative synthesis of single-subject research. *Behavioral Disorders, 23*, 193–201.

Matsumoto, D. (2002). Culture, psychology, and education. In W. J. Lonner, D. L. Dinnel, S. A., Hayes and D. N. Sattler (Eds.), *Online Readings in Psychology and Culture* (http://www.wwu.edu/~culture), Center for Cross-Cultural Research, Western Washington University. Bellingham, Washington, (Unit 2, Chapter 5).

McCoy, C. L., and Masters, J. C. (1985). The development of children's strategies for the social control of emotion. *Child Development, 56(5)*, 1214–1222.

McCullough, M. E., Bono, G., and Root, L. M. (2007). Rumination, emotion, and forgiveness: Three longitudinal studies. *Journal of Personality and Social Psychology, 92(3)*, 490–505.

McDonald, A. S. (2001). The prevalence and effects of test anxiety in school children. *Educational Psychology*, 21(1), 89–101.

McEwen, B. S. (2003). Mood disorders and allostatic load. *Biological Psychiatry, 54(3)*, 200–2007.

McLoone, J., Hudson, J. L., and Rapee, R. M. (2006). Treating anxiety disorders in a school setting. *Education and Treatment of Children, 29(2)*, 219–242.

Mehrabian, A., and Falender, C. A. (1978) A questionnaire measure of individual differences in child stimulus screening. *Educational and Psychological Measurement, 38*, 1119–1127.

Melnick, S. H., and Hinshaw, S. P. (2000). Emotional regulation and parenting in AD/HD and comparison boys: Linkages with social behaviors and peer preference. *Journal of Abnormal Child Psychology, 28(1)*, 73–86.

Mendlowitz, S. L., Manassis, K., Bradley, S., Scapillato, D., Miezitis, S., and Shaw, B. (1999). Cognitive-behavioral group treatments in childhood anxiety disorders: The role of parental involvement. *Journal of the American Academy of Child & Adolescent Psychiatry, 38(10)*, 1223–1229.

Menesini, E. (Chair) (1999). Bullying and emotions. Report of the Working Party. The TMR Network Project. Nature and Prevention of Bullying: The causes and nature of bullying and social exclusion in schools, and ways of preventing them. Retrieved March 4, 2006, from http://www.gold.ac.uk/tmr/reports/aim2_firenze2.html

Mennin, D. S. (2001). Research interests. Retrieved January 5, 2006, from http://www.yale.edu/psychology/FacInfo/Mennin.html

Mennin, D. S. (2004). An emotion regulation treatment for generalized anxiety disorder. *Clinical Psychology and Psychotherapy, 11*, 17–29.

Mennin, D. S. (2006). Emotion regulation therapy: An integrative approach to treatment-resistant anxiety disorders. *Journal of Contemporary Psychotherapy, 36(2)*, 95–105.

Mennin, D. S., Heimberg, R. G., Turk, C. L., and Fresco, D. M. (2005). Preliminary evidence for an emotion regulation deficit model of generalized anxiety disorder. *Behaviour Research and Therapy, 43*, 1281–1310.

Merrell, K. W. (1999). *Behavioral, Social, and Emotional Assessment of Children and Adolescents*. Mahwah, NJ: Lawrence Erlbaum Associates.

Merrell, K. W. (2001). Assessment of children's social skills: Recent developments, best practices, and new directions. *Exceptionality, 9(1 and 2)*, 3–18.

Merrell, K. W. (2002). Social-emotional intervention in schools: Current status, progress, and promise. *School Psychology Review, 31*, 142–147.

Merrell, K. W., Carrizales, D., Feuerborn, L., Gueldner, B. A., and Tran, O. K. (2006a). *Strong Kids: A Social and Emotional Learning Curriculum for Students in Grades 4–8*. Oregon Resiliency Project, Eugene, OR.

Merrell, K. W., Carrizales, D., Feuerborn, L., Gueldner, B. A., and Tran, O. K. ((2006b). *Strong Teens: A Social and Emotional Learning Curriculum for Students in Grades 9-12*. Oregon Resiliency Project, Eugene, OR.

Meyer, D. K., and Turner, J. C. (2006). Re-conceptualizing emotion and motivation to learn in classroom contexts. *Educational Psychology Review, 18(4)*, 377–390.

Mezulis, A. H., Hyde, J. S., and Abramson, L. Y. (2006). The developmental origins of cognitive vulnerability to depression: Temperament, parenting, and negative life events in childhood as contributors to negative cognitive style. *Developmental Psychology, 42(6),* 1012–1025.

Mifsud, C. M., and Rapee, R. M. (2005). Early intervention for childhood anxiety in a school setting: Outcomes for an economically disadvantaged population. *Journal of the American Academy of Child & Adolescent Psychiatry. 44(10),* 996–1004.

Mihalic, S., Fagan, A., Irwin, K., Ballard, D., and Elliott, D. (2004). *Blueprints for violence prevention.* Center for the Study and Prevention of Violence, University of Colorado-Boulder, U.S. Department of Justice.

Miles, B., and Simpson, R. L. (2001). Effective practices for students with Asperger Syndrome. *Focus on Exceptional Children, 34(3),* 1–14.

Miller, A. L. (2002). Dialectical behavior therapy for inpatient and outpatient parasuicidal adolescents. *Adolescent Psychiatry.* Retrieved August 2005, from http://www.findarticles.com/p/articles/mi_qa3882/is_200201/ai_n9032694

Miller, A. L., and Olson, S. L. (2000). Emotional expressiveness during peer conflicts: A predictor of social maladjustment among high-risk preschoolers. *Journal of Abnormal Child Psychology, 28(4),* 339–352.

Miller, J., Williams, S., and McCoy, E. (2004). Using multimodal functional behavioral assessment to inform treatment selection for children with either emotional disturbance or social maladjustment. *Psychology in the Schools, 41(8),* 867–877.

Miller, S. R., Murry, V. M., and Brodym, G. H. (2005). Parents' problem solving with preadolescents and its association with social withdrawal at school: Considering parents' stress and child gender. *Fathering.* Retrieved May 21, 2007, from http://findarticles.com/p/articles/mi_m0PAV/is_2_3/ai_n14738218

Minner, Sam. (1990). Use of a self-recording procedure to decrease the time taken by behaviorally disordered students to walk to special classes. *Behavioral Disorders, 15(14),* 210–215.

Mirenda, P. (2001). Autism, augmentative communication, and assistive technology: What do we really know? *Focus on Autism and Other Developmental Disabilities, 16(3),* 141–159.

Mogensen, L. L. (2005). There is preliminary evidence (level 4) that social stories are effective in decreasing challenging behaviors and may improve social interaction skills in children with Autism Spectrum Disorders. Retrieved November 6, 2005, from http:www.otcats.com

Moorhead, G., and Griffin, R.W. (2004). *Organizational Behavior: Managing People and Organizations* (7th Ed.). Boston: Houghton Mifflin Company.

Morrison, G. M., Brown, M., D'Incau, B., O'Farrell, S. L., and Furlong, M. J. (2006). Understanding resilience in educational trajectories: Implications for protective possibilities. *Psychology in the Schools, 43,* 19–31.

Moser, A. (2006, October 28). Enabling young learners to manage anger-extending the DANGEROUS ANIMAL metaphor. KOTESOL 2006 International Conference. Sookmyung Women's University. Chonnam National University. Retrieved January 20, 2007, from http://members.aol.com/adrmoser/ManageAnger.doc

Muraven, M., and Baumeister, R. F. (2000) Self-regulation and depletion of limited resources: Does self-control resemble a muscle? *Psychological Bulletin, 126(2),* 247–259.

Muris. P. (2006). Relation of attention control and school performance in normal children. *Perceptual and Motor Skills, 102(1),* 78–80.

Murphy, W. P., and Quesal, R. W. (2002) Strategies for addressing bullying with the school-age child who stutters. *Seminars in Speech and Language, 23(3),* 205–212.

Myles, B. S., Trautman, M. L., and Schelvan, R. L. (2004). *The Hidden Curriculum: Practical Solutions for Understanding Unstated Rules in Social Situations* (pp. 5–14). Shawnee Mission, KS: Austism Asperger Publishing Co.

Nacewicz, B. M., Dalton, K. M., Johnstone, T., Long, M. T., McAuliff, E. M., and Oakes, T. R. (2006). Amygdala volume and nonverbal social impairment in adolescent and adult males with autism. *Archives of General Psychiatry, 63(12),* 1417–1428.

Nansel, T. R., Haynie, D. L., and Simons-Morton, B. G. (2003). The association of bullying and victimization with middle school adjustment. *Journal of Applied School Psychology, 19(2)*, 45–61.

Napoli, M. (2004) Mindfulness training for teachers: A pilot program. *Complementary Health Practice Review, 9(1)*, 31–42.

Napoli, M., Krech, P. R., and Holley, L. C. (2005) Mindfulness training for elementary school students. The Attention Academy. *Journal of Applied School Psychology, 21(1)*, 99–109.

NASP (1998) Mini-Series: Implications of temperament for the practice of school psychology. *School Psychology Review, 27(4)*. Retrieved February 26, 2006, fromhttp://www.nasponline.org/publications/sprsum274.html

NASP (2002). Coping with crisis: Helping children with special needs. Retrieved February 28, 2007, from www.nasponline.org/NEAT/specpop_general.html

National Institute of Mental Health Meeting Summary (2006, April 3–4). Developmental and translational models of emotion regulation and dysregulation: Links to childhood affective disorders. Bethesda, MD.

National Research Council and Institute of Medicine. (2000) From neurons to neighborhoods: The science of early childhood development. Committee on Integrating the Science of Early Childhood Development. In J. P. Shonkoff and D. A. Phillips (Eds.), *Board on Children, Youth, and Families, Commission on Behavioral and Social Sciences and Education*. Washington, DC: National Academy Press.

National Scientific Council on the Developing Child (2004). *Children's emotional development is built into the architecture of their brain: Working Paper No. 2*. Retrieved January 10, 2007, from http://www.developingchild.net/reports.shtml

Newman-Carlson, D., and Horne, A. M. (2004). Bully Busters: A psychoeducational intervention for reducing bullying behavior in middle school students. *Journal of Counseling and Development, 82*, 259–267.

Nezu, A. M., Nezu, C. M., and Lombardo, E. R. (2001a). Cognitive-behavior therapy for medically unexplained symptoms: A critical review of the treatment literature. *Behavior Therapy, 32*, 537–583.

Nezu, A. M., Nezu, C. M., and Lombardo, E. R. (2001b). Managing stress through problem solving. *Stress News, 13(3)*. Retrieved October 20, 2004, from http://www.isma.org.uk/stressnw/manstrprob.htm

NICHD (2006). Policy, the family, and human development. Retrieved March 6, 2007, from http://www.nichd.nih.gov/publications/pubs/council_dbsb_2003/sub5.cfm

NIMH (2006, December 4). Brain's fear center likely shrinks in autism's most severely socially impaired. Retrieved January 8 2007, from http://www.nimh.nih.gov/press/autismamygdala.cfm

Nolen-Hoeksema, S., and Jackson, B. (2001). Mediators of the gender difference in rumination. *Psychology of Women Quarterly, 25(1)*, 37–47.

Novaco, R. W. (1996). Anger treatment and its special challenges. *NCP Clinical Quarterly, 6(3)*. National Center for Post-Traumatic Stress Disorder. Retrieved September 10, 2005, from http://www.ncptsd.org/publicationscq/v6/n3/novaco.html?printable = yes

Oaten, M., and Cheng, K. (2006) Longitudinal gains in self-regulation from regular physical exercise. *British Journal of Health Psychology, 11(4)*, 717–773.

Ochiltree, G., and Moore, T. (2001) Best start for children: The evidence base underlying investment in the early years (children 0–8 years). Department of Human Services. The Centre for Community Child Health. Melbourne. Retrieved December 12, 2006, from http://www.beststart.vic.gov.au/docs/evidence_base_project_1002v1.2.pdf

Olivera, F. and Straus, S. G. (2004). Group-to-individual transfer of learning. *Small Group Research, 35(4)*, 440–465.

Ollendick, T. H., King, N. J., and Yule, W. (1994). *International Handbook of Phobic and Anxiety Disorders in Children and Adolescents* (pp. 99–100). New York: Plenum Press.

Olweus, D. (1993). *Bullying at School: What We Know and What We Can Do*. Cambridge: Blackwell.

Olweus, D. (2004). The Olweus Bullying Prevention Programme: Design and implementation issues and a new national initiative in Norway. In P. K. Smith, D. Pepler and K. Rigby (Eds.), *Bullying in schools: How Successful Can Interventions Be?* (pp. 13–36). Cambridge, UK: Cambridge University Press.

Olweus, D., and Limber, S. (1999). Blueprints for violence prevention: Bullying Prevention Program. Institute of Behavioral Science, University of Colorado, Boulder, USA.

Olweus, D., Limber, S. P., and Mihalic, S. (1999). *The Bullying Prevention Program: Blueprints for Violence Prevention (Vol. 10)*. Center for the Study and Prevention of Violence, Boulder, CO.

Osher, D., Dwyer, K., and Jackson, S. (2004). *Safe, Supportive and Successful Schools: Step-by-Step*. Longmont, CO: Sopris West, pp. 132–133.

Oswald, D. P., and Mazefsky, C. A. (2006). Empirically supported psychotherapy interventions for internalizing disorders. *Psychology in the Schools, 43(4)*, 439–449.

Ott, J. (2002). Mindfulness meditation in pediatric clinical practice. *Pediatric Nursing*. Medscape. Retrieved April 12, 2006, from http://www.medscape.com/viewarticle/444209

Paluck, E. L., and Green, D. P. (2006). Anti-bias education and peer influence as two strategies to reduce prejudice: An impact evaluation of the Anti-Defamation League Peer Training Program. Retrieved January 21, 2007, from http://www.adl.org/awod_new/awod_peer_descr.asp

Papolos, J., and Papolos, D. (2005) Obsessional fears and aggressive behaviors in children and adolescents with Bipolar Disorder. *Bypolar Newsletter*. Retrieved August 22, 2006, from http://www.bipolarchild.com/newsletters/index.html

Paquette, V., Lévesque, J., Mensour, B., Leroux, J., Beaudoin, G., Bourgouin, P. et al. (2003). "Change the mind and you change the brain": Effects of cognitive-behavioral therapy on the neural correlates of spider phobia. *NeuroImage, 18*, 401–409.

Pardini, D., Lochman, J., and Wells, K. (2004). Negative emotions and alcohol use initiation in high-risk boys: The moderating effect of good inhibitory control. *Journal of Abnormal Child Psychology, 32(5)*, 505–518.

Park, R. D. (2004). Fathers, families and the future: A plethora of plausible predictions. *Merrill-Palmer Quarterly, 50(4)*, 456–470.

Park, R. J., Goodyer, I. M.,and Teasdale. J. D. (2004). Effects of induced rumination and distraction on mood and overgeneral autobiographical memory in adolescent Major Depressive Disorder and controls. *Journal of Child Psychology and Psychiatry, 45(5)*, 996–1006.

Parke, R. D., Simpkins, S. D., McDowell, D. J., Kim, M., Killian, K., Dennis, J. et al. (2002). Relative contributions of families and peers to children's social development. In P.K. Smith and C. H. Hart (Eds.), *Blackwell Handbook of Childhood Social Development* (pp. 156–177). Malden, MA: Blackwell Publishing.

Parsons, S., and Mitchell, P. (1999) What children with autism understand about thoughts and thought bubbles. *Autism, 3(1)*, 17–38.

Paul, J. J., and Cillessen, A. H. (2003). Dynamics of peer victimization in early adolescence: Results from a four-year longitudinal study. *Journal of Applied School Psychology, 19(2)*, 25–43.

Pecukonis, E. V. (1990). A cognitive/affective empathy training program as a function of ego development in aggressive adolescent females. *Adolescence, 25(97)*, 59–76.

Pekrun, R. (2006). The control-value theory of achievement emotions: Assumptions, corollaries, and implications for educational research and practice. *Educational Psychology Review, 18(4)*, 315–341.

Pekrun, R., Goetz, T., and Perry, R. P. (2005). *Achievement Emotions Questionnaire (AEQ)*. *User's manual*, Department of Psychology, University of Munich.

Pekrun, R., Goetz, T., Perry, R. P., Kramer, K., and Hochstadt, M. (2004). Beyond test anxiety: Development and validation of the Test Emotions Questionnaire (TEQ). *Anxiety, Stress and Coping,* , 287–316.

Pekrun, R., Goetz, T., Titz, W., and Perry, R. P. (2002). Academic emotions in students' self-regulated learning and achievement: A program of qualitative and quantitative research. *Educational Psychologist, 37(2),* 91–105.

Peled, M., and Moretti, M. M. (2007). Rumination on anger and sadness in adolescence: Fueling of fury and deepening of despair. *Journal of Clinical Child and Adolescent Psychology, 36(1),* 66–75.

Perry, K. E., and Weinstein, R. S. (1998). The social context of early schooling and children's school adjustment. *Educational Psychologist, 33,* 177–194.

Peterson, L. D., Young, K. R., Salzberg, C. L., West, R. P., and Hill, M. (2006). Using self-management procedures to improve classroom social skills in multiple general education settings. *Education and Treatment of Children, 29(1),* 1–21.

Pfaff, D. W. (2007). A brain built for fair play. In C. A. Read (Ed.), *Cerebrum 2007: Emerging Ideas in Brain Science* (pp. 41–53). New York: Dana Press.

Phillips, L. H., Henry, J. D., Hosie, J. A., and Milne, A. B. (2006). Age, anger regulation and well-being. *Aging and Mental Health, 10(3),* 250–256.

Pianta, R. C., Nimetz, S. L., and Bennett, E. (1997). Mother-child relationships, teacher-child relationships, and school outcomes in preschool and kindergarten. *Early Childhood Research Quarterly, 12(3),* 263–280.

Pierson, M. R., and Glaeser, B. C. (2005). Extension of research on social skills training using comic strip conversations to students without autism. *Education and Training in Mental Retardation and Developmental Disabilities, 40(3),* 279–284.

Pincus, D. B., and Friedman, A. G. (2004). Improving children's coping with everyday stress: transporting treatment interventions to the school setting. *Clinical Child and Family Psychology Review, 7(4),* 223–40.

Pons, F., and Harris, P. L. (2005). Longitudinal change and longitudinal stability of individual differences in children's emotion understanding. *Cognition and Emotion, 19(8),* 1158–1174.

Possell, L. E., and Abrams, K. (1993). Incorporating a brief social skills unit into the regular classroom setting. *School Psychology International, 14(2),* 149–158.

Potegal, M., and Davidson, R. J. (2003). Temper tantrums in young children: 1. Behavioral composition. *Developmental and Behavioral Pediatrics, 24(3),* 140–147.

Potegal, M., Kosorok, M. R., Richard, J., and Davidson, R. J. (2003). Temper tantrums in young children: 2. Tantrum duration and temporal organization. *Developmental and Behavioral Pediatrics, 24(3),* 148–154.

Pountain, D., and Robins, D. (2000). *Cool Rules: Anatomy of an Attitude.* London: Reaktion Books, pp. 113–132.

Powell, L. H., Shahabi, L., and Thoresen, C. E. (2003). Religion and spirituality: Linkages to physical health. *American Psychologist, 58(1),* 36–52.

Powers, M. B., Smits, J. A., Leyro, T. M., and Otto, M. W. (2006). Translational research perspectives on maximizing the effectiveness of exposure therapy. In D. C. Richard and D. Laurwebach (Eds.), *Handbook of Exposure Therapies* (pp. 109–126). Burlington, MA: Elsevier.

Printz, B. L., Shermis, M. D., and Webb, P. M. (1999). Stress-buffering factors related to adolescent coping: A path analysis. *Adolescence, 34,* 715–734.

Prizant, B. M., Wetherby, A. M., Rubin, R., and Laurent, A. C. (2003). The SCERTS Model: A transactional, family-centered approach to enhancing communication and socioemotional abilities of children with Autism Spectrum Disorder. *Infants and Young Children, 16(4),* 296–316.

Prizant, B. M., Wetherby, A. M., Rubin, E., Laurent, A. C., and Rydell, P. J. (2005). *The SCERTS™ Model: A Comprehensive Educational Approach for Children with Autism*

Spectrum Disorders. Retrieved September 26, 2006, from http://www.brookespublishing. com/store/books/prizant-8183/index.htm

Quakely, S., Coker, C., Palmer, K., and Reynolds, S. (2003). Can children distinguish between thoughts and behaviors? *Behavioural and Cognitive Psychotherapy, 31*, 159–168.

Ramsden, S. R., and Hubbard, J. A. (2002). Family expressiveness and parental emotion coaching: Their role in children's emotion regulation and aggression. *Journal of Abnormal Child Psychology, 30(6)*, 657–67.

Rassin, E. (2003). The White Bear Suppression Inventory (WBSI) focuses on failing suppression attempts. *European Journal of Personality, 17(4)*, 285–298.

Ratner, C. (2000). A cultural-psychological analysis of emotions. *Culture and Psychology, 6*, 5–39.

Raver, C. C. (2003). Young children's emotional development and school readiness. (ED-PS-03-8). Retrieved November 18, 2006, from http://ceep.crc.uiuc.edu/eecearchive/ digests/2003/raver03.pdf

Raver, C. C. (2004). Placing emotional self-regulation in sociocultural and socioeconomic contexts. *Child Development, 75(2)*, 346–353.

Reddy, R., Rhodes, J. E., and Mulhall, P. (2003). The influence of teacher support on student adjustment in the middle school years: A latent growth curve study. *Development and Psychopathology, 15*, 119–138.

Reid, R., Trout, A. L., and Schartz, M. (2005). Self-regulation interventions for children with Attention Deficit/Hyperactivity Disorder. *Exceptional Children, 71(4)*, 361–377.

Reijntjes. A., Stegge, H., and Terwogt, M. M. (2006). Children's coping with peer rejection: The role of depressive symptoms, social competence, and gender. *Infant and Child Development, 15(1)*, 89–107.

Reynolds, C. R. and Kamphaus, R. W. (2004). *Behavior Assessment System for Children – Second Edition (BASC-2), Self-Report of Personality Interview Edition (SRP-1)*. Circle Pines, MN: American Guidance Service.

Richards, J., and Gross, J. (2000). Emotion regulation and memory: The cognitive costs of keeping one's cool. *Journal of Personality and Social Psychology, 79(3)*, 410–424.

Richfield, S. (2003). Parent coaching for children with AD/HD and learning disabilities. SchwabLearning.org. Retrieved February 28, 2007, from http://www. schwablearning. org/articles.aspx?r = 704

Rielly, N. E. , Craig, W. M., and Parker, K. C. (2006). Peer and parenting characteristics of boys and girls with subclinical attention problems. *Journal of Attention Disorders, 9(4)*, 598–606.

Riggs, N. R., Greenberg, M. T., Kusche, C. A., and Pentz, M. A. (2006). The mediational role of neurocognition in the behavioral outcomes of a social-emotional prevention program in elementary school students: Effects of the PATHS curriculum. *Prevention Science, 7(1)*, 91–102.

Robinson, M. (2000). Writing well: Health and the power to make images. *Journal of Medical Ethics, 26*, 79–84.

Rodkin, P., and Hodges, E. (2003). Bullies and victims in the peer ecology: Four questions for psychologists and school professionals. *School Psychology Review, 32(3)*, 384–400.

Rosenthal, M. Z., Polusny, M. A., and Follette, V. M. (2006). Avoidance mediates the relationship between perceived criticism in the family of origin and psychological distress in adulthood. *Journal of Emotional Abuse, 6(1)*, 87–102.

Rothbart, M. K., and Derryberry, D. (1981) Development of individual differences in temperament. In M. E. Lamb and A. L. Brown (Eds.), *Advances in Developmental Psychology* (pp. 37–86). Hillsdale, NJ: Erlbaum.

Rothbart, M. K., and Jones, L. B. (1998). Temperament, self-regulation, and education. *School Psychology Review, 27(4)*, 479–491.

Rothenberg, S. (1998). Nonverbal learning disabilities and social functioning. Learning Disabilities Association of Massachusetts. Retrieved February 25, 2007, from http:// www.nldontheweb.org/Rothenberg-1.htm

Rottenberg, J., and Gross, J. J. (2003). When emotion goes wrong: Realizing the promise of affective science. *American Psychological Association, 10(2)*, 227–232.

Rubin, K. H. (1998). Social and emotional development from a cultural perspective. *Developmental Psychology, 34*, 611–615.

Rubin, K. H., Burgess, K. B., and Coplan, R. J. (2002). Social withdrawal and shyness. In P. K. Smith and C. H. Hart, *Blackwell Handbook of Child Social Development* (pp. 329–352). Oxford: Blackwell.

Rudolph, K. D., Lambert, S. F., Clark, A. G., and Kurlakowsky, K. D. (2001). Negotiating the transition to middle school: The role of self-regulatory processes. *Child Development, 72(3)*, 929–946.

Rutherford, R. B., Quinn, M. M., and Mathur, S. R. (1996). *Effective Strategies for Teaching Appropriate Behaviors to Children with Emotional/Behavioral Disorders*. Reston, VA: Council for Children with Behavior Disorders.

Salmivalli, C., Ojanen, T., Haanpaa, J., and Peets, K. (2005). 'I'm OK but you're not' and other peer-relational schemas: Explaining individual difference in children's social goals. *Developmental Psychology, 41(2)*, 363–375.

Salovey, P. (2006). Applied emotional intelligence: Regulating emotions to become healthy, wealthy, and wise. In J. Ciarrochi and J. D. Meyer (Eds.), *Emotional Intelligence in Everyday Life* (pp. 229–248). New York: Psychology Press.

Salters-Pedneault, K., Roemer, L., Tull, M. T., Rucker, L., and Mennin, D. S. (2006). Evidence of broad deficits in emotion regulation associated with chronic worry and generalized anxiety disorder. *Cognitive Therapy and Research, 30(4)*, 469–480.

SAMHSA (2003). Children's mental health facts. Children and adolescents with mental, emotional, and behavioral disorders. Retrieved January 30, 2007, from http://mentalhealth.samhsa.gov/publications/allpubs/CA-0006/default.asp

Sanderson, C. (n.d.). Brief description of Dialectical Behavior Therapy (DBT). The Borderline Personality Disorder Resource Center, White Plains, NY.

Sanson, A., Hemphill, S., and Smart, D. (2002). Temperament and social development. In P.K. Smith and C. H, Hart (Eds.), *Blackwell Handbook of Childhood Social Development* (pp. 97–116). Williston, VT: Blackwell Publishing.

Satcher, D. (2005). A Surgeon General's perspective on cultural competency: What is it and how does it affect diagnosis and treatment of major depressive disorder? CMECircle. Medscape. Retrieved February 14, 2006, from http://www.medscape.com/viewprogram/4489

Schnall, S., and Laird, J. D. (2003). Keep smiling: Enduring effects of facial expressions and postures on emotional experience and memory. *Cognition and Emotion, 17(5)*, 787–797.

Schoeberlein, D., and Koffler, T. (2005). Current status of programs using contemplative techniques in K-12 educational setting: A mapping report. *Garrison Institute report: Contemplation and education*. Garrison, NY. Retrieved October 30, 2006, from http://www.garrisoninstitute.org

Schutz, P. A., Hong, J. Y., Cross, D. I., and Osbon, J. N. (2006). Reflections on investigating emotion in educational activity settings. *Educational Psychology Review, 18(4)*, 343–360.

Schwartz, D. (2000). Subtypes of Victims and Aggressors in Children's Play Groups. *Journal of Abnormal Child Psychology, 28(20)*, 181–192.

Schwarz, J. (1999). Teaching emotional control could be the best Father's Day present. University of Washington Office of News and Information. Retrieved August 23, 2006, from http://uwnews.org/article.asp?articleID = 1627

Scime, M., Cook-Cottone, C., Kane, L., and Watson, T. (2006). Group prevention of eating disorders with fifth-grade females: Impact on body dissatisfaction, drive for thinness, and media influence. *Eating Disorder, 14*, 143–155.

Scime, M., and Norvilitis, J. M. (2006). Task performance and response to frustration in children with Attention Deficit Hyperactivity Disorder. *Psychology in the Schools, 43(3)*, 377–386.

Seeman T. E., Dubin L. F., and Seeman, M. (2003). Religiosity/spirituality and health: A critical review of the evidence for biological pathways. *American Psychologist, 58(1)*, 53–63.

Segerstrom, S. C., and Miller, G. E. (2004). Psychological stress and the human immune system: A meta-analytic study of 30 years of inquiry. *Psychological Bulletin, 130(4)*, 601–630.

Semple, R. (2005). Mindfulness-based cognitive therapy for children: A randomized group psychotherapy trial developed to enhance attention and reduce anxiety. DigitalCommons @Columbia. Retrieved October 29, 2006, fromhttp://digitalcommons.libraries.columbia. edu/dissertations/AAI3188789/

Semple, R. J., Reid, E. F. G., and Miller, L. (2005). Treating anxiety with mindfulness: An open trial of mindfulness training for anxious children. *Journal of Cognitive Psychotherapy, 19(4)*, 379–392.

Semrud-Clikeman, M., (2003). Executive function and social communication disorders. *Academic Language Therapy Association Bulletin, 1*, 3–6.

Shapiro, E. S. (2000). School psychology from an instructional perspective: Solving big, not little problems. *School Psychology Review, 29(4)*, 560–572.

Shinn, M. (2003). Understanding implementation of programs in multi-level systems. *Prevention and Treatment, 6(1)*. Article 22. Retrieved April 22, 2007, from http://journals. apa.org/prevention/volume6/pre0060022c.html

Shipman, K., Schneider, R., and Brown, A. (2004). Emotion dysregulation and psychopathology. In M. Beauregard (Ed.), *Consciousness, Emotional Self-regulation and the Brain* (pp. 61–86). Philadephia: John Benjamins Publishing Company.

Shipman, K., and Zeman, J. (2001). Socialization of children's emotion regulation in mother-child dyads: A developmental psychopathology approach. *Development and Psychopathology, 13*, 317–336.

Shipman, K. L., Zeman, J., Nesin, A. E., and Fitzgerald, M. (2003). Children's strategies for displaying anger and sadness: What works with whom? *Merrill-Palmer Quarterly, 49*, 100–122.

Shore, A. (1994). *Affect Regulation and the Origin of the Self.* Mahwah, NJ: Lawrence Erlbaum Associates.

Shortt, A. K., Barrett, P. M., and Fox, T. L. (2001). Evaluating the FRIENDS Program: A cognitive-behavioral group treatment for anxious children and their parents. *Journal of Clinical Child Psychology, 30(4)*, 525–535.

Shure, M. B. (1999, April). Preventing violence the problem-solving way. U. S. Department of Justice, Juvenile Justice Bulletin.

Shure, M. B. (2001a). I Can Problem Solve (ICPS): An interpersonal cognitive problem solving program for children. *Residential Treatment for Children & Youth, 18(3)*, 3–14.

Shure, M. B. (2001b). *I can problem solve: An interpersonal cognitive problem-solving program* (2nd Ed.), Champaign, IL: Research Press.

Silk, J. S., Shaw, D. S., Lane, T. J., Unikel, E., and Kovacs. M. (2005, April). Links between child emotion regulation, maternal response to emotion and child adjustment in children of depressed parents. Paper abstract submitted for the April 2005 biennial meeting of the Society for Research in Child Development, Atlanta, GA.

Silk, J. S., Shaw, D. S., Skuban, E. M., Oland, A.A. and Kovacs, M. (2006). Emotion regulation strategies in offspring of childhood-onset depressed mothers. *Journal of Child Psychology and Psychiatry, 47(1)*, 69–78.

Silk, J., Steinberg, L., and Morris, A. (2003). Adolescents' emotion regulation in daily life: Links to depressive symptoms and problem behavior. *Child Development, 74(6)*, 1869–1880.

Silverman, W. K. (2003). Using CBT in the treatment of social phobia, separation anxiety and GAD. *Psychiatric Times*, Vol. XX Issue 9. Retrieved November 29, 2005, from http:// www.psychiatrictimes.com/p030960.html

Sim, L., and Zeman, J. (2006). The contribution of emotion regulation to body dissatisfaction and disordered eating in early adolescent girls. *Journal of Youth and Adolescence, 35(2)*, 219–228.

Skiba, R., and McKelvey, J. (2000). What works in preventing school violence: The safe and responsive fact sheet series - Anger management. Retrieved July 23, 2003, from http://www.indiana.edu/~safeschl/AngerManagement.pdf

Sloan, D. M. (2004). Emotion regulation in action: Emotional reactivity in experiential avoidance. *Behavior Research and Therapy, 42*, 1257–1270.

Smart, D., and Sanson, A. (2001). Children's social competence: The role of temperament and behavior and their 'fit' with parents' expectations. *Family Matters, 59*, 10–15.

Smith, D. C., and Furlong, M. J. (1998). Introduction to the special issue: Addressing youth anger and aggression in school settings. *Psychology in the Schools, 35(3)*, 201–203.

Smith, P. K., Talamelli, L., Cowie, H., Naylor, P., and Chauhan, P. (2004). Profiles of non-victims, escaped victims, continuing victims and new victims of school bullying. *British Journal of Educational Psychology, 74*, 565–581.

Smith, S. (2002). Applying cognitive-behavioral techniques to social skills instruction. (ED469279). ERIC Clearinghouse on Disabilities and Gifted Education, Arlington, VA. ERIC/OSEP Special Project. Retrieved October 2, 2006, from http://www.ericdigests.org/2003-3/skills.htm

Smokowski, P. R., Fraser, M. W., Day, S. H., Galinsky, M. J., and Bacallao, M. L. (2004). School-based skills training to prevent aggressive behavior and peer rejection in childhood: Evaluating the Making Choices program. *Journal of Primary Prevention, 25(2)*, 233–251.

Smokowski, P. R., and Kopasz, K. H. (2005). Bullying in School: An overview of types, effects, family characteristics, and intervention strategies. *Children & Schools, 27(2)*, 101–110.

Snider, V. E. (1987). Use of self-monitoring of attention with LD students: Research and application. *Learning Disability Quarterly, 10(2)*, 139–151.

Spering, M., Wagener, D., and Funke, J. (2005). The role of emotions in complex problem-solving. *Cognition and Emotion, 19(8)*, 1252–1261.

Spinrad, T. L., Eisenberg, N., Cumberland, A., Fabes, R. A., Valiente, C., Shepard, S. A. et al. (2006). Relation of emotion-related regulation to children's social competence: A longitudinal study. *Emotion, 6(3)*, 498–510.

Spivack, G., and Shure, M. B. (1976). *Social Adjustment of Young Children: A Cognitive Approach to Solving Real-Like Problems.* San Francisco: Jossey-Bass Publishers, pp. 22–34, 60–65, 78–81.

Stecker, P. M. (1996). Self-recording during unsupervised academic activity: Effects on time spent out of class. *Exceptionality, 6(3)*, 133–147.

Stokes, T. F., and Baer, D. M. (1977). An implicit technology of generalization. *Journal of Applied Behavior Analysis, 10*, 349–367.

Sultanoff, B., and Zalaquett, C. (2000). Relaxation therapies. In D. Novey (Ed.), *Clinicians Complete Reference to Complementary and Alternative Medicine* (pp. 114–129). New York: Mosby.

Suveg, C., Comer, J. S., Furr, J. M., and Kendall, P. C. (2006). Adapting manualized CBT for a cognitively delayed child with multiple anxiety disorders. *Clinical Case Studies, 5(6)*, 488–510.

Suveg, C., Kendall, P. C., Comer, J. S., and Robin, J. (2006). Emotion-focused behavioral therapy for anxious youth: A multiple-baseline evaluation. *Journal of Contemporary Psychotherapy, 36(2)*, 77–85.

Suveg, C., and Zeman, J. (2004). Emotion regulation in children with anxiety disorders. *Journal of Clinical Child and Adolescent Psychology, 33(4)*, 750–759.

Suveg, C., Zeman, J., Flannery-Schroeder, E., and Cassano, M. (2005). Emotion socialization in families of children with an anxiety disorder. *Journal of Abnormal Child Psychology, 33*, 145–155.

Tangney, J. P., Baumeister, R. F., and Boone, A. L. (2004). High self-control predicts good adjustment, less pathology, better grades, and interpersonal success. *Journal of Personality*, *72*, 271–324. Retrieved October 26, 2006, from http://www.psy.fsu.edu/~baumeistertice/pubs.html

TARA-APD (2004). Understanding Borderline Personality Disorder. Retrieved December 12, 2006, from http://www.tara4bpd.org/dyn/index.php?option = content & task = view & id = 12

Taub, J., and Pearrow, M. (2005). Resilience through violence prevention in schools. In S. Goldstein and R. B. Brooks (Eds.), *Handbook of Resilience in Children* (pp. 357–371). New York: Springer Science + Business Media, Inc.

Taylor, S, and the Psychosocial Working Group (1998). Coping strategies. John D. and Catherine T. MacArthur Research Network on Socioeconomic Status and Health. Retrieved October 21, 2006, from http://www.macses.ucsf.edu/Research/Psychosocial/notebook/coping.html

Teglasi, H. (1995). *Assessment of Temperament*. [ED389963]. Greensboro, NC: ERIC Clearinghouse on Counseling and Student Services.

Teglasi, H. (1998a). Temperament constructs and measures. *School Psychology Review*, *27(4)*, 562–583.

Teglasi, H. (1998b). Introduction to the mini-series: Implications of temperament for the practice of school psychology. *School Psychology Review*, *27(4)*, 475–478.

Teicher, M. H., Samson, J. A., Polcari, A., and McGreenery, C. E. (2006). Verbal abuse and witnessing violence in childhood are highly associated with psychiatric symptoms: A viewpoint. *American Journal of Psychiatry*, *163*, 993–1000.

Thayer, J. F., Rossy, L. A., Ruiz-Padial, E., and Johnsen, B. H. (2003). Gender differences in the relationship between emotional regulation and depressive symptoms. *Cognitive Therapy and Research*, *27(3)*, 349–364.

Thienemann, M., Moore, P., and Tompkins, K. (2006). A parent-only group intervention for children with anxiety disorders: Pilot study. *Journal of the American Academy of Child & Adolescent Psychiatry*, *45(1)*, 37–46.

Thomas, A., and Chess, S. (1977). *Temperament and Development*. New York: Brunner & Mazel.

Thompson, R. A. (1991). Emotional regulation and emotional development. *Educational Psychology Review*, *3(4)*, 269–307.

Toblin, R. L., Schwartz, D., Hopmeyer, G. A., and Abouezzeddine, T. (2005). Social-cognitive and behavioral attributes of aggressive victims of bullying. *Journal of Applied Developmental Psychology*, *26(3)*, 329–346.

Tice, D., Bratslavsky, E., and Baumeister, R. (2001). Emotional distress regulation takes precedence over impulse control: If you feel bad, do it! *Journal of Personality and Social Psychology*, *80(1)*, 53–67.

Travis, F. T., Grosswald, S. J., and Stixrud, W. (2006). ADHD, brain functioning, and the Transcendental Meditation Program. Poster presented at the Annual Meeting of the Society for Psychophysiological Research, Vancouver, British Columbia.

Trentacosta, C. J., Izard, C. E., Mostow, A. J., and Fine, S. E. (2006). Children's emotional competence and attentional competence in early elementary school. *School Psychology Quarterly*, *21(2)*, 148–170.

Tsai, J. L., and Chentsova-Dutton, Y. (2002). Understanding depression across cultures. In I. Gotlib and C. Hammen (Eds.), *Handbook of Depression* (pp. 467–491). New York: Guilford Press.

Tsai, J. L., and Levenson, R. W. (1997). Cultural influences on emotional responding: Chinese American and European American dating couples during interpersonal conflict. *Journal of Cross-Cultural Psychology*, *28*, 600–625.

Turecki, S. (2003). The behavioral complaint: Symptom of a psychiatric disorder or a matter of temperament? *Contemporary Pediatrics*, *20(3)*, 111–119.

Twenge, J. M., Baumeister, R. F., DeWall, C. N., Ciarocco, N. J., and Bartels, J. M. (2007). Social exclusion decreases prosocial behavior. *Journal of Personality and Social Psychology*, *92*, 56–66.

Uebuchi, H. (2004). The new coping-model of self-regulated learning. *Shinrigaku Kenkyu*, *75(4)*, 359–364.

Underwood, M. K., and Bjornstad, G. J. (2001). Children's emotional experience of peer provocation: The relation between observed behaviour and self-reports of emotions, expressions, and social goals. *International Journal of Behavioral Development*, *25(4)*, 320–330.

Underwood, M. K., Hurley, J. C., Johanson, C. L., and Mosley, J. E. (1999). An experimental, observational investigation of children's responses to peer provocation: Developmental and gender differences in middle childhood. *Child Development*, *70(6)*, 1428–1446.

Venham, L. L., and Gaulin-Kremer, E. (1979). A self-report measure of situational anxiety for young children. *Pediatric Dentistry*, *1*, 91–96.

Ventis, W. L., Higbee, G., and Murdock, S. A. (2001). Using humor in systematic desensitization to reduce fear. *Journal of General Psychology*, *128(2)*, 241–253.

Verissimo R. (2005). Emotional intelligence, social support and affect regulation. *Acta Medica Portuguesa*, *18*, 345–352.

Verplanken, B., Friborg, O., Wang, C. E., Trafimow, D., and Woolf, K. (2007). Mental habits: Metacognitive reflection on negative self-thinking. *Journal of Personality and Social Psychology*, *92(3)*, 526–554.

Voeller, K. (2004) Attention deficit hyperactivity disorder (ADHD). *Journal of Child Neurology*, *19(10)*, 798–814.

Vreeman, R. C., and Carroll, A. E. (2007). A systematic review of school-based interventions to prevent bullying. *Archives of Pediatric & Adolescent Medicine*, pp. 161–78 and 88.

Waber, D., Gerber, E., Turcios, V., and Wagner, E. R. (2006). Executive functions and performance on high-stakes testing in children from urban schools. *Developmental Neuropsychology*, *29(3)*, 459–477.

Walcott, C. M., and Landau, S. (2004). The relation between disinhibition and emotion regulation in boys with Attention Deficit Hyperactivity Disorder. *Journal of Clinical Child & Adolescent Psychology*, *33(4)*, 772–782.

Wall, R. B. (2005). Tai Chi and mindfulness-based stress reduction in a Boston public middle school. *Journal of Pediatric Health Care*, *19(4)*, 230–237.

Wallace, B. A., and Truelove, J. E. (2006). Monitoring student cognitive-affective processing through reflection to promote learning in high-anxiety contexts. *Journal of Cognitive Affective Learning*, *3(1)*, 22–27.

Waller, E., and Scheidt, C. E. (2006). Somatoform disorders as disorders of affect regulation: A development perspective. *International Review of Psychiatry*, *18(1)*, 13–24.

Watt, D. F. (2004). Consciousness, emotional self-regulation and the brain. *Journal of Consciousness Studies*, *11(9)*, 77–82.

Weber, C. J., and Bizer, G. Y. (2006). The effects of immediate forewarning of test difficulty on test performance. *Journal of General Psychology*, *133(3)*, 277–285.

Wegner, D. M. (1992). You can't always think what you want: Problems in the suppression of unwanted thoughts. *Advances in Experimental Social Psychology*, *25*, 193–222.

Wegner, D. M. (1994). *White Bears and Other Unwanted Thoughts: Suppression, Obsession, and the Psychology of Mental Control* (pp. 59–60 and 96–98). New York: Guilford Press.

Wegner, D. M., Schneider, D. J., Carter, S. R., and White, T. L. (1987). Paradoxical effects of thought suppression. *Journal of Personality and Social Psychology*, *53(1)*, 5–13.

Weiten, W., and Lloyd, M. A. (2006). Psychology applied to modern life: Adjustment in the 21st century. Canada: Thompson Learning, Inc.

Wellman. H. M., Baron-Cohen, S., Caswell, R., Gomez, J. C., Swettenham, J., and Toye, E. et al. (2002). Thought-bubbles help children with autism acquire an alternative to a theory of mind. *Autism*, *6(4)*, 343–363.

Wells, A. (2003). Anxiety disorders, metacognition, and change. In R. L. Leahy (Ed.), *Roadblocks in Cognitive-Behavioral Therapy: Transforming Challenges into Opportunities for Change* (pp. 69–90). New York: Guilford Publications.

Wells, A. (2004). Metacognitive therapy: Elements of mental control in understanding and treating generalized. Anxiety Disorder and Posttraumatic Stress Disorder. In R. L. Leahy (Ed.), *Contemporary Cognitive Therapy: Theory Research and Practice* (p. 200). New York: The Guilford Press.

Wentzel, K. R. (1991). Relations between social competence and academic achievement in early adolescence. *Child Development, 62(5)*, 1066–1078.

Wentzel, K. R. (1998). Social relationships and motivation in middle school: The role of parents, teachers, and peers. *Journal of Educational Psychology, 90(2)*, 202–209.

Wenzlaff, R. D., and Eisenberg, A. R. (1998). Parental restrictiveness of negative emotions: Sowing the seeds of thought suppression. *Psychological Inquiry, 9(4)*, 310–313.

Wenzlaff, R. M., and Wegner, D. M. (2000). Thought suppression. *Annual Review of Psychology, 51*, 59–91.

Westphal, M., and Bonanno, G. A. (2004). Emotional self-regulation. In M. Beauregard (Ed.), *Consciousness, Emotional Self-Regulation and the Brain* (pp. 1–33). Philadelphia: John Benjamins Publishing Company.

White, D. R., and Howe, N. (1998). The socialization of children's emotional and social behavior by day care educators. In D. Pushkar, W. M. Bukowski, A. E. Schwartzman, D. M. Stavck, and D. R. White (Eds.), *Improving Competence Across the Lifespan: Building Interventions Based on Theory and Research*. New York: Plenum Press.

Whiteside, U.S., Hunter, D. A., Dunn, E. C., Palmquist, R. M., and Naputi, L. M. (2003). Severity of eating disorder pathology in relation to difficulties in emotion regulation. Retrieved November 5, 2006, from http://staff.washington.edu/dhunter/2003%20 Severity%20of%20ED%20Pathology.pdf

Williams, K. D. (2007). Ostracism. *Annual Review of Psychology, 58*, 425–452.

Williams, S., Waymouth, M., Lipman, E., Mills, B., and Evans, P. (2004). Evaluation of a children's Temper-Taming Program. *The Canadian Journal of Psychiatry, 49*, 607–612.

Wilson, S. J., and Lipsey, M. W. (2004). The effects of school-based social information processing interventions on aggressive behavior: A Campbell Collaboration Systematic Review. Education Review Group. Retrieved February 27, 2007, from http://www. campbellcollaboration.org/doc-pdf/agbhprt.pdf

Wilton, M. M., Craig, W. M., and Pepler, D. J. (2000). Emotional regulation and display in classroom victims of bullying: Characteristic expressions of affect, copying styles and relevant contextual factors. *Social Development, 9(2)*, 227–245.

Winslow, E. B., Sandler, I. N., and Wolchik, S. A. (2005). Building resilience in all children: A public health approach. In S. Goldstein and R. B. Brooks (Eds.), *Handbook of Resilience in Children* (pp. 337–356). New York: Springer Science + Business Media, Inc., NY.

Woller, W. (2006). Psychotherapeutic intervention for disturbed emotional regulation in complex post-traumatic stress disorder. *Nevenarzt, 77(3)*, 327–332.

Wood, J. J. (2006). Effect of anxiety reduction on children's school performance and social adjustment. *Developmental Psychology, 42(2)*, 345–349.

Wood, J. J., Piacentini, J. C., Southam-Gerow, M., Chu, B., and Sigman, M. (2006). Family cognitive behavioral therapy for child anxiety disorders. *Journal of the American Academy of Child and Adolescent Psychiatry, 45*, 314–421.

Ysseldyke, J., Burns, M., Dawson, P., Kelley, B., Morrison, D., Ortiz, S. et al. (2006). *School Psychology: A Blueprint for Training and Practice*. Bethesda, MD: National Association of School Psychologists.

Zbornik, J. (2001). Test anxiety: Conceptualization and remediation strategies. *Today's School Psychologist*. Retrieved February 8, 2007, from http://.lkwdpl.org/schools/ specialed/zbornik1.htm

Zeidner, M., Matthews, G., and Roberts, R. D. (2006). Emotional intelligence, coping with stress, and adaptation. In J. Ciarrochi and J. D. Meyer (Eds.), *Emotional Intelligence in Everyday Life* (pp. 100–125). New York: Psychology Press.

Zeman, J., Shipman, K., and Penza-Clyve, S. (2001). Development and initial validation of the Children's Sadness Management Scale. *Journal of Nonverbal Behavior*, 25, 187–205.

Zhang, J.S., Jin, X. M., and Shen, X. M. (2006). Development of children's self-regulation competence and its relationship with behavioral problems. Abstract. *Zhonghua Er Ke Za Zhi, 44(1)*, 31–36.

Zins, J. E., Bloodworth, M. R., Weissberg, R. P., and Walberg, H. J. (2004). The scientific base linking social and emotional learning to school success. In J. E. Zins, M. R. Bloodworth, R. P. Weissberg, and H. J. Walberg (Eds.), *Building Academic Success on Social and Emotional Learning: What Does the Research Say?* Teachers College, Columbia University, pp. 3–22.

Postscript

There is no doubt that intervening early with young children who are demonstrating weak emotion regulation or having problems with emotion regulation is important. Difficulties with self-regulation are seen as early as age three. Some of these early problems that cause so much stress include:

- Difficulties in calming oneself.
- Overreaction to sensory input.
- Difficulties regulating mood.
- Poor emotional control.

DeGangi, Breinbauer, Roosevelt, Porges, and Greenspan (2000) found that as many as 95 percent of the infants they followed who exhibited moderate regulatory disorders were demonstrating developmental delays and difficult family relationships by the time they were three years of age. Children first come to the attention of school psychologists by three years of age. Interventions for children and their parents designed to facilitate the development of emotion regulation can be expected to make a considerable difference in children's lives, particularly if we intervene early.

Although we may be well aware of the need to address emotion regulation abilities, school psychologists may not have a large repertoire of tools to address these concerns because emotion regulation has only recently come to the attention of researchers and there remain many unknowns. On April 3 and 4, 2006, the National Institute of Mental Health sponsored a meeting of scientists engaged in research on emotion regulation to explore links among behavior science, neuroscience, and clinical studies (National Institute of Mental Health Meeting Summary (2006, April 3–4). This collaborative effort summarized much of what is known about emotion regulation and what is needed if goals include intervention approaches. The discussion was quite fruitful.

Neuroscience has demonstrated that patterns of neural activity in the brains of children appear to differ from those in adults. Researchers further reported that emotion regulation can occur both voluntarily and automatically. Clinical researchers noted that self-regulation of emotion is a powerful social mediator. There are some promising intervention approaches in the literature. These relate to (a) the critical role of parents, (b) the child's developmental level, and (c) the context in which emotion regulation or dysregulation occurs, and they are maximally engaging.

A great deal remains unknown particularly in regard to interventions, identifying emotion regulation risk profiles, determining how emotion dysregulation emerges, and implementing emotion regulation work among schoolchildren. This text is a first attempt to raise awareness of the need for emotion regulatory work in schools.

Given the intense interest in emotion regulation, there is every reason to be optimistic in regard to the likelihood that we will soon have more knowledge and more tools to help children and adolescents develop 'good enough' emotion regulation. Although current knowledge suggests that work with children be initiated as early as possible, the brain continues to be plastic during the entire school-age period. For example, Forrest and Hay (2000) recently demonstrated that about 60 percent of students from age seven to fifteen have high levels of self-control from age seven or earlier. These students will remain well controlled through age fifteen. Those students who exhibited low self-control by age seven continued to be poorly controlled. However, one in five to one in six students showed changes in degrees of self-control between the ages of eleven and fifteen.

Parenting was the key. Negative home factors during this period could interfere with students' high self-control or could guarantee that a student with low self-control would do even less well. Parental socialization continues to affect self-control during adolescence. There is no reason to believe that self-control of emotion would not also follow this pattern. Close, caring relationships with adults other than parents might also positively influence young people dealing with family stress and contribute positively to the development of the child's emotion regulation as he or she goes through school.

It is clear that there is a great deal of work to be done to help children who are demonstrating weaknesses in emotion regulation. We have to carefully consider the literature available and use the current research to design interventions using best practices. However, we must also focus on prevention. We are aware of the value of implementing universal social-emotional programs in schools. We have to add an emotion regulation component to these curricula to benefit all children.

This is an exciting time in regard to both prevention and intervention work. School psychologists are better trained, have greater access to research, and have more tools than ever before. The likelihood that our work will truly make a difference is increasingly secure.

Subject Index